THE COMPLETE PARTNERSHIP MANUAL AND GUIDE —

With Tax, Financial and Managerial Strategies

Daniel L. McKnight, Jr.

PRENTICE-HALL, INC.
ENGLEWOOD CLIFFS, NEW JERSEY

Prentice-Hall International, Inc., *London*
Prentice-Hall of Australia, Pty. Ltd., *Sydney*
Prentice-Hall Canada, Inc., *Toronto*
Prentice-Hall of India Private Ltd., *New Delhi*
Prentice-Hall of Japan, Inc., *Tokyo*
Prentice-Hall of Southeast Asia Pte. Ltd., *Singapore*
Whitehall Books, Ltd., *Wellington, New Zealand*

© 1982 by
Prentice-Hall, Inc.
Englewood Cliffs, N.J.

This publication is designed to provide accurate and authoritative information in regard to the subject matter covered. It is sold with the understanding that the publisher is not engaged in rendering legal, accounting, or other professional service. If legal advice or other expert assistance is required, the services of a competent professional person should be sought.

. . . From the Declaration of Principles jointly adopted by a Committee of the American Bar Association and a Committee of Publishers and Associations.

Library of Congress Cataloging in Publication Data

McKnight, Daniel L.
    The complete partnership manual and guide.

    Includes index.
        1. Partnership—United States.   2. Partnership—
Taxation—United States.   I. Title.
KF1375.M33   346.73'0682   82-5799
                              347.306682   AACR2

ISBN 0-13-162230-7

Printed in the United States of America

To my wife, Renee,
my marriage partner of 35 years and
the best thing that ever happened to me.

About the Author

Daniel L. McKnight, Jr., has been a practicing Certified Public Accountant since 1948. In addition to his duties as managing partner, he has been partner in charge of a substantial segment of the auditing and tax practice of McKnight, Frampton, Buskirk and Co., CPAs, Charleston, South Carolina.

Mr. McKnight has written on partnership taxation and has been a discussion leader on advanced partnership taxation for several years.

He has served his profession as president of the South Carolina Association of Certified Public Accountants, and as chairman of several of its committees. He has been a member of Council of the American Institute of Certified Public Accountants, and president of the Estate Planning Council of Charleston, South Carolina.

Introduction

This book is an "operator's manual" providing the core information needed to select, organize, manage and eventually terminate the partnership.

You will find what you need to know to understand what a partnership is and how it differs from other business entities. You will find facts to help you decide whether the partnership form is the proper choice, and may find that some commonly accepted ideas about partnerships and corporations lack substance. In these pages you will find suggestions for crucial clauses in the partnership agreement, the "charter" of the unincorporated venture. You will be told how much structure a partnership needs, how to employ capital effectively, and how to keep people from working at cross purposes. Advice will be given on how to reorganize or terminate the venture when it has served its purpose or has outgrown its shell.

The opening sections of the Uniform Partnership Act say that a partnership is organized for profit. No matter how carefully you select your partners, no matter how precisely you word the agreement or operate the venture, you have failed in your purpose of maximizing profit if you have given inadequate thought to the *tax* aspects. It is in the tax area that the partnership really shines. It is itself not a taxable entity; its advantages include a flexibility as to who will be taxed and when and how he will be taxed, that corporations cannot match. This book will cover the tax angle of each facet of partnership formation and operation. Without going into the great detail available in the several fine works devoted exclusively to partnership taxation, these chapters will alert you to the most attractive opportunities and to the most common pitfalls arising from Subchapter K, the partnership section of the Internal Revenue Code.

You will find this to be a useful reference work for partnerships of any kind. It also goes beyond the appearances of the tax-shelter partnership to help you decide whether these ventures are effective in tax avoidance and, if so, for how long.

The author, from his long experience with and study of professional partnerships, relates how these ventures, probably more numerous than any other kind of partnership, can get well-educated, frequently aggressive and sometimes "prima donna-ish" people to work for their common good.

The rapid economic rise (and sometimes fall) of these well-paid professionals and their tendency to regroup as concepts change make management difficult and pose problems of entry and exit. Unless plans to provide for growth are well laid, the almost inevitable split-up can leave a battleground as bloody as the site of a hotly contested divorce.

Partnerships have a place in the estate planning field. The author shows ways to use partnerships when tax planning is a major reason for the partnership's existence. He shows how to arrange a partnership organized for solid business reasons alone to make the choices that will best serve those most interested in conserving their estates without placing an undue burden on those whose principal assets are their brains and youthful vigor.

In sum, this book is a storehouse of tax planning, financial and managerial ideas and information on partnerships.

EDITOR'S NOTE

Readers may wish to know the authority for specific legal rules found in this book. The author has provided such information without allowing footnotes to monopolize the book. He cites references, when appropriate, in the body of the text.

Acknowledgments

The author would like to acknowledge his indebtedness to Mrs. James. L. Gaillard, his secretary of 26 years service. Without her patience, and her willingness to accommodate her incredibly busy schedule to this additional need, the project could not have succeeded.

Contents

Introduction   vii

CHAPTER ONE

The Technical Points of View of Statute and Income Tax Law • 1

INTRODUCTION   3

1.1 THE UNIFORM PARTNERSHIP ACT — THE STATUTORY VIEW   3

     1.1.1   Intent to Form a Partnership is Required – 3
     1.1.2   Partnerships Are Organized to Make a Profit – 3
     1.1.3   General and Limited Partnerships – 4
     1.1.4   A Partnership Interest Is Personal Property – 4

1.2 THE INTERNAL REVENUE CODE — THE TAX COLLECTOR'S VIEW   4

     1.2.1   The Internal Revenue Service Regulations Expand Upon the Code – 5
     1.2.2   The Brevity of the Tax Law and Regulations Can Be Misleading – 5

1.3 GENERAL PARTNERSHIPS IMPOSE UNLIMITED LIABILITY ON THEIR PARTNERS   5

     1.3.1   Evaluating the Risks of Unlimited Liability – 6

1.4 LIMITED PARTNERSHIPS REQUIRE FORMALITY IN THEIR CREATION AND OPERATION   6

     1.4.1   Comparison of General and Limited Partnerships – 7

1.5 BENEFITS AND PITFALLS OF GENERAL AND LIMITED PARTNERSHIPS   8

1.6 THE PARTNERSHIP AS A MERE CONDUIT   9

     1.6.1   Dangers in Accepting the Conduit Concept – 9

1.7 THE PARTNERSHIP AS AN ENTITY OR AS AN AGGREGATE OF PARTNERS   9

1.8   DISTINCTION BETWEEN PARTNERSHIPS, TENANCIES,
       AND INCOME-SHARING ARRANGEMENTS   10

       1.8.1   How to Reduce Uncertainty as to Status as a Partner-
                ship, Tenancy or Other Arrangements – 13
       1.8.2   Legal and Economic Considerations Carry Weight – 13
       1.8.3   Advantages and Disadvantages of Partnerships
                Vs. Tenancies – 14
       1.8.4   Silent Partners – 13

1.9   A TAX TRAP — PENALTIES FOR FAILURE TO RECOGNIZE
       EXISTENCE OF A PARTNERSHIP   15

1.10   PARTNERSHIP RETURN FILING REQUIREMENTS   15

1.11   THE PARTNERSHIP, SEEMINGLY SIMPLE, IS COMPLEX   16

1.12   CHAPTER ONE IN SUMMARY   16

CHAPTER TWO

When to Choose
The Partnership Form • 17

INTRODUCTION   19

2.1   ADVANTAGES AND DISADVANTAGES OF PARTNERSHIPS
       COMPARED WITH CORPORATIONS — NONTAX   19

       2.1.1   Limited Liability of Stockholders – 19
       2.1.2   Ease of Partnership Formation and Operation – 20
       2.1.3   Nontax Disadvantages of Partnerships – 20
       2.1.4   Transferability of Corporate Stock – 21
       2.1.5   Conclusions – 21

2.2   ADVANTAGES AND DISADVANTAGES OF PARTNERSHIPS
       COMPARED WITH CORPORATIONS — TAX   21

       2.2.1   The Partnerships Pays No Taxes and Partners Have
                Discretion in Allocating Taxability Among
                Themselves – 22
       2.2.2   Examples of How the Same Income Can Produce
                Different Tax Results, Depending on Whether It Is Earned
                by a Partnership or by a Subchapter S Corporation – 23
       2.2.3   Partnerships Are at a Disadvantage in Accumulating
                Earnings, in Retirement Plans, in Deducting Loss on
                Investment, and in Selecting a Business Year – 24
       2.2.4   Comparison of Partnerships and Corporations – 25

2.3   FAMILY PARTNERSHIPS CAN SHIFT INCOME TO LOW-
       BRACKET FAMILY MEMBERS   32

       2.3.1   IRS Weapons for Challenging the Family Partnership – 32
       2.3.2   "Damn the IRS Torpedoes" — The Family Partnership
                Is Worth a Try – 33
       2.3.3   Gift Tax Returns May Be Required – 33
       2.3.4   Examples of How a Family Partnership Can Save
                Taxes – 33

2.4   PARTNERSHIPS TAXABLE AS ASSOCIATIONS   34

       2.4.1   The Danger in Having Too Many Corporate
                Characteristics – 34
       2.4.2   The Danger Lurks in Both Directions – 35
       2.4.3   Conclusion – 36

2.5   CHAPTER TWO IN A NUTSHELL   36

CHAPTER THREE

How to Organize
A Partnership • 37

       INTRODUCTION   39

3.1   THE PARTNERSHIP AGREEMENT   39

3.2   THE TAXABLE YEAR   43

       3.2.1   Adoption of a Fiscal Year Can Defer Taxation
                Significantly – 43
       3.2.2   How to Get IRS Permission to Adopt a Fiscal Year – 43
       3.2.3   Reporting Requirements for the New Partnership – 44

3.3   RIGHTS, DUTIES AND RESPONSIBILITIES OF PARTNERS   44

       3.3.1   Duties and Responsibilities of a Partner – 44
       3.3.2   Rights of a Partner – 44

3.4   CAPITAL SOURCES   45

       3.4.1   The Combination of Cash and Property – 45
       3.4.2   Contribution of Encumbered Property – 46

3.5   PARTNERSHIP INTEREST PURCHASED WITH INFUSIONS
       OF PROPERTY   46

       3.5.1   Contribution of High-Value, Low-Basis Property Does
                Not Result in Immediately Taxable Income – 46

3.5.2   Distinction Between Capital Account and Basis of
Partnership Interest – 47

3.5.3   Contribution of Mortgaged Property – 48

3.5.4   The Tax Trap in Contribution of Mortgaged Property – 49

3.5.5   Special Allocation Rule for Contribution of Undivided
Interests in Property – 50

3.5.6   Depreciation and Credit Recapture – 52

3.5.7   Holding Period of Contributed Property – 52

3.5.8   How to Escape from the Tax Problems Associated with
Contribution of Property – 52

3.6   PARTNERSHIP INTEREST ACQUIRED IN EXCHANGE FOR
SERVICES   52

3.6.1   The Tax Distinction Between Property and Services – 53

3.6.2   A Solution to the Problem – 54

3.6.3   The IRS Attacks Its Own Regulations – 54

3.6.4   Avoiding Income from Contribution of Services Is Not
Always Desirable – 54

3.6.5   Conclusion – 55

3.7   ORGANIZATION EXPENSES AND SYNDICATION FEES   55

3.8   A REVIEW OF CHAPTER THREE   55

CHAPTER FOUR

Normal Operations
Of a Partnership • 57

INTRODUCTION   61

4.1   WHO MANAGES THE PARTNERSHIP?   61

4.1.1   The Managing Partner – 62

4.1.2   The Executive Committee – 62

4.2   LIMITATION ON OUTSIDE ACTIVITIES   63

4.2.1   The Case for Outside Activities – 63

4.2.2   There Can Be Too Much of a Good Thing – 63

4.2.3   A Negative Defense – 64

4.2.4   A Positive Defense – 64

4.2.5   Outside Activities Can Be an Embarrassment – 64

4.2.6   An Ounce of Prevention – 64

4.3   CAPITAL AND DRAWING ACCOUNTS   64

4.3.1   The Distinction Between Capital and Drawing
Accounts – 65

4.3.2   The Partnership Agreement Defines Capital and
         Drawing Accounts – 65
4.3.3   How the Capital Account Is Created – 65
4.3.4   Shares of Capital and Shares of Profits – 66
4.3.5   Not All Capital Is on the Books – 67
4.3.6   "Off-Balance Sheet" Capital – 68

4.4   INCREASES IN CAPITAL   69

4.4.1   Varying Ratios Offer a Solution to the Capital Problem
         – 69
4.4.2   Varying Ratios Present a Problem – 69
4.4.3   Illustration of Accounting for Both the Cash Basis
         and Accrual Basis Capital Accounts – 70
4.4.4   Capital Accounts May Permanently Reflect an Opening
         Inequality – 71
4.4.5   Changing Circumstances May Erase or Reverse the
         Inequality – 71

4.5   COMPENSATION FOR SERVICES   71

4.5.1   Partners' Salaries Are a "Must" – 71
4.5.2   Partners' Salaries and Payroll Taxes – 72

4.6   INTEREST ON CAPITAL ACCOUNTS   72

4.6.1   The Tax Aspect of Interest on Capital Accounts – 72

4.7   GUARANTEED PAYMENTS   73

4.7.1   Receipt of Guaranteed Payments Does Not Make an
         Employee out of a Partner or Affect His Status as a
         Principal Partner – 74
4.7.2   Guaranteed Payments and Capital Gains – 74
4.7.3   Guaranteed Payments Must Be Reasonable – 75
4.7.4   Guaranteed Payments Are Deductible Only if They Are
         Expenses – 75
4.7.5   Guaranteed Payments to Former Partners – 75

4.8   PROFIT AND LOSS SHARING RATIOS   75

4.8.1   Profit Sharing Is Not a Substitute for Compensation – 75
4.8.2   The Remaining Profit Is Shared – 76
4.8.3   Losses Must Be Shared, Too! – 77
4.8.4   Profit Sharing Ratios and Capital Ratios—Statutory
         Rules – 77
4.8.5   The Internal Revenue Code Permits Income and Deductions
         to Be Allocated According to the Ratios Specified in the
         Agreement – 78
4.8.6   The Tests for Substantial Economic Effect – 78

4.8.7   Other Tax Effects of the Profit Sharing and Capital
         Ratios – 79

4.9   ALLOCATION OF TAX EFFECTS OF CONTRIBUTIONS OF
       PROPERTY   80

4.9.1   The Internal Revenue Code Permits Allocation – 80
4.9.2   The Internal Revenue Code Provides Automatic
         Allocation – 80
4.9.3   How and When the Undivided Interests Rule Applies – 81
4.9.4   When the Undivided Interests Rule Doesn't Apply – 81
4.9.5   Allowable Depreciation Is Limited to Total Depreciation
         – 82
4.9.6   Tax Treatment When the Contributed Asset Is Sold – 82

4.10   SIGNIFICANCE OF GROSS INCOME   83

4.10.1   How a Partner's Share of Partnership Gross Income Is
         Computed – 83

4.11   SPECIAL TREATMENT ITEMS OF INCOME   84

4.12   TIME FOR INCLUSION OF ITEMS OF INCOME   86

4.13   ELECTIONS HAVING AN EFFECT ON COMPUTATION OF
       TAXABLE INCOME   86

4.14   RETROACTIVE ALLOCATIONS AND VARYING INTERESTS   87

4.14.1   A Superb Tax-Planning Opportunity Survived the Ban
         on Retroactive Allocations – 88

4.15   DISTRIBUTIONS   88

4.15.1   Ordinarily, No Gain or Loss Is Recognized Upon a
         Distribution – 88
4.15.2   The Exception to the General Rule – 89
4.15.3   How the Partnership Is Affected by Distributions – 89
4.15.4   The Nature of Gain Upon a Nonliquidating Distribution
         – 89
4.15.5   Guaranteed Payments as Distributions – 89
4.15.6   Constructive Distributions – 89

4.16   TAXATION OF DISTRIBUTIVE SHARES   89

4.16.1   When a Distributive Share Is Taxed – 89
4.16.2   How a Distributive Share Is Taxed – 90
4.16.3   To Whom a Distributive Share Is Taxed – 90

4.17   DEALINGS BETWEEN PARTNERSHIP AND PARTNERS   90

4.17.1   Regulation 1.707.1 Defines Certain Transactions as
         Being Transactions Between Partnership and Partner as
         Outsider – 90

4.17.2   Losses Between a Partner and a Controlled Partnership
            May Be Disallowed – 91
4.17.3   Gains Between a Partner and Controlled Partnership Are
            Treated as Ordinary Income – 91

4.18   DISABILITY OF PARTNERS   91

4.19   SUMMATION OF CHAPTER FOUR   92

CHAPTER FIVE

**Transfers of Interest
In a Partnership • 93**

INTRODUCTION   97

5.1   ADMISSION OF PARTNERS   97

        5.1.1   The Founding Partners – 97
        5.1.2   Admission of New Partners – 98
        5.1.3   Employees as a Source of New Partners – 98
        5.1.4   Relatives as a Source of New Partners – 98
        5.1.5   Be Thorough and Objective in Screening Applicants – 98
        5.1.6   What to Do When You Find the Right Person – 99
        5.1.7   The Partnership Agreement Spells Out the Terms for
                  Admission of New Partners – 99

5.2   BUY-SELL AGREEMENTS   100

        5.2.1   Why a Written Agreement Is Needed – 101
        5.2.2   Essential Provisions of the Buy-Sell Agreement – 101

5.3   FUNDING THE BUY-SELL AGREEMENT WITH LIFE
        INSURANCE   101

        5.3.1   The Kind and Amount of Insurance Needed – 102
        5.3.2   Cash Values Are a Resource and a Temptation – 102
        5.3.3   Policies May Be Owned by a Partnership or by Partners
                  – 102
        5.3.4   Disposition of Policies for Which an Urgent Need No
                  Longer Exists – 104
        5.3.5   Insurance Proceeds Used to Fund a Deferred Payout – 105

5.4   PURCHASE AND SALE OF GOOD WILL   105

        5.4.1   Guaranteed Payments Are the Normal Choice – 105
        5.4.2   Guaranteed Payments May Not Be the Best Choice – 105
        5.4.3   Good Will Does Not Include Unrealized Receivables
                  and Inventory Items – 107

5.5   RETIREMENT OF A PARTNER   107

5.5.1   Retirement Can Be a Reward or Exile – 107
5.5.2   Retirement Should Be Scheduled – 107
5.5.3   Transition Should Be Controlled – 108

5.6   DISABILITY OF A PARTNER   108

5.6.1   Causes of Disability – 108
5.6.2   Defining Disability – 108
5.6.3   Disability Compensation – 109
5.6.4   The Tax Aspects of Disability Pay – 109
5.6.5   When Disability Invokes the Buy-Sell Agreement – 109

5.7   DEATH OF A PARTNER   110

5.7.1   Payments for a Deceased Partner's Interest – 110
5.7.2   Life Insurance as a Security Device – 111

5.8   DISAGREEMENT WITH OR EXPULSION OF A PARTNER   111

5.8.1   Contumacy Can Be a Weapon – 111
5.8.2   Submission of Disputes to Arbitration – 111

5.9   HOW AND WHEN THE DEPARTING PARTNER WILL BE PAID FOR HIS INTEREST   112

5.10   DETERMINATION OF THE PRICE TO BE PAID TO THE DEPARTING PARTNER   113

5.10.1   Determination of Fair Value – 113
5.10.2   Valuing Tangible Assets – 113
5.10.3   Valuing Intangible Assets – 114
5.10.4   Setting the Price – 114

5.11   GUARANTEED PAYMENTS TO RETIRED PARTNERS OR TO A DECEASED PARTNER'S SUCCESSOR IN INTEREST   115

5.11.1   Guaranteed Payments Defined – 115
5.11.2   The Good (Tax) News and the Bad (Tax) News About Guaranteed Payments – 115

5.12   INCOME IN RESPECT OF DECEDENT   115

5.13   CLOSING PARTNERSHIP YEAR UPON TRANSFER OF INTEREST   116

5.13.1   Death Does Not Necessarily Terminate a Partnership – 116
5.13.2   When the Partnership Year Closes for Tax Purposes – 116
5.13.3   Death Ordinarily Does Not Close the Partnership Year – 117
5.13.4   Select the Estate's First Fiscal Year-End to Minimize Taxes – 117

5.13.5   A Deceased Partner Can Have Two Partnership Closings in His Final Year – 118

5.14   APPRECIATED INVENTORIES AND UNREALIZED RECEIVABLES   118

5.14.1   "Appreciated Inventories" Can Be a Misleading Term – 119
5.14.2   When the Sale of a Partnership Interest Produces Ordinary Income – 119
5.14.3   How Section 751 Is Applied – 119
5.14.4   The Paradoxical Definitions of Section 751 – 120
5.14.5   Inventories Must be Substantially Appreciated to Invoke Section 751 – 120
5.14.6   Tax Effect to the Transferee Partner – 122
5.14.7   Tax Effect to the Transferor Partner – 123
5.14.8   Tax Effect to the Remaining Partners – 123
5.14.9   The Tax Effect to the Partners Giving Up an Interest in Property of a Character Different from the Property Received – 124
5.14.10   The Tax Effect to the Partnership of Giving Up an Interest in Property of a Character Different from the Property Retained – 124
5.14.11   The Tax Effect When the Partners Do Not Specify What Will Be Exchanged – 125
5.14.12   Preplanning the Distribution Can Improve the Tax Consequences – 126

5.15   PARTNERSHIP ELECTIONS TO ADJUST BASIS OF PARTNERSHIP ASSETS   126

5.15.1   The Logic of Opportunity to Adjust Basis of Partnership Assets – 127
5.15.2   An Election Can Be Beneficial Whether Partners Are Coming or Going – 127
5.15.3   Elections to Adjust Basis of Partnership Assets Upon Transfer of Interests – 128
5.15.4   An Election, Once Made, Is Binding Upon Future Transfers – 129
5.15.5   Elections to Adjust Basis of Partnership Assets Upon a Distribution in Liquidation – 129
5.15.6   How an Election Under Section 754 Is Made – 131
5.15.7   Section 755 Provides for Designation of the Assets Whose Basis Is to Be Adjusted – 131

5.16   PARTNER'S ELECTION TO ADJUST BASIS OF DISTRIBUTED PROPERTY (SECTION 732)   132

5.16.1   The Partnership's Failure to Make a Section 754 Election Works Against the Withdrawing Partner – 132

5.16.2   Where the Tax Advantage to the Withdrawing Partner
Lies – 132

5.16.3   How the Election Under Section 732 Is Made – 133

5.16.4   An Election Under Section 732(d) May Be Required – 133

5.17   THE MAIN POINTS OF CHAPTER FIVE   134

CHAPTER SIX

Bases of Partnership Assets
And of Partnership Interests • 135

INTRODUCTION   37

6.1   DISTINCTION BETWEEN BASIS OF PARTNERSHIP ASSETS
AND BASIS OF PARTNERSHIP INTERESTS   137

6.1.1   How a Partnership Asset's Basis Is Determined – 138

6.1.2   How the Basis of a Partnership Interest Is Determined – 138

6.1.3   The Significance of Basis of a Partnership Interest – 139

6.1.4   The Sums of the Partnership Asset Bases and Partnership
Interest Bases Frequently Are Identical – 140

6.2   SOURCES OF BASIS OF PARTNERSHIP INTEREST   141

6.3   EFFECTS OF LIABILITIES ON BASIS OF PARTNERSHIP
INTEREST   141

6.3.1   Increases in Liabilities Increase Basis of Partnership
Interests – 142

6.3.2   Decreases in Liabilities Decrease Basis of Partnership
Interests – 142

6.3.3   Special Rule for Nonrecourse Liabilities – 142

6.4   OTHER CAUSES OF CHANGES IN BASIS OF PARTNERSHIP
INTEREST   143

6.5   ALTERNATE RULE FOR DETERMINING BASIS OF
PARTNERSHIP INTEREST   143

6.6   BASIS OF PARTNERSHIP ASSETS AND BASIS OF
PARTNERSHIP INTERESTS FREQUENTLY RUN "IN SYNC"   144

6.7   DATES ON WHICH BASIS OF PARTNERSHIP INTEREST
MUST BE DETERMINED   146

6.8   LOST BASIS OF PARTNERSHIP INTEREST UPON
DISTRIBUTION   146

6.9   CHAPTER SIX IN RETROSPECT   147

CHAPTER SEVEN
Termination of a Partnership • 149

INTRODUCTION   151

7.1   STATUTORY PROVISIONS FOR TERMINATION   151

7.2   CONTINUATION OF A PARTNERSHIP UNDER THE
      INTERNAL REVENUE CODE   152

7.3   INCORPORATION OF A PARTNERSHIP   153

    7.3.1   Tax Implications of Incorporation – 153
    7.3.2   Arranging for Tax-Free Incorporation – 153
    7.3.3   Importance of Competent Legal Counsel for
            Incorporation – 154
    7.3.4   Methods of Transferring Assets in Incorporation of a
            Partnership – 154

7.4   DISPOSITION OF ASSETS AND LIABILITIES   154

    7.4.1   Dividing the Partnership's Business So That Former
            Partners Continue the Business as Sole Proprietors – 155
    7.4.2   Dividing the Partnership's Business So That One Partner
            May Retire and the Other Partner May Continue the
            Business – 157
    7.4.3   Dividing the Partnership's Business by Selling All or Part
            of the Assets – 158

7.5   AVOIDING UNWANTED TERMINATION OF A PARTNERSHIP 159

7.6   TAX HAZARDS OF TERMINATION OF A PARTNERSHIP   160

    7.6.1   Recapture of Investment Credit Upon Termination
            of a Partnership – 161

7.7   CHAPTER SEVEN SUMMARIZED   162

CHAPTER EIGHT
Branch Offices
Of Professional Partnerships • 165

INTRODUCTION   167

8.1   HOW BRANCH OFFICES ARE ACQUIRED   167

8.2   STAFFING BRANCH OFFICES   168

    8.2.1   Staffing Branch Offices of Large Firms – 168

8.2.2   Staffing Branch Offices of Small Firms – 169
8.2.3   Staffing with Recruits or Transferees – 169
8.2.4   The Pros and Cons of Rotation of Personnel – 170
8.2.5   Potential Personnel Problems of the Branch Office – 171
         A Case Study in Opening A Branch Office – 172

8.3   DEFECTIONS BY BRANCH OFFICE PERSONNEL   174

8.3.1   Prevention of Defection – 174
         A Case Study on Branch Partner Defection – 175

8.4   COMMUNICATION BETWEEN MAIN AND BRANCH OFFICES 176

8.4.1   The Vices of Written Communication – 176
8.4.2   Verbal Communication Must Supplement Written
         Communication – 177
8.4.3   The Engagement as a Communication Medium – 177
8.4.4   Illustration of the Engagement as a Mixer – 177
8.4.5   Seminars to Build Business and Cement Relations – 178
8.4.6   Introductions Are a Two-Way Street – 178

8.5   CONTROL OVER IMAGE AND QUALITY   179

8.5.1   Constant Vigilance Is Required – 179
8.5.2   Specific Controls Are Needed – 179

8.6   THE BRANCH OFFICE SYNDROME   180

8.6.1   Estrangement Strains Loyalty – 181
8.6.2   Prevention of Estrangement and Disloyalty – 181

8.7   DUPLICATION OF EXPENSES IN BRANCH OFFICES   182

8.8   CHAPTER EIGHT IN REVIEW   183

CHAPTER NINE
Management of the Partnership • 185

INTRODUCTION   187

9.1   DICTATORSHIP, OLIGARCHY, OR DEMOCRACY?   187

9.1.1   Dictatorship, Genesis of Many Partnerships – 187
9.1.2   Dominant Partner Resists Change – 187
9.1.3   Partnerships Spawn Oligarchies – 188
9.1.4   Partnership Democracy Is an Idle Fancy – 188

9.2   DISTINCTION BETWEEN THEORY AND REALITY IN
       MANAGEMENT OF A PARTNERSHIP   188

       9.2.1   How Partners Say They Want to Be Managed – 188
       9.2.2   What Partners Really Want from Management – 189
       9.2.3   Management Technique Recognizes Individual
                Capabilities – 189

9.3   MANAGING PARTNER OR ADMINISTRATIVE PARTNER   189

       9.3.1   Assigning Responsibility for Chores – 189
       9.3.2   Upgrading Routine Tasks Improves Performance – 190
       9.3.3   Upgrading the Payroll Function – 190
       9.3.4   Upgrading the Bookkeeping Function – 190
       9.3.5   Make a Clean Sweep for Profit – 191

9.4   THE MANAGING PARTNER   191

       9.4.1   How the Managing Partner Functions – 191
       9.4.2   Qualities of the Managing Partner – 192
       9.4.3   The Managing Partner Leads Toward Well-Defined
                Goals – 192
       9.4.4   Meetings as Goal-Setters – 192
       9.4.5   Individual Characteristics and Partnership Goals – 193
       9.4.6   Individual Goals Subordinated to Firm Goals – 194
       9.4.7   There Are No "Born Subordinators" – 195
       9.4.8   Partners Have Different Attitudes Towards Work – 195
       9.4.9   Management Must Recognize Productivity – 195

9.5   WHO SHOULD BE A MANAGING PARTNER?   196

       9.5.1   A Managing Partner Must Be a Good Administrator – 196
       9.5.2   Requisites of a Managing Partner – 196

9.6   ORGANIZATION BY FUNCTION   197

9.7   COMMUNICATIONS   197

       9.7.1   The Hazards of Lack of Communication – 197
       9.7.2   Communication Should Be Systematic – 198
       9.7.3   The Absorption of Communication – 198

9.8   RECONCILING CONFLICTING MOTIVES   198

       9.8.1   Partnership Motivators – 199
       9.8.2   Conflicts in Motivations – 199
       9.8.3   Resolution of Conflicts in Motivation – 200

9.9   PROVISION FOR SHIFTS IN RELATIVE POSITIONS OF
       PARTNERS   200

9.10 RECORD-KEEPING   202

    9.10.1   Records Which a Partnership Should Keep – 202
    9.10.2   Records and Partner Compensation – 203
    9.10.3   Records to Maximize Profitability – 204

9.11 SUMMARY OF CHAPTER NINE   216

CHAPTER TEN
Estate Planning and
Administration Aspects
Of a Partnership Interest • 217

INTRODUCTION   219

10.1 VALUATION OF A PARTNERSHIP INTEREST   219

    10.1.1   Valuing a Partnership Interest When There Is No
             Established Market – 219
    10.1.2   IRS Rules for Valuing an Interest in a Partnership – 220
    10.1.3   The Practical Aspects of Valuing a Partnership
             Interest – 220
    10.1.4   Value of Underlying Assets Alone Is Seldom
             Determinative of Value of a Partnership Interest – 221
    10.1.5   Income and Cash Flow Are Determinants of Value
             of a Partnership Interest – 221
    10.1.6   Economic Circumstances of the Partner Influence the
             Value of This Interest – 221
    10.1.7   Valuing an Interest in a Tax Shelter Partnership Presents
             Special Problems – 222
    10.1.8   Timing and Security Factors in Valuing a Partnership
             Interest – 222

10.2 PARTNERSHIP INCOME AS INCOME IN RESPECT OF A
      DECEDENT   223

    10.2.1   Income in Respect of a Decedent Is Taxed Twice – 223
    10.2.2   Double Taxation of Partnership Income – 224
    10.2.3   Reducing the Double Tax on Income in Respect of a
             Decedent – 225
    10.2.4   Tax-Saving Options Concerning Guaranteed Payments
             Are Available to a Partner – 225
    10.2.5   Payments for an Interest in the Partnership as Income
             in Respect of a Decedent – 226

10.3 GIFTS OF PARTNERSHIP INTERESTS   227

10.4 A WRAP-UP OF CHAPTER TEN   228

CHAPTER ELEVEN
Tax-Shelter Partnerships • 229

INTRODUCTION   231

11.1 WHY TAX SHELTERS ARE ATTRACTIVE   232

    11.1.1   Tax Savings Alone Are Not Enough – 232
    11.1.2   Who Can Benefit from Tax Shelters? – 233
    11.1.3   The Benefits of a Tax-Sheltered Investment – 233

11.2 COMPARISON OF THE LIMITED PARTNERSHIP WITH
     OTHER ARRANGEMENTS FOR ORGANIZING TAX
     SHELTERS   236

    11.2.1   Sole Proprietorships, General Partnerships, and
             Corporations Don't Quite Have It – 236
    11.2.2   Limited Partnerships Fill the Bill – 237
    11.2.3   Limitations on the Limited Partner – 237

11.3 HOW TAX SHELTERS ARE SOLD   237

    11.3.1   Tax Shelters Bring Money and Talent Together – 237
    11.3.2   Tax Shelters and the Securities Laws – 238
    11.3.3   The Prospectus of a Tax Shelter – 239
    11.3.4   Participation in a Tax Shelter May Draw IRS Fire – 239
    11.3.5   Buying Tax Shelters on the Easy Payment Plan – 240

11.4 ORGANIZATION AND OPERATION OF THE LIMITED
     PARTNERSHIP   240

    11.4.1   Limited Partners Are Excluded from Management – 240
    11.4.2   Characteristics of the General Partner – 241
    11.4.3   Compensation of the General Partner – 241
    11.4.4   How Costs Are Shared and Deductions Are Allocated in
             the Real Estate Partnership – 242
    11.4.5   How Costs Are Shared and Deductions Are Allocated in
             an Oil and Gas Drilling Program – 242
    11.4.6   Allocations Should Not Unduly Place General and
             Limited Partners in Adversary Roles – 243
    11.4.7   How Costs Are Shared and Deductions Are Allocated in
             an Oil and Gas Income Program – 244
    11.4.8   Sharing of Income and Cash Flow – 246
    11.4.9   The General Partner's Potential Conflict of Interest – 246
    11.4.10 The Limited Partners' Defense Against Conflicts of
             Interest – 247
    11.4.11 Prospectuses Disclose Conflicts of Interest – 247

11.5 LEVERAGE   248

11.6   ECONOMIC HAZARDS OF A LIMITED PARTNERSHIP   248

11.7   OTHER KINDS OF TAX-SHELTER LIMITED PARTNERSHIPS   249

11.8   CHAPTER ELEVEN REVIEWED   249

CHAPTER TWELVE

**Income Tax Aspects
Of a Tax-Shelter Partnership • 251**

INTRODUCTION   253

12.1   SAVING TAXES OR DEFERRING TAXES   254

   12.1.1   Deferring Taxes Has the Effect of an Interest-Free
               Government Loan – 254
   12.1.2   Use of a Partnership Increases the Size of the Government
               Loan and Has Other Advantages for a Lessor of
               Equipment – 256
   12.1.3   Equipment Leasing Invites IRS Attack – 258
   12.1.4   Saving Taxes by Changing the Form of Taxation – 258
   12.1.5   Economic Advantages of Real Estate Investment
               Complement the Tax Advantages – 260

12.2   PASS-THROUGH OF TAX ATTRIBUTES   261

   12.2.1   Partners' Distributive Share Items – 261
   12.2.2   Schedule K-1 Contains Other Information – 262
   12.2.3   Disclosure Reveals Adverse Features of a Tax Shelter – 262

12.3   WHAT TO DO WHEN THE PASS-THROUGH OF TAX
        ATTRIBUTES TURNS THE VENTURE INTO A NEGATIVE
        TAX SHELTER   264

12.4   AT-RISK RULES   265

   12.4.1   At-Risk Rules Prior to 1976 – 265
   12.4.2   1978 Changes in the At-Risk Rules – 265
   12.4.3   At-Risk Rules Can Have Delayed Effect – 266
   12.4.4   Other Effects of the At-Risk Rules – 266
   12.4.5   Real Estate and the At-Risk Rules – 267

12.5   PRE-OPENING EXPENSES   268

   12.5.1   Organization Expenses, but Not Syndication Expenses
               Are Amortizable – 268
   12.5.2   Construction Period Interest Is Capitalized and May
               Be Amortized – 269

12.5.3   Start-up Costs Are Capitalized and May Be Amortized – 270
12.5.4   Costs of Obtaining Financing Generally Are Capitalized
         and May Be Amortized – 270

12.6 A LIMITED PARTNERSHIP RISKS BEING TAXED AS AN
      ASSOCIATION   271

12.7 CHAPTER TWELVE SUMMARIZED   272

APPENDIX A

**Sample Partnership Agreement:
Professional Partnership • 275**

APPENDIX B

**Sample Partnership Agreement:
Nonprofessional General
Partnership • 285**

APPENDIX C

**Sample Partnership Agreement:
Agreement of Limited Partnership • 289**

Index   **297**

CHAPTER ONE

The Technical Points of View of Statute and Income Tax Law

CONTENTS

	INTRODUCTION	3
1.1	THE UNIFORM PARTNERSHIP ACT — THE STATUTORY VIEW	3
	1.1.1 Intent to Form a Partnership is Required – 3	
	1.1.2 Partnerships Are Organized to Make a Profit – 3	
	1.1.3 General and Limited Partnerships – 4	
	1.1.4 A Partnership Interest Is Personal Property – 4	
1.2	THE INTERNAL REVENUE CODE — THE TAX COLLECTOR'S VIEW	4
	1.2.1 The Internal Revenue Service Regulations Expand Upon the Code – 5	
	1.2.2 The Brevity of the Tax Law and Regulations Can Be Misleading – 5	
1.3	GENERAL PARTNERSHIPS IMPOSE UNLIMITED LIABILITY ON THEIR PARTNERS	5
	1.3.1 Evaluating the Risks of Unlimited Liability – 6	

1

1.4   LIMITED PARTNERSHIPS REQUIRE FORMALITY
        IN THEIR CREATION AND OPERATION   6

        1.4.1   Comparison of General and Limited Part-
                  nerships – 7

1.5   BENEFITS AND PITFALLS OF GENERAL AND
        LIMITED PARTNERSHIPS   8

1.6   THE PARTNERSHIP AS A MERE CONDUIT   9

        1.6.1   Dangers in Accepting the Conduit Concept
                  – 9

1.7   THE PARTNERSHIP AS AN ENTITY OR AS AN
        AGGREGATE OF PARTNERS   9

1.8   DISTINCTION BETWEEN PARTNERSHIPS,
        TENANCIES, AND INCOME-SHARING
        ARRANGEMENTS   10

        1.8.1   How to Reduce Uncertainty as to Status as a
                  Partnership, Tenancy or Other Arrange-
                  ments – 13
        1.8.2   Legal and Economic Considerations Carry
                  Weight – 13
        1.8.3   Advantages and Disadvantages of Partner-
                  ships Vs. Tenancies – 14
        1.8.4   Silent Partners – 13

1.9   A TAX TRAP — PENALTIES FOR FAILURE TO
        RECOGNIZE EXISTENCE OF A PARTNERSHIP   15

1.10   PARTNERSHIP RETURN FILING REQUIREMENTS   15

1.11   THE PARTNERSHIP, SEEMINGLY SIMPLE, IS
        COMPLEX   16

1.12   CHAPTER ONE IN SUMMARY   16

INTRODUCTION

The person who proposes that a business take the partnership form is immediately faced with an identity problem. Corporations are generally understood to have specific attributes conferred upon them by law. Everyone knows that a sole proprietorship is owner and manager embodied in one person. The public is less sure about a partnership. The term conjures up the image of the two guys who operate the neighborhood gas station, an unsophisticated sharing of the wealth and management in a situation where there is very little of either. To someone else, partnership brings to mind the highly structured, highly leveraged tax-sheltered oil well or shopping center venture. To others, a partnership is the three doctors who have banded together to share a receptionist, a nurse, and the work schedule so that a fellow can get an undisturbed night's sleep once in a while. All of these varied business units could operate effectively as partnerships and so could the vast majority of all American businesses; the flexibility of the partnership is one of its strongest points. In order to see the role of this much misunderstood entity, we start by precisely defining it from the technical points of view of statute law and of income tax law.

1.1 THE UNIFORM PARTNERSHIP ACT — THE STATUTORY VIEW

The statutory definition of a partnership is "an association of two or more persons to carry on as co-owners of a business for profit." "Persons" means more than human beings, natural persons. The term includes corporations, trusts, estates, government units and even other partnerships.

1.1.1 Intent to Form a Partnership Is Required

This association may be created by formal written agreement, or it may result from actions that cause the participants to appear to the public as partners. Taking title to property in a partnership name may be evidence of the existence of a partnership, whereas taking title as tenants in common clearly shows the lack of such an intention. The sharing of net profits indicates a partnership, but the sharing of gross receipts does not.

1.1.2 Partnerships Are Organized to Make a Profit

The intention to make a profit is a requisite for the creation of a partnership. There are nonprofit corporations and eleemosynary trusts that were designed to be that way; many partnerships turn out to be nonprofit ventures, but they were not and could not have been formed for that purpose.

3

1.1.3 General and Limited Partnerships

The statute provides for general partnerships, in which each partner is liable for all the actions and all the debts of the partnership even though he personally did not commit the acts or incur the debt, or even know of their existence. It also provides for limited partnerships, in which the general partner, or partners, have unlimited responsibility and in which limited partners are liable for financial loss only up to the amounts of their investments.

1.1.4 A Partnership Interest Is Personal Property

The Uniform Acts provide that an interest in either a general or limited partnership is personal property, even though the partnership's assets are substantially all real estate. The Internal Revenue Code takes the position that the portion of an individual partner's interest that is attributable to certain partnership non-capital assets (defined in IRC Section 751) is an ordinary asset; under Section 741, the remainder of the interest is a capital asset.

1.2 THE INTERNAL REVENUE CODE — THE TAX COLLECTOR'S VIEW

The Internal Revenue Code (IRC) covers partnerships in Subchapter K, which includes IRC Sections 701 through 761. Typically perverse, the Code waits until its last section to tell you how it defines a partnership, using these words:

> For purposes of this sub-title, the term "partnership" includes a syndicate, group, pool, joint venture or other unincorporated organization through or by means of which any business, financial operation or venture is carried on, and which is not, within the meaning of this title [subtitle], a corporation or a trust or estate. Under regulations, the Secretary or his delegate may, at the election of all the members of an unincorporated organization, exclude such organization from the application of all or parts of this sub-chapter, if it is availed of –
>
> (1) for investment purposes only and not for the active conduct of a business, or
>
> (2) for the joint production, extraction, or use of property, but not for the purpose of selling services or property produced or extracted if the income of the members of the organization may be adequately determined without the computation of partnership taxable income.

Though it hardly seems necessary, the IRC proceeds immediately to define a partner, using this untypically brief sentence, "For purposes of this sub-title, the term "partner" means a member of a partnership."

1.2.1 The Internal Revenue Service Regulations Expand Upon the Code

The Regulations (1.761.1(a)) contain helpful explanatory comment to help determine when a partnership exists, and include these words:

> (a) Partnership – The term "partnership" includes a syndicate, group, pool, joint venture, or other unincorporated organization through or by means of which any business, financial operation, or venture is carried on, and which is not a corporation or a trust or estate within the meaning of the Code. The term "partnership" is broader in scope than the common law meaning of partnership, and may include groups not commonly called partnerships. See section 7701(a) (2). See regulations under section 7701(a) (1), (2), and (3) for the description of those unincorporated organizations taxable as corporations or trusts. A joint undertaking merely to share expenses is not a partnership. For example, if two or more persons jointly construct a ditch merely to drain surface water from their properties, they are not partners. Mere co-ownership of property which is maintained, kept in repair, and rented or leased does not constitute a partnership. For example, if an individual owner, or tenants in common, of farm property lease it to a farmer for a cash rental or a share of the crops, they do not necessarily create a partnership thereby. Tenants in common, however, may be partners if they actively carry on a trade, business, financial operation, or venture and divide the profits thereof. For example, a partnership exists if co-owners of an apartment building lease space and in addition provide services to the occupants either directly or through an agent.

1.2.2 The Brevity of the Tax Law and Regulations Can Be Misleading

The entire federal tax law on partnerships, Subchapter K, is printed in the Prentice-Hall edition of the Internal Revenue Code in only 13 pages. The Prentice-Hall Federal Tax Service prints all the regulations on Sections 701 through 761 in slightly over 200 pages. This apparent brevity and the common misconception that a partnership is only a conduit for information can lead to expensive errors and lost opportunities; few practitioners have the familiarity they should have with the income taxation of partnerships, or, stated more correctly, the taxation of their partners.

1.3 GENERAL PARTNERSHIPS IMPOSE UNLIMITED LIABILITY ON THEIR PARTNERS

By far the most numerous partnerships are general partnerships. The principal distinguishing feature of a general partnership is that each partner is liable for the acts of the partnership. All partners are liable jointly and severally for wrongful acts or omissions of any partner acting in the ordinary course of business of the partnership or with the authority of his co-partners, and for a partner's or the partnership's breach of trust. "Breach of trust" includes receiving money or property of a third person and misapplying it. Partners are jointly liable for all other debts and obligations of the partnership. A person admitted as a partner into an existing partnership is liable for all the obligations of the partnership arising before his admission as though he had been a partner when such obligations were incurred, except that this liability shall be satisfied only out of partnership property.

1.3.1 Evaluating the Risks of Unlimited Liability

This broad liability of a general partner, which can hold him responsible for acts of which he does not even have knowledge and extends beyond his investment in the partnership, is frequently cited as the principal objection to doing business in the general partnership form. It is a danger that should not be taken lightly; an investor should never submit himself to the risks inherent in associating with others who might be lacking in mature judgment or the highest moral standards unless he is willing and has the time and the capability to be effective in monitoring and controlling acts performed in the name of the partnership. However, the many advantages of the partnership form of doing business should not be cast aside out of an unreasonable fear of personal liability. The successful businessman must exercise a high degree of caution in running his business, regardless of legal form. The prudent entrepreneur carries adequate insurance, regardless of the legal form by which he does business. When the question is raised as to how much insurance is enough, particularly for a professional, personal service or construction partnership, the answer is frequently found in another question: "How much can you get?"

1.4   LIMITED PARTNERSHIPS REQUIRE FORMALITY IN THEIR CREATION AND OPERATION

A limited partnership is defined in the Uniform Limited Partnership Act as "a partnership formed by two or more persons . . . having as members one or more general partners and one or more limited partners. The limited partners as such shall not be bound by the obligations of the partnership."

Whereas a general partnership may be based upon a written or a verbal agreement, a limited partnership may be formed only by the preparation of a certificate that shall be signed and sworn to and filed in such public record as state law requires. The requirements are specific:

"Two or more persons desiring to form a limited partnership shall:

    (a) Sign and swear to a certificate, which shall state –
        I. The name of the partnership,
        II. The character of the business,

III. The location of the principal place of business,

IV. The name and place of residence of each member; general and limited partners being respectively designated,

V. The term for which the partnership is to exist,

VI. The amount of cash and a description of and the agreed upon value of the other property contributed by each limited partner,

VII. The additional contributions, if any, agreed to be made by each limited partner and the times at which or events on the happening of which they shall be made,

VIII. The time, if agreed upon, when the contribution of each limited partner is to be returned,

IX. The share of the profits or the other compensation by way of income which each limited partner shall receive by reason of his contribution,

X. The right, if given, of a limited partner to substitute an assignee as contributor in his place, and the terms and conditions of the substitution,

XI. The right, if given, of the partners to admit additional limited partners,

XII. The right, if given, of one or more of the limited partners to priority over other limited partners, as to contributions or as to compensation by way of income, and the nature of such priority,

XIII. The right, if given, of the remaining general partner or partners to continue the business on the death, retirement or insanity of a general partner, and

XIV. The right, if given, of a limited partner to demand and receive property other than cash in return for his contribution."

1.4.1 Comparison of General and Limited Partnerships

A reading of the Uniform Limited Partnership Act will reveal these similarities with or differences from a general partnership:

A limited partnership may carry on any business that a partnership without limited partners may carry on;

A limited partner may not receive his partnership interest in exchange for services;

Generally, the surname of a limited partner may not appear in the name of the partnership and improperly including a limited partner's surname in the partnership may cause him to assume the liability of a general partner;

1.5 BENEFITS AND PITFALLS OF GENERAL AND LIMITED PARTNERSHIPS

	General Partnership	Limited Partnership
Exposure to Liability	Each partner has unlimited liability for all acts or omissions of the partnership or of its partners, employees, or others acting in its name.	General partners have unlimited liability for all acts or omissions of the partnership or of its partners, employees, or others acting in its name. The liability of a limited partner is limited to the amount of his investment.
Form of agreement required	None	Very specific provisions are required by the Uniform Limited Partnership Act.
Admission of partners	Requires consent of all partners; may be altered by agreement.	As specified in the agreement.
Death, retirement, or bankruptcy of a partner	Partnership terminates; may be altered by agreement.	Agreement may give the right to admit additional partners or to continue the business upon the death, retirement or insanity of a general partner.
Term of partnership	May be specified in agreement; for all practical purposes, unlimited life can be obtained.	Must be specified in the partnership agreement.
Name of partnership	No restriction on name, except as provided under ethics rules.	May not contain the surname of a limited partner unless it is also the surname of a general partner.
Income taxation	The partnership; as such, is not a taxable entity; income and deductions are passed through to the partners with losses limited to the basis of the partner's interest. Basis includes a partner's share of partnership liabilities as well as his capital investment.	Same as a general partnership; however, since the limited partner is responsible for partnership liabilities only up to a certain amount, his basis usually is lower than it would be if he were a general partner.

A limited partner who takes part in the control of the business may assume the liability of a general partner;

Upon dissolution of a limited partnership, limited partners have a prior claim to those of general partners;

The same person may be both a limited partner and a general partner.

1.6 THE PARTNERSHIP AS A MERE CONDUIT

The partnership is considered by many to be a mere conduit of tax information. This idea gets its roots from the opening sentence of the Internal Revenue Code's Subchapter on partnerships, Section 701, which provides

> a partnership as such shall not be subject to the income tax imposed in this chapter. Persons carrying on business as partners shall be liable for income tax only in their separate or individual capacities.

The Internal Revenue Service apparently condones the conduit concept. The author has filed amended individual income tax returns to correct information obtained from the Partnership Return of Income, Schedule K-1, when the income or credits originally reported on the Partnership Return of Income was found to be incorrect. Upon examination of the amended individual returns, the Service's representative, upon being asked if they would require filing an amended Partnership Return of Income replied "Don't bother; a partnership return is only an information return."

1.6.1 Dangers in Accepting the Conduit Concept

The "conduit" concept is a handy one, and most practitioners will hold to it to minimize useless paper work, as in the above example. It is, however, a dangerous concept. The partnership is an entity separate from its partners; many elections that are beneficial to the partners must be made only by the partnership, in some cases only upon the original, timely filed partnership return. The alert practitioner will be aware of the distinctions between partners and partnership and will not be lulled into a false sense of security by believing that any partnership filing error can be corrected at the level of the partner's return.

1.7 THE PARTNERSHIP AS AN ENTITY OR AS AN AGGREGATE OF PARTNERS

The tax law is ambivalent as to whether a partnership is an entity or an aggregation of partners. This ambivalence is expressed in Section 701 which says "a partnership as such shall not be subject to the income tax imposed in this chapter. Persons carrying on business as partners shall be liable for income tax only in their separate or individual capacities" and in Section 703(a) which says "The taxable income of a partnership shall be computed in the same manner as in the case of an individual" (with exceptions not germane to this discussion). Section 701 exemplifies the aggregate approach by clearly providing that the partners are the payers of any tax on partnership income. Section 703 then provides that an entity, the partnership, is responsible for determining partnership income. A quick glance at the U.S. Partnership Return of Income, Form 1065, Schedule K-1, shows that the following items may be omitted from the Page 1 computation of ordinary income (or loss) of the partnership, separately stated and carried directly to the partner's return: qualifying dividends, capital gains and losses, involuntary conversions, gains or losses from sales of land or depreciable property used in a trade or business, charitable contributions, and interest on investment debt. If appropriate, even gross receipts may have to be separately stated (so that a partner will know if he has enough gross income to be required to file a return).

Credits, such as investment or jobs credit, are allocated directly to the partners; since the partnership pays no income tax, it has no use itself for credits against the income tax.

The logic is easy to follow: the entity approach places responsibility in one place for management decisions (such as elections) and reporting requirements; the aggregate approach provides partners with ample information to properly report tax-favored items such as capital gains and dividends and to meet limitations such as those imposed by laws changing investment interest.

1.8 DISTINCTION BETWEEN PARTNERSHIPS, TENANCIES AND INCOME-SHARING ARRANGEMENTS

Partnerships are similar to other kinds of joint ownership or arrangements for the pooling of or sharing income.

The most common is joint ownership of property. The Uniform Partnership Act (Section 7) provides that joint tenancy, tenancy in common, tenancy by the entireties, joint property, common property or part ownership does not of itself establish a partnership, whether or not such co-owners do or do not share any profits made by the use of the property.

The Act goes on to provide that the sharing of gross receipts does not of itself establish a partnership, whether or not the persons sharing them have a joint or common right or interest in the property from which the returns are derived.

A profit-sharing arrangement with an employee does not make him a partner. Sharing of common expenses such as rent and the receptionist's salary does not make a partnership out of a group of people who find it advantageous to share office space.

IRS Regulation 1.761.1(a), quoted earlier in this chapter, mentions other examples of joint undertakings that are not partnerships for federal tax purposes. It refers specifically to an area likely to invite confusion, that of co-ownership of property when services are rendered. The key issue is how substantial the services are.

Illustration: Partnership or Expense-Sharing Arrangement in a Medical Practice

Heckle and Jekyll are specialists in internal medicine who are agreeable to sharing space, facilities, and staff, as well as taking turns in handling night and weekend calls. They have been unable to agree on any formula for sharing net income because Jekyll is more hard-nosed about accepting patients who are not comfortable with his rates, which are higher than Heckle wants to charge, and is more insistent on payment than Heckle, who, in his wife's opinion is a "softie" who is too easy on the patients financially. They accept as fact that all expenses should be borne equally.

They can solve their problem in any of three ways. They can operate two practices, with Heckle and Jekyll sending separate bills, recording receipts separately, and paying every expense with two checks, one from each doctor. This is a clerical nuisance, also involving two sets of payroll tax returns (with double the unemployment taxes, since each staff member's salary is at least twice the covered amount for state and federal unemployment taxes.)

Heckle and Jekyll can set up a partnership to pay expenses and each may reimburse the partnership to the penny for expenses. There is one employer, so the amount of check writing is minimized. The financial statements will always show neither profit nor loss. Is this a partnership? Possibly not. The Uniform Partnership Act, Section 6, defines a partnership as an association of two or more persons to carry on as co-owners a business for profit. This "business" will never make a profit, although the co-owners separately will profit from the efficiency of the arrangement. However, Section 16 of the UPA indicates that persons who hold themselves out to third parties as partners (to the landlord, the copying machine lessor) admit to the existence of a partnership. In the author's opinion, one would encounter no problem with state law in claiming that a partnership exists. Section 761 of the Internal Revenue Code defines a partnership as an "unincorporated organization through or by means of which any business, financial operation or venture is carried on, and which is not, within the meaning of this title, a corporation or a trust or an estate." The Regulations

1.761.1 clearly state that "a joint undertaking merely to share expenses is not a partnership." This forthright declaration is then clouded by an illustration of sharing expenses in a far less sophisticated venture and then goes on to indicate that the degree of activity (services rendered) is a determinant of the existence of a partnership. If this is the arrangement the doctors want, your author believes that they have sufficient support to file partnership tax returns, including payroll tax returns.

The third solution, and the preferred solution, is to draw a partnership agreement specifying that the net profits, to the extent that one doctor's net collections exceed the other doctor's net collections, shall be allocated to the high-receipts doctor and all other profits (or losses) shall be shared equally.

A choice of options should be made only after careful consideration of the legal liability resulting from one arrangement or another.

Illustration: Tenancy in Common or Partnership in Ownership of Real Estate

Fred and Joe own a duplex which is rented to unrelated tenants. The rent checks come to Fred, who makes the mortgage payments and handles matters such as occasionally finding new tenants and hiring and paying a plumber. Although Fred performs minimal services for their mutual benefit, they divide the cash flow equally. This is not a partnership.

The duplex works out well and Fred and Joe acquire several other properties. They find that tenants will pay higher rents if the landlords have the grass cut and provide maid service. Fred is willing to handle the extra work of administration and perform handyman chores for 10 percent of the gross rent. Since Fred retired from his job, he welcomes an excuse to get out of the house (and away from his wife with whom relations have become stormy). Fred and Joe create a partnership and transfer their undivided interests in the realty to the partnership. The degree of services rendered seems to qualify this venture as a partnership under IRC Section 761; holding the realty in partnership name and filing a partnership tax return should be enough to convince the Internal Revenue Service that a partnership exists. As a practical matter, the realty operation seems to be the same as it was before. There are these differences:

1. The partnership must make elections, such as methods of accounting and depreciation;
2. Fred, under prior law, could use the share of income which does not depend on profits to qualify for an individual retirement account;
3. Mrs. Fred may find the partnership interest to be out of her reach for dower purposes, and she may have lesser rights in his partnership interest than she had in his tenancy in real estate.

1.8.1 How to Reduce Uncertainty as to Status as a Partnership, Tenancy, or Other Arrangements

Although, as in so many areas in tax practice, some doubt may still remain, reasonable certainty as to classification as a partnership can be had by researching the question and making a decision based on the relevant cases. Generally, the IRS accepts the entity for what it purports to be; this may indicate acquiescence or it may indicate benign neglect of the issue. Since filing a partnership return is one of the indicia of the existence of a partnership, this frequently will clinch the case. On the other hand, if the joint venturers definitely do not want to be considered partners for tax purposes and can support their contention that they are not subject to the provisions of Subchapter K, they may file for exclusion from the application of all or part of Subchapter K by following the procedures set forth in Regulations 1.761-2.

1.8.2 Legal and Economic Considerations Carry Weight

Legal and economic considerations should have great weight in arriving at a decision to affirmatively create a partnership, when otherwise the co-ownership of property clearly would be a tenancy in common. Examples of such considerations are the ability to centralize management and decision-making, such as permitting a designated partner to buy, sell or mortgage property without the consent of all co-owners; and the partnership's ability to circumvent state laws concerning dower or curtesy rights and the rights of minors. Obviously, legal counsel should participate in the evaluation of such criteria.

1.8.4 Silent Partners

For various reasons, a person may enter into a joint venture with another with the intention of sharing in the profits but not wanting to be publicly identified with the business. For example, Moneybags, a general construction contractor, may want to participate in the profits of a building materials business selling to the construction trade. His contractor competitors would be unlikely to buy from the materials company if they knew that they were thereby enriching their competitor.

Since Moneybags must remain invisible, he cannot openly participate in management. A limited partnership seems appropriate, but to achieve the cloak of limited liability, a written agreement must be prepared and a copy filed with the state's Secretary of State and perhaps in the local Court house; such a filing would "blow his cover."

If Moneybags holds himself out to no one as a partner, he can probably avoid the liability of a general partner. However, if he confides the relation-

1.8.3 Advantages and Disadvantages of Partnerships Vs. Tenancies

	Partnership	Tenancies
Requirement for filing income tax return	A partnership must file Form 1065, except as provided in Revenue Procedure 81–11.	Tenancies require no return; usually a schedule showing the income and expenses of the tenancy and the allocation to each return is filed with the return of each tenant.
Legal nature of the interest	A partnership interest is always personal property.	A tenancy is an undivided interest in the property itself, and takes the nature of the property.
Valuation for estate or gift tax purposes	All factors affecting the valuation of the partnership, aside from the value of the underlying property, must be taken into consideration.	The value of the proportional interest in the property, probably reduced by lack of control by the joint tenant.
Management	May be managed by a managing partner or committee so that partners under a legal disability (underage, incompetence) do not present barriers to acts such as mortgaging or disposing of property.	Each tenant must be legally competent to transfer property or to incur obligations, or a legal representative must be authorized to act in his stead.
Inclusion in probate estate	All personal property, including partnership interests, is includible in the probate estate and accordingly is subject to the debts of the estate, including estate taxes.	Real estate generally passes outside the probate estate, directly to the heirs. Normally this causes the estate tax burden to fall on the residue of the probate estate.
Requirement for elections to allocate depreciation or gain or loss on sale	IRC Section 704(c)(3) provides that depreciation, depletion or gain or loss with respect to undivided interests in property contributed to a partnership shall be determined as though such undivided interests had not been contributed to the partnership. Election to adjust basis of partnership assets upon transfer of partnership interests must be made under IRC Section 754.	Each undivided interest is treated as if it were a separate parcel of property; tenants have no control over tax consequences of transactions as they relate to interests other than their own.

14

ship to anyone for business purposes, he would then be liable as a general partner at least to that third party—for instance, a bank that made loans on the basis of his participation in the business.

As long as Moneybags and his partner actually operate as a partnership and file a partnership return with the Internal Revenue Service, they should experience no tax problems solely because of Moneybags' reluctance to be identified publicly with the business.

As a practical matter, Moneybags and partner would be well advised to form a corporation and elect tax treatment under Subchapter S of the Internal Revenue Code, since a corporation can be formed with "dummy" incorporators and there is no requirement of public notice as to who are stockholders, directors, or officers of a corporation.

1.9   A TAX TRAP — PENALTIES FOR FAILURE TO RECOGNIZE EXISTENCE OF A PARTNERSHIP

Despite the uncertainty that may exist as to whether a joint venture is a partnership under the income tax definition, harsh results can occur if the decision is upset by the Internal Revenue Service. Taxpayers who report as co-owners and later are found to be partners can find that they have not made valid elections, because the election must be made by the partnership, not by the partners (Section 703(b)). These may include elections of accounting method, such as cash or accrual method, reserve method for charging off bad debts, depreciation methods, cost recovery methods, LIFO inventory, intangible drilling and development costs of oil and gas wells and deferral of recognition of gain on involuntary conversions. Subchapter K itself provides for elections that must be made by the partnership, under Section 709 to amortize organization and syndication fees; under Section 754 to elect optional adjustments to basis of partnership property; and under Section 195 to amortize start-up costs.

As will be pointed out in later chapters, certain flexible features of partnerships, such as those provided under Section 704 to specially allocate items of income and to allocate pre-contribution appreciation, and for guaranteed payments under Section 707, are available only to those ventures which establish to the satisfaction of the IRS that they are qualified to file returns as partnerships. Earlier filing as co-owners may make these privileges harder to come by in borderline cases.

1.10   PARTNERSHIP RETURN FILING REQUIREMENTS

Section 6031 of the Internal Revenue Code requires every partnership to file an annual income tax return, using forms and providing information that the Secretary of the Treasury may specify. Prior to 1978 there was no penalty for failure to file a partnership return. Absence of a penalty encouraged the relaxed attitude toward partnership returns referred to in 1.6.

Section 6698 was added to the Code in 1978 to impose penalties of $50 per partner per month for failure to file a return. Although the penalty can be waived for cause, a partnership that fails to file a return risks a stiff penalty under the Revenue Act of 1978.

By using Revenue Procedure 81-11, the Internal Revenue Service recognized that the penalties were too harsh for application to the smaller, simpler partnership. This procedure permits certain partnerships with ten or fewer partners to avoid penalty for failure to file returns provided that all of the partners have reported their shares of the income, deductions and credits of the partnership on their timely-filed income tax returns.

Considering that this saving provision does not apply to limited partnerships or to partnerships with corporate partners, and that all partners must have reported what a form K-1, if provided, would have shown, Revenue Procedure 81-11 should not be considered an invitation to forego filing partnership returns.

1.11   THE PARTNERSHIP, SEEMINGLY SIMPLE, IS COMPLEX

The typical tax practitioner sees the partnership as an aggregate of sole proprietors, filing an income tax return as a conduit for information. This is true only in the sense that the tax burden ultimately is borne by the proprietors. The practitioner who thinks of his partnership client as sort of an information system, devoid of separate tax personality, risks overlooking superb tax-planning opportunities. Its complexity, once understood, can be turned into a series of profitable planning opportunities.

1.12   CHAPTER ONE IN SUMMARY

A builder does not pick up hammer and saw until he has drawn plans, and he doesn't draw plans until he has studied the site. So it is with selecting or designing the structure of your business. Learn the statute and tax requirements of each potential form; these constitute the "building code" with which you must comply. There will be trade-offs; accepting a disadvantage to gain some desired advantage. Being forewarned is being forearmed; there are enough hazards in the business world without trusting to chance to set you up in the most effective arrangement.

CHAPTER TWO

When to Choose
The Partnership Form

CONTENTS

INTRODUCTION   19

2.1 ADVANTAGES AND DISADVANTAGES OF
PARTNERSHIPS COMPARED WITH
CORPORATIONS — NONTAX   19

     2.1.1   Limited Liability of Stockholders – 19

     2.1.2   Ease of Partnership Formation and Opera-
tion – 20

     2.1.3   Nontax Disadvantages of Partnerships – 20

     2.1.4   Transferability of Corporate Stock – 21

     2.1.5   Conclusions – 21

2.2 ADVANTAGES AND DISADVANTAGES OF
PARTNERSHIPS COMPARED WITH
CORPORATIONS — TAX   21

     2.2.1   The Partnerships Pays No Taxes and
Partners Have Discretion in Allocating
Taxability Among Themselves – 22

     2.2.2   Examples of How the Same Income Can
Produce Different Tax Results, Depending
on Whether It Is Earned by a Partnership or
by a Subchapter S Corporation – 23

17

2.2.3   Partnerships Are at a Disadvantage in Accumulating Earnings, in Retirement Plans, in Deducting Loss on Investment, and in Selecting a Business Year – 24

2.2.4   Comparison of Partnerships and Corporations – 25

2.3   FAMILY PARTNERSHIPS CAN SHIFT INCOME TO LOW-BRACKET FAMILY MEMBERS   32

2.3.1   IRS Weapons for Challenging the Family Partnership – 32

2.3.2   "Damn the IRS Torpedoes" — The Family Partnership Is Worth a Try – 33

2.3.3   Gift Tax Returns May Be Required – 33

2.3.4   Examples of How a Family Partnership Can Save Taxes – 33

2.4   PARTNERSHIPS TAXABLE AS ASSOCIATIONS   34

2.4.1   The Danger in Having Too Many Corporate Characteristics – 34

2.4.2   The Danger Lurks in Both Directions – 35

2.4.3   Conclusion – 36

2.5   CHAPTER TWO IN A NUTSHELL   36

INTRODUCTION

All too often a business is organized as a partnership or as a corporation with little more thought than goes into selecting the proper tie to wear with today's suit. Too often, the business drifts into a form through failure to think through the options or selects one form or another because of a predilection of an owner or attorney or accountant.

The form of business organization should be selected with at least as much care as the geographical location or the architectural style of the physical plant. In most cases, there are only two choices—partnership or corporation. There is then an additional choice of a decision to set up the corporation to make it eligible to elect partnership treatment under Subchapter S of the Internal Revenue Code. Both tax and nontax considerations should be given appropriate weight when choosing the form in which to carry on a business.

2.1 ADVANTAGES AND DISADVANTAGES OF PARTNERSHIPS COMPARED WITH CORPORATIONS — NONTAX

The nontax consideration of partnership versus corporation is easier because the differences are few.

2.1.1 Limited Liability of Stockholders

The most frequently cited advantage of the corporation over the partnership—limited legal liability for the corporate stockholder—has been covered in Chapter One under "General Partnerships." Although the corporation clearly wins this round when only theoretical considerations are given weight, a practical consideration of the facts will establish that the limited liability of the corporation is more imaginary than real. Bankers and other creditors aren't naive; they are aware that the shaky businessman will attempt to protect himself from personal liability by hiding behind the corporate veil. The unsophisticated think that bankers are in the business of lending money; bankers know that they are in the business of getting it back. For their self-preservation they require backers of small corporations to guarantee corporate debt. Creditors take similar steps to protect themselves. In dealing with construction contractors, customers and bonding companies frequently require more capital from a corporate contractor than they would require from a noncorporate contractor, and they may require endorsement. State licensing boards set fairly high minimum permanent capital for corporate contractors. Franchisors likewise take appropriate steps to be sure that they are dealing with something more substantial than a corporate shell.

Example of an Unintended Effect of Incorporation

Accountants who suggest incorporation to small clients who must furnish financial statements to state licensing boards, particularly licensing boards for contractors, may find themselves in an embarrassing bind when the client's net worth is founded on assets with substantial fair market value but low tax basis. The unincorporated builder may furnish a personal financial statement showing all his assets, whether used in the business or not, and licensing boards and insurance companies frequently accept personal financial statements prepared by the applicant or by his bookkeeper. Upon incorporation, a certified financial statement is frequently required, at least for the first application. The public accountant immediately comes face-to-face with generally accepted accounting principles which require that the assets be shown in financial statements at cost to the stockholder who contributed them, less depreciation allowed prior to contribution. If he ignores this rule, he must state that the financial statements are not prepared in accordance with generally accepted accounting principles; if he follows the rule, net worth per the financial statements may be inadequate for the needed bond or line of credit. This does not present a major problem, as the users of such statements will usually accept the statements, provided an explanation is furnished. The same question of the value at which assets are carried on the books and on financial statements would arise upon the formation of a partnership, but automatic reliance upon the financial strength of the partners would make the question less likely to be raised or easier to dispose of.

2.1.2 Ease of Partnership Formation and Operation

Advantages of the partnership over the corporation include ease of formation and operation. Although a written partnership agreement is advisable, there is no statutory requirement for one. Since the corporation is a creature of statutory origin and is subject to supervision by the state, it must have a charter and bylaws and must issue stock certificates and hold meetings. A close look at this so-called advantage of the partnership suggests that it is not an advantage. First, closely held corporations are frequently operated so loosely that they are, except for the name, indistinguishable from partnerships or sole proprietorships; second, almost every partnership would be improved by more formality in its creation and operation.

2.1.3 Nontax Disadvantages of Partnerships

Partnerships have nontax disadvantages when compared to corporations having other than unlimited liability of general partners. A corporation has unlimited life. Sections 31 and 32 of the Uniform Partnership Act list causes of dissolution of a partnership, including death, bankruptcy or incompetence of a partner. These misfortunes, the occurrence or timing of which cannot be predicted or controlled, do not cause the demise of a corporation. Involuntary dissolution of the partnership can be prevented by including appropriate provisions in the partnership agreement, so the lack of unlimited life by statute should not be a principal reason for deciding against operating in the partnership form.

2.1.4 Transferability of Corporate Stock

Shares of stock in a corporation are easier to transfer than are interests in a partnership. Easy transferability, coupled with the ability to issue various classes of stock, make the corporation a more useful tool for dividing ownership in a business that cannot be conveniently broken into smaller units. This corporate advantage assumes most importance in the estate planning area.

2.1.5 Conclusions

Almost every corporate advantage mentioned here can be achieved for the relatively inactive owner by making him a limited partner in a limited partnership. The subject of limited partnerships will be dealt with in a later chapter.

The author believes that there are certain high-risk businesses, such as transportation and manufacture of products with a high risk of injury or adverse side effects to users, in which nontax considerations mandate the corporate form. In most businesses, the nontax considerations, properly hedged, are not paramount factors in the decision to conduct the business in partnership or corporate form.

2.2 ADVANTAGES AND DISADVANTAGES OF PARTNERSHIPS COMPARED WITH CORPORATIONS — TAX

Whereas there may be few cases in which the partnership beats out the corporation when the score is based on nontax considerations, the partnership form clearly offers tax advantages which the corporation lacks and avoids many tax disadvantages inherent in the corporation. Perhaps the best evidence of congressional and public acceptance of the idea that the partnership "is the way to go" came to light when Congress added Subchapter S to the Internal Revenue Code to give certain corporations many of the tax advantages which partnerships already had.

2.2.1 The Partnership Pays No Taxes and Partners Have Discretion in Allocating Taxability Among Themselves

The primary tax advantage of a partnership is that the entity is never subject to income taxes. Thus, there can be no imposition of double taxation; once when earned by a corporation and again when distributed. Also, the favorably taxed income retains that status on the partner's returns.

Capital gains lose their identity when passed through as dividends by the regular corporation and are included in ordinary dividends. Even though municipal bond interest is not taxable income to the corporation, it is included in "earnings and profits," resulting in taxability to the shareholders of the regular corporation.

Partners can, within limitations, plan their own tax destinies. Subchapter K permits wide latitude in setting profit and loss sharing ratios, including changing them without a corresponding change in the level of investment. Depreciation and gain or loss on sale of contributed property may be allocated to the partner from whom the property was received.

Illustration

A business entity was formed on January 2, 19X0. In the year ended December 31, 19X1, its income is:

1. Net income operating a retail business $10,000
2. Interest income from New York City bonds   15,000
3. Long term gain on sale of New York City bonds   50,000

This illustration compares results in:

1. A partnership,
2. A corporation which elected in January, 19X1 to be taxed under Subchapter S of the Internal Revenue Code, and
3. A corporation which did not elect to be taxed under Subchapter S, each of which promptly distributes all of its income to its owners.

	Partnership	Subchapter S Corporation	Regular Corporation
Income			
Retail business	$10,000	$10,000	$10,000
New York City bonds	none	none	none
Capital gain (long-term)	50,000	50,000	50,000
Taxable income	none	25,000	60,000
Tax paid (1983 rates)	none	7,000	11,250
Income taxable to owners:			
Ordinary income	10,000	25,000	
Long-term capital gain	50,000	43,000	

The calculations are based on the fact that a Subchapter S corporation, which has had its election in effect for less than three years, pays tax on capital gains in excess of $25,000 at the alternate rate of 28 percent. The entire amount of the capital gain, reduced by the corporate tax thereon, is passed through to the shareholders. In this illustration, the tax to the Subchapter S corporation is based on $25,000 at 28 percent. The regular corporation pays tax on $60,000.

Basis of partnership assets may be adjusted to reflect increased (or decreased) basis of a partner's interest. A partnership has almost complete freedom to select ordinary income or capital gain treatment of payments to a retiring partner or to his estate. There can be no "thin capitalization" problems with a partnership and there is no limitation on the pass-through of charitable contribution deductions. Losses are passed through without limitation except for being limited by the amount of the partner's basis in his partnership interest. Since a general partner's basis includes his share of liabilities, there is seldom a practical limit. A disallowed partnership expense can increase the taxable income of a partnership and therefore of its partners; a disallowed corporate expense increases corporate taxable income and is frequently also taxed to the benefited stockholder as a constructive dividend. Accumulated income may be retained in the partnership without fear of a Section 531 tax on unreasonable accumulations. Funds for working capital may be invested or withdrawn at times appropriate to the needs of the partnership or partner without risk of dividend treatment or of the funds being locked in as contributions to corporate capital. A partnership can be liquidated without risk of the double taxation which only elections under Code Sections 333 or 337 can prevent in a corporate liquidation. A partnership cannot be subject to the 50 percent personal holding company tax, as corporations sometimes are.

2.2.2 Examples of How the Same Income Can Produce Different Tax Results, Depending on Whether It Is Earned by a Partnership or by a Subchapter S Corporation

Example 1: Long-term capital gain $10,000; ordinary loss $10,000. The partnership passes through $10,000 of long-term capital gain, which appears on the returns of the partners (all individuals) as $4,000 taxable income. The $10,000 ordinary loss appears on Schedules 1040E as $10,000 loss, for an effective reduction of taxable income of $6,000. On a Subchapter S return on Form 1120S the long-term capital gain would exactly offset the ordinary loss so that there would be zero effect on the income tax returns of the shareholders.

Example 2: Ordinary income $10,000; long-term capital loss $10,000. The partnership passes through $10,000 of ordinary income, fully taxable on the partners' returns, and $10,000 of long-term capital loss which offsets capital gains on the partners' return, reducing income which is only 40 percent taxable. This has the effect of increasing the partners' adjusted gross income by $6,000. The $10,000 ordinary income would be the only item appearing on Form 1120S; since a net capital loss is not deductible on a corporate return, the only benefit of the loss comes from a carryover to a future year.

Example 3: Long-term capital gain $10,000; ordinary loss $5,000. Using the same principles as in Example 1, the effect on the partners' taxable income is a reduction of $1,000. Since capital gain pass-through from a Subchapter S Corporation is limited to taxable income, $5,000 of long-term capital gain is passed through to the shareholders for an increase in taxable income of $2,000.

Note: for years beginning after 1982, these examples are not valid.

2.2.3 Partnerships Are at a Disadvantage in Accumulating Earnings, in Retirement Plans, in Deducting Loss on Investment and in Selecting a Business Year

Partners are at a disadvantage compared with stockholders in some situations. Since all income is taxable to the partners at rates appropriate to their income level, there is no opportunity to build up working capital at the low rates available to corporations with taxable incomes of under $50,000. Partnerships are limited to Keogh-type retirement plans which are generally niggardly when compared to the retirement plan deductions available to a corporation that has not elected to be taxed under Subchapter S. Other corporate fringe benefits such as medical reimbursement plans, stock options and deferred compensation are not available to partners. A sale of a partnership interest at a loss results in a capital loss, whereas Section 1244 gives ordinary loss treatment to many losses on disposition or worthlessness of corporate stock. At first glance, this seems like a corporate advantage. In practice, it is more an attempt to equalize a corporate disadvantage. If the corporation had been qualified under Subchapter S, the investor probably would have gotten an ordinary loss deduction arising from the business losses which caused the stock to decline in value. Therefore, Section 1244 is usually of greatest value to investors who did not take advantage of a Subchapter S election. In many cases, a partner would have gotten an ordinary loss deduction for the partnership losses that caused the drop in value of his partnership interest.

A new "regular" (Subchapter C) corporation can elect any tax year it chooses and can change to a different year (in some cases) by merely filing a timely return with the new closing date; almost all partnerships and Subchapter S corporations are limited to the calendar year.

2.2.4 Comparison of Partnerships and Corporations

Characteristic	Partnership	Subchapter S Corporation	Other Corporations
Ease of formation	No formality required (though a written partnership agreement is desirable).	Must be chartered by a state, have bylaws and minutes of meetings.	Same as Subchapter S corporations.
Limits of liability	General partners have joint and several personal liability for partnership obligations. The liability of a limited partner is limited to his investment in the partnership.	Limited to capital stock.	Same as Subchapter S corporations.
Duration of entity	Terminated upon death, bankruptcy or incompetence of a partner, though provisions of the partnership agreement may overcome this provision of the statute.	Charter is usually granted in perpetuity, and death or bankruptcy of stockholder has no effect on the life of the corporation.	Same as Subchapter S corporations.
Transferability of shares permissible number of participants	No person can become a member of the partnership without the consent of all partners. Provisions of the partnership agreement may modify this. There is no limit on the number of partners.	Shares are freely transferable, but the permissible number of shareholders is limited and only one class of stock may be issued.	Shares are freely transferable. There is no limit on number of stockholders. Various classes of stock may be issued.
Management responsibility of owners	All general partners share in responsibility for management. Limited partners may not participate in management.	Stockholders as such do not have management duties or responsibility. The board of directors, elected by stockholders perform the management functions.	Same as Subchapter S corporations.

2.2.4 Comparison of Partnerships and Corporations, continued

Characteristic	Partnership	Subchapter S Corporation	Other Corporations
Taxability of earnings	A partnership never pays income tax.	A Subchapter S corporation pays a tax only on certain capital gains (IRC Section 1378).	Pays tax on its taxable income
Election not to be taxed	None required.	Must be made in accordance with IRC Section 1327.	Not available.
Person upon whom tax is imposed	Partners	Shareholders, except for capital gains cited above.	Corporation.
Nature of income passed through	Capital gains and losses, charitable contributions, dividends eligible for exclusion, foreign taxes and ordinary income are passed through to the partners, separately stated.	Capital gains and losses, charitable contributions, dividends eligible for exclusion, foreign taxes and ordinary income are passed through to the shareholders, separately stated.	Capital gains and ordinary income taxable to the corporation.
Use of credits	Passed through to partners.	Passed through to shareholders.	Claimed by corporation.
Limitation on losses	Pass-through of losses, limited to partners' basis plus his share of liabilities of partnership.	Pass-through of ordinary losses limited to basis of shareholders' stock plus shareholders' loans to corporation.	Losses may be carried back for refund or forward to reduce future taxable income of corporation.

26

2.2.4 Comparison of Partnerships and Corporations, continued

Characteristic	Partnership	Subchapter S Corporation	Other Corporations
Limitation on charitable contribution deduction	No limit.	No limit.	10 percent of taxable income before contributions; excess may be carried forward.
Taxation of distributions	Generally not taxed, as income to be distributed is taxed when earned.	Generally not taxed, as income to be distributed is taxed when earned.	Dividends are taxed unless they are distributions not out of earnings and profits.
Personal Holding company tax	Not applicable.	Not applicable.	Undistributed personal holding company income taxed at rate of 50 percent.
Penalty tax on unreasonable accumulations of earnings	Not applicable.	Not applicable.	Earnings accumulated beyond the reasonable needs of the business are taxed at 27-½ percent or 38-½ percent.
Eligibility for qualified employee benefit plans	Eligible only for Keogh-type plans.	Deduction limited to 15 percent of compensation of shareholder-employees, up to a limit of $15,000. New dollar limits apply in years beginning after 1983.	Very high dollar limit on amount deductible for contribution for any employee, including shareholder-employees.

2.2.4 Comparison of Partnerships and Corporations, continued

Characteristic	Partnership	Subchapter S Corporation	Other Corporations
Other fringe benefits	Partners receive no fringe benefits such as group insurance or death benefit.	Shareholders holding more than 2 percent of the stock receive no fringe benefits such as group insurance or death benefit.	Stockholder-employees are eligible for benefits as are any other employees.
FICA tax	Applicable to salary and share of income, unless income is from rents or interest.	Not applicable to dividends or to distributions of previously taxed income.	Not applicable to dividends.
Exclusion of dividends received	Partners may exclude up to $100 of dividend income passed through partnership.	Shareholders may exclude up to $100 of dividend income passed through corporation.	Subject to exclusion up to $100 for each shareholder. Corporate shareholders may exclude up to 85 percent of dividends received.
Capital gains	Capital gains and Section 1231 gains retain their character when passed through to partners. Partnership can pass through an operating loss and a capital gain.	Capital gains and Section 1231 gains retain their character when passed through to shareholders. Corporation can pass through an operating loss and a capital gain.	Are taxed to the corporation. Alternate calculation may be used.

28

2.2.4 Comparison of Partnerships and Corporations, continued

Characteristic	Partnership	Subchapter S Corporation	Other Corporations
Tax-exempt income	Tax-exempt income is passed through to partners as tax-exempt income.	Tax-exempt income is passed through to shareholders as tax-exempt income.	Same as Subchapter S corporations.
Net operating losses	Operating losses pass through to each partner, limited to the basis of his partnership interest. The excess may be deducted in a later year when basis is restored.	Operating losses are passed through to shareholders up to the amount of the shareholder's basis. The excess may be deducted in a later year when basis is restored.	Net operating losses do not pass through to stockholders, but may be carried backward or forward.
Adjustment of basis of entity's assets upon change of ownership interest	Basis of assets may be stepped up for benefit of transferee partner with higher basis than transferor party.	Basis of corporate assets not affected by basis of stockholder interests.	Same as Subchapter S corporations.
Business in which engaged	Can engage in any business for profit.	Limited in amount of "passive" income which it may receive without forfeiting Subchapter S status if it has any "regular" corporation earnings and profits at the close of the taxable year.	May engage in any business.

29

22.4 Comparison of Partnerships and Corporations, continued

Characteristic	Partnership	Subchapter S Corporation	Other Corporations
Services in exchange for interest in business	Nontaxable if only an interest in profits is received. Taxable income from exchange of services for an interest in capital may be negated by allocating the deductions for the services to the partner performing the services.	Results in income to shareholder.	Results in income to shareholder.
Choice of taxable year	Must be same as that of principal partner(s).	Must be same as that of principal shareholders.	May end on last day of any month.
Person who must report income or losses	Partner reports income or loss for period for which he was a partner.	Shareholder reports income or loss for period which he was a shareholder.	Neither taxability of gains nor deductibility of losses is passed through to stockholders.
Liquidation	Limited tax consequences.	Similar to liquidation of other corporations but with less danger of double taxation.	May be very complex, with possibility of substantial dividend income and of double taxation on sale of assets which is part of liquidation process.

30

2.2.4 Comparison of Partnerships and Corporations, continued

Characteristic	Partnership	Subchapter S Corporation	Other Corporations
Effect of disallowance of expenses	Disallowed expenses increase partnership income.	Disallowed expenses which are held to benefit a stockholder are added to taxable income of corporation so as to increase taxable income spread among all stockholders.	Disallowed expenses which are held to benefit a stockholder increase taxable income of corporation and may also be added to taxable income of that stockholder as a constructive dividend.
Worthlessness of interest or sale of interest at a loss	Capital loss.	Capital loss unless deductible as ordinary loss under IRC Section 1244.	Same as Subchapter S corporations.

2.3   FAMILY PARTNERSHIPS CAN SHIFT INCOME TO LOW-BRACKET FAMILY MEMBERS

A favorite ploy in the old game of outwitting the tax collector is that of dividing income among family members so as to have some of it taxed to members in the lowest income tax brackets. The family partnership provides an apt arena in which this game can be played. Section 704(e)(1) of the Code invites participation when it says "a person shall be recognized as a partner for purposes of this subtitle if he owns a capital interest in a partnership in which capital is a material income-producing factor, whether or not such interest was derived by purchase or gift from any other person." Notice that there is no requirement that the partner render services, participate in management, or even have the capacity to do so; an infant (probably through a trustee) can be a bona fide partner. There is also no stipulation that capital must be the only income-producing factor. A farm, a hotel, or a retail store seem suited for operation by a family partnership, even though substantial management is required in addition to a material amount of capital. The temptation to siphon off too much of the father's income to the low-bracket returns of his offspring could become very tempting. As if reading the minds of taxpayers with avoidance in their hearts, the Code immediately goes on to say that the distributive share of the donee shall be includible in his gross income unless the share is determined without allowance of reasonable compensation for services rendered to the partnership by the donor. The Code also disallows allocation to the donee partner of a share of income which is proportionately greater than the share of the donor attributable to the donor's capital. To further narrow the opportunities for an unduly favorable transfer of taxable income, the Code tightens the rules by providing that a share purchased by one member of a family from another "shall be considered to be created by gift from the seller."

2.3.1   IRS Weapons for Challenging the Family Partnership

If tax avoidance is the primary motive for creating a family partnership, the defenses which the Regulations mount probably are too formidable to justify the effort. These defenses include a requirement that the property interests be genuinely vested in the donee and that the property interests be real; the mere right to participate in the profits of the partnership does not constitute a capital interest in the partnership. The donor must not have retained so much control that he may require retention of capital beyond the reasonable needs of the business to the detriment of the donee partner. The donee partner must have the right to withdraw his capital interest and should participate in the control and management of the business, including participation in major policy decisions. Except where a minor child is shown to be competent to manage his own property and to participate in the partnership activities, the minor's interest should be held by a fiduciary who is neither the donor nor a person who is amenable to the will of the donor. The child's share of partnership income should not be used to discharge the donor's obligation of support. There must be a written partnership agreement, the donee partner must be accepted as a partner by customers and creditors, and a partnership agreement naming all the partners must be filed.

2.3.2 "Damn the IRS Torpedoes" — The Family Partnership Is Worth a Try

Despite these restrictions, the family partnership can have good results. A husband-wife partnership can, in some states, split state taxable income. It can permit Individual Retirement Account or Keogh plan contributions for a spouse who otherwise might not be eligible. A family partnership can bring younger members of the family into the family business with a real sense of being part of the team. It can have estate planning benefits because an increase in value of the donee's interest in many cases would have resulted in an increase in the taxable estate of the donor if the partnership had not existed.

2.3.3 Gift Tax Returns May Be Required

Donation of a partnership interest, or donation of the cash or property to acquire or increase an interest may require the filing of gift tax returns.

2.3.4 Example of How a Family Partnership Can Save Taxes

Here is an example of how a family partnership can save income and estate taxes. A high-bracket father needs a building in which to conduct his business. He finds that a suitable facility can be purchased for $100,000, or can be rented for $15,000 per year, at which rent the tenant pays all operating expenses, such as repairs, utilities, insurance and property taxes. He gives his three children $18,000 which, along with the lease, is enough to support the acquisition of a $100,000 building with an $82,000 mortgage, in the name of a partnership including only the three children. If we assume $3,000 per year depreciation and $8,000 interest, the property produces $4,000 per year net income, which causes the children to pay little or no tax. Had the partnership not existed, the father would have had $4,000 more taxable income. Since the rent covers the mortgage payments, no further investment is needed by or for the children. Assuming that the building holds its value, eventually it will be worth $100,000 free and clear of mortgage, $100,000 which would have been in the father's estate if he had not set up a family partnership. *Warning*: The rent must be reasonable, the father's services to the partnership must not be such that a salary can be imputed to him, and the partnership earnings should not be used to fulfill his support obligation.

2.4 PARTNERSHIPS TAXABLE AS ASSOCIATIONS

IRC Section 7701(a)(3) says that the definition of a corporation includes "associations." An organization is classified as an association if it is more like a corporation than like a trust or partnership.

These factors must be considered in determining whether a partnership has so many corporate characteristics that it must be taxed as a corporation:

1. Associates;
2. An objective to carry on a business and divide the gains therefrom;
3. Continuity of life;
4. Centralization of management;
5. Liability for debts limited to property;
6. Free transferability of interests.

The above criteria obviously describe the associations of doctors, lawyers and other professionals, that are known as professional associations or professional corporations. Since such organizations are in fact corporations they have no need to be concerned about the potential tax trap of Section 7701(a)(3).

2.4.1 The Danger in Having Too Many Corporate Characteristics

Since the attractive features of partnership taxation appeal to those who would pool their resources in capital-intensive, frequently large ventures with others whom they do not know in the same sense that operating partners know each other, and since they have no intention of participating in operations or management, such investors and their advisors must be leary of obtaining too many corporate characteristics.

The danger, of course, is that the partners may find themselves retroactively classed as stockholders, with tax upon their withdrawals, reclassified as dividends, after a tax has been imposed at the level of the entity, now reclassified as a corporation. It is not inconceivable that such taxation could be imposed or threatened at a time when the entity's assets have been distributed and there are no funds to pay a tax or to fight an assessment.

Regulation 301.7701-2(a)(1) concedes that all partnerships and all corporations have the common characteristics of associates and an objective to carry on a business for profit. Therefore, these two characteristics are not considered in determining whether an entity has more corporate than noncorporate characteristics. That leaves the last four characteristics as the determinants of association status. An example under this Regulation says that a limited partnership that has centralized management and free transferability of interests but lacks continuity of life and limited liability (and if the limited partnership has no other characteristics that are significant in determining its classification), is not classified as an association.

Here follows another example under this Regulation. A group of twenty-five persons forms an organization for the purpose of engaging in real estate investment activities. Under their agreement, the organization is to have a life of twenty years, and under the applicable local law, no member has the power to dissolve the organization prior to the expiration of that period. The management of the organization is vested exclusively in an executive committee of five members elected by all the members, and under the applicable local law, no one acting without the authority of this committee has the power to bind the organization by his acts. Under the applicable local law, each member is personally liable for the obligations of the organization. Every member has the right to transfer his interest to a person who is not a member of the organization, but he must first advise the organization of the proposed transfer and give it the opportunity, by a vote of the majority, to purchase the interest at its fair market value. The organization has associates and an objective to carry on business and divide the gains therefrom. While the organization does not have the corporate characteristic of limited liability, it does have continuity of life, centralized management, and a modified form of free transferability of interests. The organization will be classified as an association for all purposes of the Internal Revenue Code.

These two examples illustrate the "numbers game" which one must play to avoid the "Association" trap. In the first example, the partnership had two characteristics and lacked two; since two isn't more than two, it passed the test. In the second example, the partnership had three corporate characteristics and lacked one; since three is more than one, it flunked.

2.4.2 The Danger Lurks in Both Directions

There is a danger that a partnership having more noncorporate characteristics than corporate characteristics could, by changing its structure or operating procedures, tip the scales the other way. This inadvertent conversion to an association is equivalent to incorporation; if the "incorporation" does not meet the tests of IRC Section 351, a taxable incorporation has occurred. Conversely, an entity operating as an association could lose enough corporate characteristics to be classified as a partnership. Such reclassification might be held to be a liquidation under Section 331, too late to elect the benefits of Section 333 or Section 337.

2.4.3 Conclusion

It seems clear that a general partnership organized under the Uniform Partnership Act has no fear of classification as an association because the partners do not have limited liability. A limited partnership with a corporate general partner having substantial assets (and therefore exposed to liability), or with a noncorporate general partner, is probably safe from classification as an association. The limited partnership that seeks to obtain many of the advantages normally accruing to the corporate form is well advised to seek a ruling to the effect that it will be taxed as a partnership.

2.5   CHAPTER TWO IN A NUTSHELL

The prospective investor and his advisors should know the choices of form available to them. They should weigh the tax and nontax characteristics of each legal form and select the one that comes closest to fulfilling their need. They should closely examine the resulting structure to be sure that it is sufficiently well planned to survive the hard knocks of prolonged operations; is flexible enough to change as circumstances change; and that its classification will not be successfully challenged by the tax authorities. In this quest for the best vehicle, they should avoid the temptation to incorporate because that's what everybody does, and they should avoid the delusion that a partnership is so simple that it requires no forethought. Think beyond the immediate present; what effect will your choice have on your estate planning, or the income pattern within the family five or ten years from now?

CHAPTER THREE

How to Organize
A Partnership

CONTENTS

INTRODUCTION 39

3.1 THE PARTNERSHIP AGREEMENT 39

3.2 THE TAXABLE YEAR 43

    3.2.1 Adoption of a Fiscal Year Can Defer Taxation Significantly – 43

    3.2.2 How to Get IRS Permission to Adopt a Fiscal Year – 43

    3.2.3 Reporting Requirements for the New Partnership – 44

3.3 RIGHTS, DUTIES AND RESPONSIBILITIES OF PARTNERS 44

    3.3.1 Duties and Responsibilities of a Partner – 44

    3.3.2 Rights of a Partner – 44

3.4 CAPITAL SOURCES 45

    3.4.1 The Combination of Cash and Property – 45

    3.4.2 Contribution of Encumbered Property – 46

3.5   PARTNERSHIP INTEREST PURCHASED WITH
       INFUSIONS OF PROPERTY   46

       3.5.1   Contribution of High-Value, Low-Basis
                Property Does Not Result in Immediately
                Taxable Income – 46
       3.5.2   Distinction Between Capital Account and
                Basis of Partnership Interest – 47
       3.5.3   Contribution of Mortgaged Property – 48
       3.5.4   The Tax Trap in Contribution of Mort-
                gaged Property – 49
       3.5.5   Special Allocation Rule for Contribution of
                Undivided Interests in Property – 50
       3.5.6   Depreciation and Credit Recapture – 52
       3.5.7   Holding Period of Contributed Property –
                52
       3.5.8   – How to Escape from the Tax Problems As-
                sociated with Contribution of Property – 52

3.6   PARTNERSHIP INTEREST ACQUIRED IN
       EXCHANGE FOR SERVICES   52

       3.6.1   The Tax Distinction Between Property and
                Services – 53
       3.6.2   A Solution to the Problem – 54
       3.6.3   The IRS Attacks Its Own Regulations – 54
       3.6.4   Avoiding Income from Contribution of
                Services Is Not Always Desirable – 54
       3.6.5   Conclusion – 55

3.7   ORGANIZATION EXPENSES AND SYNDICATION
       FEES   55

3.8   A REVIEW OF CHAPTER THREE   55

INTRODUCTION

All too often, people in business combine their resources with inadequate planning, if any planning at all. They believe that they have a common interest and fully expect that to be sufficient to insure a long and profitable relationship as partners. The spirit of the Three Musketeers, "all for one and one for all," pervades their thinking. In this honeymoon stage, problems of waning enthusiasm, increased capital needs, or even divorce are far away.

The U. S. Declaration of Independence may assert that all men are created equal, but it does not guarantee that they will remain equal as partners, despite the fact that so many partnerships start that way. The partner who brings in capital may start out as an equal partner with the fellow who has only his talent to share; the talented person will soon establish his own relationships, develop the ability to raise capital, and will be reluctant to continue to do all the work and get half the profit. Because of increasing age, decreasing inclination or failing health, one partner may fail to carry his share of the load. A partner who likes to live the good life now may want to draw out more of the profits than his future-oriented partner thinks proper.

No one can anticipate all of the problems that a business will face but it is prudent to plan for as many as you can and to assure the flexibility of the business so that it can change as circumstances change, without each required decision becoming the cause of a new battle.

3.1 THE PARTNERSHIP AGREEMENT

A written partnership agreement is essential. The draft should be prepared by the partners, because it should reflect their concept of what they want to do and how they want to do it. The agreement should then be reviewed or rewritten by an attorney, because laymen's language tends to be unclear. If an attorney prepares the document himself, he should do so only after listening carefully to the partners and drawing out their ideas, particularly regarding such potential trouble spots as future infusions of capital and those things we don't like to plan for, such as death, disability, retirement, withdrawal or expulsion of a partner.

Obviously, the agreement must give the partnership a name and a term of existence and must list the initial partners. Capital contribution required from each partner must be specified. If interest is to be paid on capital accounts, the rate and time of payment must be made clear.

The method of management, including provision for a managing partner and/or executive committee, must be stated. The accounting year to be followed and the method of accounting must be selected. Responsibility for accounting records and for filing of tax returns must be assigned. Dates and times of stated meetings and procedure for calling special meetings, as well as the method of allocating votes among the partners, must be included in the agreement. If any vote other than a simple majority is required, the percentage of votes necessary to carry a motion must be specified. If absentee or proxy voting is to be permitted, this should be provided for. If notice of special or major issues, such as admission of new partners or incurring of substantial debt, requires notice, the amount of notice and the method by which notice is to be given must be specified. A quorum should be defined, and if there are to be any restrictions on the right of any partner to vote (such as preventing the presiding partner from voting) it must be spelled out. A quorum should be specified.

As the Uniform Partnership Act says, the purpose of a partnership is to make a profit and divide it among the partners. Therefore, a formula for dividing profits and losses, including salaries, is necessary. Drawing accounts, partners' expenses to be paid by the partnership, and the times for distribution of profits (or recoupment of losses) must be covered.

The composition of the partnership will change, and the relative positions within the partnership will change. Provision should be made for admission of new partners, illness, disability, retirement and death of partners. The terms under which a partner may retire or withdraw or be expelled, and the conditions under which a leave of absence may be granted, should be in the agreement. The portion of normal compensation to be continued during an absence must be specified, as well as the method of compensating partners for time spent in activities that produce no billable time but that otherwise carry out the purpose of the partnership.

The proportion of a partner's time to be devoted to the partnership interests and any prohibitions against activities in competition with the partnership, or which are considered to be contrary to the best interests of the firm, must be described.

Because of the exposure to liability which falls on each partner in a general partnership, a partner should have the right to be informed of and object to any proposed partnership action that increases the risks to which the business is exposed. This could include acceptance of new clients, commencement of litigation, entering a new business or offering a new product.

The agreement must have provision for its amendment and for the dissolution of the partnership, and the distribution of partnership assets and liabilities upon dissolution or contraction. Disposition of client or patient files upon dissolution or upon the departure of a partner must be covered, as well as the requirement that the person obtaining custody of the files must provide for their security and must give former partners access to the files for proper purposes.

The price to be charged for an interest granted to a new partner, or the price to be paid to an outgoing partner, including terms of payment, is one of the most important areas to be covered.

There will be disputes and differences of opinion as to interpretation of even the most carefully written agreement. There should be provision for interpretation of ambiguous provisions and for arbitration of disputes.

Life insurance, the instant creator of an estate, should be considered to protect the partnership and its creditors from the untimely loss of a partner's contacts, services or capital. Insurance may be owned by the partnership, or the partners may "cross-own" the policies, an arrangement under which a partner has no equity (and no incidents of ownership) in the policy on his life. Life insurance premiums are not tax deductible even if the policies are carried for business purposes; the partnership agreement should specify how the premium burden shall be borne, how increases in cash value shall be allocated, and provide for the disposition of the policy if the insured partner leaves the firm before his death.

Disability insurance serves a similar purpose and raises the same questions as life insurance.

There should be a provision requiring a disabled or retired partner or the legal representative of the estate of a deceased partner to sell his or its interest at a specified price, and the provision must require the partnership to buy the interest at that price. Such a provision should be drafted so that the value of the interest will be clearly fixed for estate tax purposes.

Careful consideration should be given to the need for a covenant not to compete, in the case of a withdrawn or retired partner.

If the partnership will not fund its retirement plan, there should be a clear understanding of the obligations of a withdrawing partner who might, without such a provision, walk out on his obligations to disabled, retired, or deceased partners or partners who are nearing retirement age.

To organize your thoughts and to be sure you haven't overlooked anything, a partnership agreement drafting checklist is useful. Such a list includes:

1. Name and address of the partnership
2. Business of the partnership
3. Initial partners
4. Term and termination

5. Capital contribution from each partner
6. Management
7. Replacement of the general partner
8. Voting
9. Accounting and records
10. Fiscal year
11. Bank accounts
12. Special allocations
13. Partners' compensation
14. Guaranteed payments
15. Division of profit and loss
16. Interest on capital accounts, including unpaid capital accounts
17. Drawing accounts
18. Distribution of net cash flow
19. Leaves of absence
20. Expenses incurred by partners
21. Admission of partners
22. Limits on transfer of partnership interests
23. Withdrawal of partners
24. Determination and assessment of damages against withdrawing partner
25. Expulsion of partners
26. Retirement of partners
27. Requirement that retired partner exercise "best efforts" for partnership and refrain from competition
28. Disability, incompetence or bankruptcy of a partner
29. Payments to retired or deceased partners
30. Estate of deceased partner as a partner
31. Right to require adjustment of basis of partnership assets
32. Duties and powers of partners
33. Limitations on partners' powers
34. Prohibited acts
35. Review of reports and correspondence and acceptance of clients/patients
36. Life insurance

37. Notices
38. Arbitration
39. Amendments
40. Binding nature of the Agreement
41. Controlling Law

3.2 THE TAXABLE YEAR

A corporation or a trust or estate can select the calendar year or any fiscal year. This permits the selection of a natural business year; that is, a year that ends when inventories are lowest (and therefore easiest to count) or accounts receivable are lowest, or at a time when the office staff can most easily handle the extra work of year-end closing.

3.2.1 Adoption of a Fiscal Year Can Defer Taxation Significantly

Selection of a fiscal year ending early in the calendar year, for instance January 31, also permits the deferring of income reporting for as much as eleven months when taxability of the income passes through to the stockholders or beneficiaries. To prevent this obvious opportunity for recurring tax deferral, Congress inserted Section 706(b)(1) into the Internal Revenue Code. This states that "The taxable year of a partnership shall be determined as though the partnership were a taxpayer. A partnership may not change to, or adopt, a taxable year other than that of all its principal partners unless it establishes, to the satisfaction of the Secretary, a business purpose therefor." The Section goes on to define a principal partner as a partner having a 5 percent or greater interest in partnership profits or capital.

3.2.2 How to Get IRS Permission to Adopt a Fiscal Year

Regulation 1.706-1(b)(4) says that permission may be granted if a business purpose can be shown for adoption of a change to a fiscal year, and cites an example in which a partnership was permitted to select the fiscal year ending September 30 to make its tax year coincide with its natural business year.

Application for change to a different tax year is made on Form 1128, to be filed on or before the 15th day of the second calendar month following the close of the short taxable period. Application for adoption of a fiscal year for a newly formed partnership is made by using Form 1128, suitably modified. A copy of the Commissioner's approval must accompany the return for the year of change.

3.2.3 Reporting Requirements for the New Partnership

A newly formed partnership must file with its first return either:

1. A copy of the letter from the Commissioner approving the adoption of a partnership taxable year which is not the same as the taxable year of all its principal partners; or

2. A statement indicating that the taxable year it has adopted is the same as the taxable year of all its principal partners or that all its principal partners are concurrently changing to the taxable year it has adopted; or

3. A statement that all its principal partners are not on the same taxable year and that it is adopting a calendar year without prior approval.

The closing of the partnership's tax year, either upon the termination of the partnership or upon a change of partnership interests, will be discussed in Chapters Five and Seven.

3.3 RIGHTS, DUTIES AND RESPONSIBILITIES OF PARTNERS

The rights, duties and responsibilities of partners are specified in the Uniform Partnership Act.

3.3.1 Duties and Responsibilities of a Partner

The first obligation of a general partner is to realize the awesome responsibility that he carries. Every partner is an agent of the partnership for the purpose of its business, and the act of every partner binds the partnership, unless the partner so acting has no authority to act for the partnership in that particular matter, and the person with whom he is dealing has knowledge of the fact that he has no such authority. This agency includes the execution in the partnership name of any instrument for apparently carrying on in the usual way the business of the partnership of which he is a member.

A partner has a duty to share in the losses of the partnership. He has a duty to render true and full information on all things affecting the partnership to any partner or the legal representative of a deceased or disabled partner.

3.3.2 Rights of a Partner

A partner has a right to be repaid for his contributions to the capital of the partnership, as well as his advances, and to share in the profits and surplus remaining after all liabilities are paid. He is entitled to draw interest on his loans to the partnership and on any delinquent repayments of his capital account. He has a right to a voice in management. He has a right to prevent any person from being admitted to the partnership. He must have access to the books and has a right to an accounting. He has a right to use partnership property for partnership purposes, but has no other rights in the property. A partner has a right to obtain, upon cause shown, a winding up of the partnership's affairs. He has a right to damages from any of his partners who wrongfully cause the dissolution of the partnership, and to be protected against fraud committed by his partners.

3.4   CAPITAL SOURCES

A partnership may obtain its capital by investment of cash, by investment of property, and by investment of services, or any combination thereof.

3.4.1 The Combination of Cash and Property

This can be illustrated by the creation of a partnership to share equally in the profits from operating a newly formed business in which Allen, who has ideas and energy but empty pockets, enlists Babcock, who has equipment used in a business operated as a sole proprietorship, and Cannon, who has money and who believes that the three of them can get a good thing going. The equipment has been appraised at $10,000; they agree that it is worth $10,000 to have Allen put things together and agree to enter into copartnership. Cannon is willing to risk $10,000 in cash.

The partnership agreement has been drawn and an accountant is engaged to set up books for the partnership. The opening entry, as first drafted, looks like this:

	Debit	Credit
?	$10,000	
Equipment	10,000	
Cash	10,000	
Capital – Allen		$10,000
Capital – Babcock		10,000
Capital – Cannon		10,000

The accountant tries to replace the question mark with "Goodwill" or "Organization Expense" but discards them as inappropriate.

He rethinks the matter, and drafts this:

	Debit	Credit
Equipment	$10,000	
Cash	10,000	
Capital – Allen		$ 6,666
Capital – Babcock		6,667
Capital – Cannon		6,667

Cannon vetoes this entry, on the reasonable assertion that he put up 10,000 good dollars and expects to get back those $10,000 at some future date. Babcock takes a similar position, but his adamancy is shaken by the recollection that his equipment has been depreciated to a book value and tax basis of $5,000.

After a little research, the accountant concludes that the proper entry is:

	Debit	Credit
Equipment	$10,000	
Cash	10,000	
Capital – Babcock		$10,000
Capital – Cannon		10,000

The explanation lies in the fact that the entry is intended to record shares of partnership *capital*, and Allen receives only a share in partnership *profits*. There is an important difference, as explained later in this chapter.

3.4.2 Contribution of Encumbered Property

If property encumbered by a mortgage or with a tax basis different from the value at which it will be placed on the partnership books is involved, the problems mentioned in "Partnership Interest Purchased With Infusions of Property," later in this chapter, should be dealt with in the partnership agreement. IRC Section 704 should be consulted for guidance in drafting appropriate provisions.

3.5 PARTNERSHIP INTEREST PURCHASED WITH INFUSIONS OF PROPERTY

3.5.1 Contribution of High-Value, Low-Basis Property Does Not Result in Immediately Taxable Income

Even though the books are in balance with the entry shown in the preceding section, the accountant is uncomfortable with it because he knows that he cannot take tax deductions for more than the $5,000 remaining tax basis of the equipment which he has just placed on the books at

$10,000. Is the answer that Babcock must recognize $5,000 worth of income immediately, all taxable as ordinary income under Internal Revenue Code Section 1245, so as to restore a depreciable basis of $10,000? Babcock declines to agree with that.

The correct answer is found in Internal Revenue Code Section 721, which, with uncharacteristic brevity, says:

> No gain or loss shall be recognized to a partnership or to any of its partners in the case of a contribution to the partnership in exchange for an interest in the partnership.

Since no gain is recognized, the recapture provisions of Section 1245 do not enter the picture.

3.5.2 Distinction Between Capital Account and Basis of Partnership Interest

At this point, a distinction must be made between the tax basis of a partnership interest and the capital account as it appears on the partnership's books. Although the difference will be discussed in more detail in a later chapter, it should be pointed out here that capital accounts on the books start out with an agreed-upon figure and are increased by profits and by additional contributions to capital and are decreased by losses and by distributions and can be less than zero. Basis of an interest in a partnership starts out, as provided in IRC Section 722, as the amount of money contributed plus the adjusted basis of contributed property increased by the amount of any gain recognized to the contributing partner. Section 705 provides for changes in the basis of a partnership interest in these words:

> General Rule – The adjusted basis of a partner's interest in a partnership shall, except as provided in subsection (b), be the basis of such interest determined under section 722 (relating to contributions to a partnership) or section 742 (relating to transfers of partnership interests) –
>
> (1) Increased by the sum of his distributive share for the taxable year and prior taxable years of –
>
> (A) taxable income of the partnership as determined under section 703(a),
>
> (B) income of the partnership exempt from tax under this title, and
>
> (C) the excess of the deductions for depletion over the basis of the property subject to depletion;
>
> (2) Decreased (but not below zero) by distributions by the partnership as provided in section 733 and by the sum of his distributive share for the taxable year and prior taxable years of –
>
> (A) losses of the partnership, and

(B) expenditures of the partnership not deductible in computing its taxable income and not properly chargeable to capital account; and

(3) Decreased (but not below zero), by the amount of the partner's deduction for depletion under section 611 with respect to oil and gas wells.

If the Code's definition of basis stopped there, there would be no practical difference between capital account and tax basis of the partnership interest. However, Section 752 introduces what could be the most significant distinction between partnership and corporation taxation when it permits basis to be increased by increases in the partner's share of partnership liabilities and decreased by decreases in the partner's share of partnership liabilities.

Getting back to the example, the basis of Babcock's interest is $5,000. IRC Section 723 provides that the basis of property contributed to a partnership by a partner shall be the adjusted basis of the property increased by the amount (if any) of gain recognized to the contributing partner. Since no gain is recognized to Babcock, the partnership, assuming a 10-year life with calculation on the straight-line method, will book an annual depreciation expense of $1,000 and claim an annual tax deduction of only $500. Cannon, having contributed $10,000 in money for a $10,000 interest, will feel that his pockets have been picked when he finds that the partnership income taxable to him will be higher than it would have been if Babcock's $10,000 equipment had had the same tax basis as Cannon's cash, a feeling which Allen may share. It may dawn on them that a sale of the equipment at its fair market value will produce a gain, taxable under IRC Section 1231, a gain that may result in each of them paying more tax than if the equipment's basis had been $10,000. Section 704(c)(2) offers at least a partial palliative by permitting the partnership to alleviate some of its outrage by allocating all of the depreciation to the "innocent" partners, Allen and Cannon, or allocating all of the gain on sale to Babcock, whose sin of having inadequate basis caused all the trouble. A truly creative accountant might conclude that he could take $1,000 depreciation on the tax return, making up the difference by crediting Babcock with $500 additional taxable income. That idea won't work; allocable depreciation in this instance is limited to $500. If divided equally between Allen and Cannon, each gets a deduction for $250, less than the $333.33 deduction each might have expected.

3.5.3 Contribution of Mortgaged Property

The foregoing example covers contributed property unencumbered by debt. To illustrate the effect of assumed debt, we shall have another partnership formed, in which Ajax puts in $5,000 cash and Bojangles puts in machinery with fair market value and tax basis of $10,000, encumbered by a chattel mortgage with a balance of $5,000. The opening entry is:

	Debit	Credit
Cash	$ 5,000	
Equipment	10,000	
Chattel·mortgage		$5,000
Capital – Ajax		5,000
Capital – Bojangles		5,000

There is no depreciation problem here, since fair market value and tax basis are the same. However, the partners might be surprised at the tax bases of their partnership interests. Section 752, to which we referred in a preceding paragraph, says that any increase in a partner's individual liabilities by assumption of partnership liabilities is treated as if that partner had contributed money to the partnership, and any decrease in a partner's individual liabilities by reason of the assumption by the partnership of such individual liabilities shall be considered as a distribution of money to the partner by the partnership. Put into numbers, Ajax, by assuming one-half of the $5,000 debt and investing $5,000 cash, has acquired a tax basis for his partnership interest of $7,500. Bojangles, who had a tax basis of $10,000 in the contributed property, has his basis reduced to $7,500. This does, however, illustrate again the basic difference between capital accounts and bases of partnership interest; capital accounts total $10,000 and basis totals $15,000.

3.5.4 The Tax Trap in Contribution of Mortgaged Property

IRC Section 752(b) says that "any decrease in a partner's individual liabilities by reason of the assumption by the partnership of such individual liabilities shall be considered as a distribution of money to the partner by the partnership." The constructive receipt of money reduces the partner's basis in the contributed property; if the mortgage exceeds the basis, the partner will be deemed to have a taxable gain from the sale or exchange of a partnership interest. The Regulations furnish this example:

A contributes property with a basis to him of $1,000 to equal partnership AB. The property is subject to a mortgage of $2,500 and its value exceeds $2,500. Under paragraph (b) of this section, A will be treated as receiving a distribution in money of $1,250, one-half of the liability of $2,500 assumed by the partnership. Since the basis of A's partnership interest is $1,000 (the basis of the property contributed by him), the distribution to him of $1,250 results in his realizing a capital gain of $250 under Section 731(a). A's basis for his partnership interest is zero. Although as a partner A has a $1,250 share of the $2,500 partnership liability, this $1,250 is not added to the basis of A's partnership interest since it does not represent an increase in liabilities as to him.

3.5.5 Special Allocation Rule for Contribution of Undivided Interests in Property

IRC Section 704(c)(3) says "If the partnership agreement does not provide otherwise, depreciation, depletion, or gain or loss with respect to undivided interests in property contributed to a partnership shall be determined as though such undivided interest had not been contributed to the partnership. This paragraph shall apply only if all the partners had undivided interest in such property prior to contribution and their interests in the capital and profits of the partnership correspond with such undivided interests."

Regulation 1.704(1)(c)(3) offers three helpful examples of how this works:

> Example (1). A and B are tenants in common owning undivided one-half interests in improved real estate consisting of land on which a factory is situated. They each contribute their respective undivided interests in the real estate to a partnership in which the profits are to be divided equally and, because the partners have equal shares in the capital, the assets will be divided equally on dissolution. A's basis for his undivided one-half interest is $4,000, of which $1,000 is allocable to the land and $3,000 to the factory. B's basis for his undivided one-half interest is $10,000 of which $3,000 is allocable to the land and $7,000 to the factory. The partnership agreement contains no provisions as to the allocation of depreciation or gain or loss on disposition of the property by the partnership. The factory depreciates at a rate of 5 percent a year. The annual partnership allowance for depreciation of $500 (5 percent of $10,000) will be allocated between the partners by allowing A a deduction of $150 (5 percent of $3,000, his basis for his undivided interest in the factory, and by allowing B a deduction of $350 (5 percent of $7,000, his basis for his undivided interest in the factory). At the end of the first year of partnership operation, A's adjusted basis for his undivided interest in the factory is $2,850 ($3,000 less $150), and B's adjusted basis is $6,650 ($7,000 less $350).

> Example (2). If, in example (1) of this subdivision, the partnership at the end of the first year's operation sells the factory and land for $12,000, each partner's share of the gain or loss would be determined as follows: Since the undivided interests in the factory and the land are to be treated as though held by the partners outside the partnership, A's share of the proceeds of the sale is $6,000. His adjusted basis in the contributed property is $3,850 ($1,000 for the land and $2,850 for the factory). Therefore, his gain from the sale is $2,150. Since B's share of the proceeds is also $6,000, and his adjusted basis in the contributed property is $9,650 ($3,000 for the land and $6,650 for the factory), his loss is $3,650.

Example (3). Assume the same facts as in examples (1) and (2) of this subdivision, except that A and B do not enter into a partnership agreement. Assume further that they are found to be a partnership for income tax purposes because of their joint business activity, but that the factory and the land are not actually contributed by them to the partnership. Although A and B have permitted the partnership to use such properties, they continue to own the factory and the land in their individual capacities (as tenants in common), and the same tax consequences result as in examples (1) and (2) of this subdivision.

Partners, having taken advantage of the special provisions of Section 704(c)(3), should recognize that it is effective only as long as there is no change in the relative shares of capital and profits. Unless the partnership agreement specifically provides that the allocation provided by Section 704 (c)(3) is to be continued, then the depreciation, depletion and gain or loss upon disposition of property contributed as undivided interests henceforth will be allocated according to the ratios currently in effect. Again, the same regulations illustrate how the income and expenses may continue to be allocated in the same manner as prior to the change:

Example (1). C and D are tenants in common, each owning an undivided one-half interest in certain unimproved land. Each contributes his respective undivided interest in the land to a partnership in which each has an equal interest in capital and profits. C's basis for his one-half interest is $4,000; D's basis is $10,000. The fair market value of the land is $20,000. Subsequently, C contributes $5,000 cash to his share of partnership capital. As a result of C's additional contribution, he now has a 60-percent interest in partnership capital and D, a 40-percent interest, although profits and losses still are to be shared equally. Since the interests of the partners in the capital and profits of the partnership no longer correspond to their undivided interests in the land, the method of allocation prescribed by Section 704(c)(3) no longer applies. Therefore, if the land is sold for $12,000, the partnership will have a loss of $2,000 ($14,000 partnership basis minus $12,000). Since the partnership agreement contains no special allocation for gain or loss with respect to contributed property, the $2,000 loss is allocated as if such property had been purchased by the partnership, i.e. $1,000 to each partner.

Example (2). Assume in example (1) of this subdivision that the partners agree that, because of C's additional contribution of $5,000 cash, he is to have a 60-percent interest in partnership capital. Profits and losses still are to be shared equally, except that gain or loss with respect to the land is, under Section 704(c)(2), to continue to be allocated in the same manner as it had been allocated under Section 704(c)(3) prior to the additional contribution. The land is sold for $12,000. C's share of the proceeds is $6,000. His basis for the land is $4,000. Therefore, he has a $2,000 gain. D's loss is $4,000 ($10,000 basis less $6,000 proceeds).

3.5.6 Depreciation and Credit Recapture

Property contributed to a partnership continues to bear any stigma placed upon it when it was owned by the contributing partner, such as vulnerability to depreciation recapture under IRC Sections 1245 and 1250 and to investment credit recapture.

A premature disposition of property on which investment credit has been claimed usually results in a recapture of all of the credit that has not been earned. This principle can apply to the contribution of Section 38 property to a partnership. If the entire business of the partner is contributed and the partner acquires a substantial interest in the partnership, IRC Section 47(b) seems to offer protection from recapture.

3.5.7 Holding Period of Contributed Property

Since IRC Section 721 provides for nonrecognition of gain or loss upon contribution of property to a partnership in exchange for an interest in the partnership, IRC Section 1223 adds the holding period of the partner to the holding period of the partnership to determine if any gain or loss upon disposition of the property by the partnership is long-term or short-term.

3.5.8 How to Escape from the Tax Problems Associated with Contribution of Property

The prospective partner and his advisors must be aware of the potential tax problems of contributing property to a partnership. Recognized in time, the problems can be dealt with without unreasonable complexity or adverse consequences. The problem of fair market value exceeding tax basis can be resolved by having the person who would have contributed the property sell it instead, contribute the cash and then have the partnership buy the property, at its fair market value, from the purchaser.

This technique results in taxation to the seller, in many cases at ordinary income tax rates, and the nuisance of two possibly simultaneous sales. There may be cases where the sale-purchase should be used, as when the seller has low income otherwise, or has a capital or operating loss carryover to the year of sale. The problem of property encumbered by debt can be resolved by getting rid of the debt, either by payment or by having the contributing partner substitute other collateral.

3.6   PARTNERSHIP INTEREST ACQUIRED IN EXCHANGE FOR SERVICES

Services rendered in the past, including those rendered in the organization of the partnership, or to be rendered in the future, can be the consideration for receipt of a partnership interest in a general partnership. The Uniform Limited Partnership Act prohibits granting a limited partnership interest in exchange for services. The first illustration in "Capital Sources" has Allen contributing only services and receiving a $10,000 interest in the partnership. After doing a little research, we concluded that the intention was to give him an interest in profits only. Whereas he will share equally in profits and losses, he has no capital subject to withdrawal or on which interest will be paid, if the partnership agreement provides for interest on capital accounts. This decision was based partly on the logic that Allen had put no money or property into the partnership, and has nothing to draw out until the existence of profits establishes that his services really have value. Another reason for the decision to limit Allen's interest to an interest in profits is the tax effect of allocating a capital interest to him.

3.6.1 The Tax Distinction Between Property and Services

When we discussed acquiring a partnership interest in exchange for property, we found that such an exchange is nontaxable because IRC Section 721 says that no gain or loss is recognized upon the receipt of a partnership interest in exchange for the contribution of property. Services, however, are not property and therefore do not fall under the protection of Section 721.

If Allen had received a capital interest of $6,667 (one-third of total capital of $10,000 cash and $10,000 equipment) there is very little doubt that he would have had income of $6,667 taxable as compensation. IRS Regulation 1.721-1(b)(1) is the authority for this conclusion when it says:

> Normally, under local law, each partner is entitled to be repaid his contributions of money or other property to the partnership (at the value placed upon such property by the partnership at the time of the contribution) whether made at the formation of the partnership or subsequent thereto. To the extent that any of the partners gives up any part of his right to be repaid his contributions (as distinguished from a share in partnership profits) in favor of another partner as compensation for services (or in satisfaction of an obligation), section 721 does not apply. The value of an interest in such partnership capital so transferred to a partner as compensation for services constitutes income to the partner under section 61. The amount of such income is the fair market value of the interest in capital so transferred, either at the time the transfer is made for past services, or at the time the services have been rendered where the transfer is conditioned on the completion of the transferee's future services. The time when such income is realized depends on all the facts and circumstances, including any substantial restrictions or conditions on the compensated partner's right to withdraw or otherwise dispose of such interest. To the extent that an interest in capital representing compensation for services rendered by the dece-

dent prior to his death is transferred after his death to the decedent's successor in interest, the fair market value of such interest is income in respect of a decedent under section 691.

3.6.2 A Solution to the Problem

IRS Regulation 1.721-1 (b) (2) immediately provides at least a partial solution to the problem of receipt of a partnership interest in exchange for services constituting ordinary income to the recipient of the interest when it says "To the extent that the value of such interest is: (1) compensation for services rendered to the partnership, it is a guaranteed payment for services under Section 707(c)." Since the partnership gets a deduction of $6,667, Allen's income from the partnership is reduced by $2,222 because of his own services, leaving him with net income for his services of $4,445. Under IRC Section 704(b), the deduction for the guaranteed payment could be allocated entirely to Allen, giving him salary income equal to the reduction in his share of profits (or increase in his share of loss) creating a washout.

·   If the services rendered by Allen are of such a nature that they must be capitalized, he has salary income but the partnership does not have an immediate deduction.

Assuming that the property in our example had a tax basis of $5,000, the receipt of a $3,333 interest by Allen in property with a tax basis of $1,667 might be held to have resulted in a taxable gain to the partnership of $1,666.

3.6.3 The IRS Attacks Its Own Regulations

Despite the language of the Regulations cited above, the Internal Revenue Service has successfully contended that receipt of an interest in *profits only* gives rise to taxable income. Why the Service would take a position contrary to its own Regulations is not hard to see. A partnership interest is a capital asset (except for the provisions of IRC Section 751, discussed in a later chapter). This was especially true before 1977, when the holding period necessary for long-term capital gain treatment was only six months; there were obvious advantages to being paid for services with a partnership interest followed by a sale of the interest.

3.6.4 Avoiding Income from Contribution of Services Is Not Always Desirable

There may be situations in which a person wants to have receipt of a partnership interest in exchange for services and receive currently taxable income. Income so created could be brought into taxable income in a year when the new partner otherwise had low income or an operating loss carryover, or when the normal loss pass-through from the partnership could be used against the compensation for services to the partner to good tax advantage.

3.6.5 Conclusion

The problems arising from receipt of a partnership interest in exchange for services seldom are such that they cannot be prevented or mitigated by timely planning. This is an area where being forewarned is being forearmed.

3.7 ORGANIZATION EXPENSES AND SYNDICATION FEES

Prior to 1977, a partnership could neither deduct organization expenses, nor could it elect to amortize them, as IRC Section 248 has permitted corporations to do since 1954.

Section 709 denies to a partnership or to its partners the right to deduct any amounts paid or incurred to organize a partnership or to promote the sale of an interest in a partnership. However, the Section goes on to permit the partnership to treat organization expenses as deferred expenses, to be allowed as a deduction ratably over such period of not less than 60 months as may be selected by the partnership. The deduction, if elected, begins with the month in which the partnership begins business. If the partnership is liquidated before the end of the amortization period, the unamortized portion may be deducted as a loss under IRC Section 165.

To be deductible under Section 709, the organizational expenses must be incidental to the creation of the partnership, be chargeable to capital account, and be of a character which, if expended incident to the creation of a partnership having an ascertainable life, would be amortized over such life.

Expenses of selling partnership interests must be capitalized and are not deductible under Section 709. Such expenses include commissions, professional fees and printing costs.

3.8 A REVIEW OF CHAPTER THREE

A partnership is a team. How successfully it plays the game, whatever the game may be, depends not only on what it does after the starting whistle blows but also on what it has done to get itself into shape to play.

A team has members with varied talents. The talents, however different, must complement each other. The members of our partnership team have talents called Capital, Experience, Contacts, Expertise. There must be a proper balance of these talents. There must be a clear understanding among the team members that each is to use his talent for the benefit of the team. In the business team, this set of rules for the team's composition and operation is called a partnership agreement.

The members of our team are professionals; they accept their duties and responsibilities in exchange for rewards. The potential rewards must be proportionate to the obligations borne by the player-partners.

Equipped, organized, motivated, a team has been formed and stands ready to take on the competition and come out a winner.

CHAPTER FOUR

Normal Operations
Of a Partnership

←——————————————————→

CONTENTS

INTRODUCTION   61

4.1   WHO MANAGES THE PARTNERSHIP?   61

    4.1.1   The Managing Partner – 62
    4.1.2   The Executive Committee – 62

4.2   LIMITATION ON OUTSIDE ACTIVITIES   63

    4.2.1   The Case for Outside Activities – 63
    4.2.2   There Can Be Too Much of a Good Thing – 63
    4.2.3   A Negative Defense – 64
    4.2.4   A Positive Defense – 64
    4.2.5   Outside Activities Can Be an Embarrassment – 64
    4.2.6   An Ounce of Prevention – 64

4.3   CAPITAL AND DRAWING ACCOUNTS   64

    4.3.1   The Distinction Between Capital and Drawing Accounts – 65
    4.3.2   The Partnership Agreement Defines Capital and Drawing Accounts – 65
    4.3.3   How the Capital Account Is Created – 65
    4.3.4   Shares of Capital and Shares of Profits – 66

4.3.5   Not All Capital Is on the Books – 67

4.3.6   "Off-Balance Sheet" Capital – 68

4.4   INCREASES IN CAPITAL   69

4.4.1   Varying Ratios Offer a Solution to the Capital Problem – 69

4.4.2   Varying Ratios Present a Problem – 69

4.4.3   Illustration of Accounting for Both the Cash Basis and Accrual Basis Capital Accounts – 70

4.4.4   Capital Accounts May Permanently Reflect an Opening Inequality – 71

4.4.5   Changing Circumstances May Erase or Reverse the Inequality – 71

4.5   COMPENSATION FOR SERVICES   71

4.5.1   Partners' Salaries Are a "Must" – 71

4.5.2   Partners' Salaries and Payroll Taxes – 72

4.6   INTEREST ON CAPITAL ACCOUNTS   72

4.6.1   The Tax Aspect of Interest on Capital Accounts – 72

4.7   GUARANTEED PAYMENTS   73

4.7.1   Receipt of Guaranteed Payments Does Not Make an Employee out of a Partner or Affect His Status as a Principal Partner – 74

4.7.2   Guaranteed Payments and Capital Gains – 74

4.7.3   Guaranteed Payments Must Be Reasonable – 75

4.7.4   Guaranteed Payments Are Deductible Only if They Are Expenses – 75

4.7.5   Guaranteed Payments to Former Partners – 75

4.8   PROFIT AND LOSS SHARING RATIOS   75

4.8.1   Profit Sharing Is Not a Substitute for Compensation – 75

4.8.2   The Remaining Profit Is Shared – 76

4.8.3   Losses Must Be Shared, Too! – 77

4.8.4   Profit Sharing Ratios and Capital Ratios —Statutory Rules – 77

4.8.5   The Internal Revenue Code Permits Income and Deductions to Be Allocated According to the Ratios Specified in the Agreement – 78

4.8.6 The Tests for Substantial Economic Effect – 78

4.8.7 Other Tax Effects of the Profit Sharing and Capital Ratios – 79

4.9 ALLOCATION OF TAX EFFECTS OF CONTRIBUTIONS OF PROPERTY 80

4.9.1 The Internal Revenue Code Permits Allocation – 80

4.9.2 The Internal Revenue Code Provides Automatic Allocation – 80

4.9.3 How and When the Undivided Interests Rule Applies – 81

4.9.4 When the Undivided Interests Rule Doesn't Apply – 81

4.9.5 Allowable Depreciation Is Limited to Total Depreciation – 82

4.9.6 Tax Treatment When the Contributed Asset Is Sold – 82

4.10 SIGNIFICANCE OF GROSS INCOME 83

4.10.1 How a Partner's Share of Partnership Gross Income Is Computed – 83

4.11 SPECIAL TREATMENT ITEMS OF INCOME 84

4.12 TIME FOR INCLUSION OF ITEMS OF INCOME 86

4.13 ELECTIONS HAVING AN EFFECT ON COMPUTATION OF TAXABLE INCOME 86

4.14 RETROACTIVE ALLOCATIONS AND VARYING INTERESTS 87

4.14.1 A Superb Tax-Planning Opportunity Survived the Ban on Retroactive Allocations – 88

4.15 DISTRIBUTIONS 88

4.15.1 Ordinarily, No Gain or Loss Is Recognized Upon a Distribution – 88

4.15.2 The Exception to the General Rule – 89

4.15.3 How the Partnership Is Affected by Distributions – 89

4.15.4 The Nature of Gain Upon a Nonliquidating Distribution – 89

4.15.5   Guaranteed Payments as Distributions – 89
4.15.6   Constructive Distributions – 89

4.16   TAXATION OF DISTRIBUTIVE SHARES   89

4.16.1   When a Distributive Share Is Taxed – 89
4.16.2   How a Distributive Share Is Taxed – 90
4.16.3   To Whom a Distributive Share Is Taxed – 90

4.17   DEALINGS BETWEEN PARTNERSHIP AND
PARTNERS   90

4.17.1   Regulation 1.707.1 Defines Certain Transactions as Being Transactions Between
Partnership and Partner as Outsider – 90
4.17.2   Losses Between a Partner and a Controlled
Partnership May Be Disallowed – 91
4.17.3   Gains Between a Partner and Controlled
Partnership Are Treated as Ordinary Income – 91

4.18   DISABILITY OF PARTNERS   91

4.19   SUMMATION OF CHAPTER FOUR   92

INTRODUCTION

Remember the phrases which started our childish games,

> One for the money,
> two for the show
> three to get ready
> and four to go!

Our first three chapters have told us what a partnership is, why you choose partnership as your way to do business, and how to organize it. We are now at four, and ready to go!

A partnership stays organized and follows the game plan only so long as someone or some group plans, leads and controls its activities. Besides players, the partnership team must have equipment. In our world of business, we call that "capital." Unlike a corporation, where the source of capital (stockholders) is not necessarily the same as the players (directors, officers and employees), the members of the partnership are also the source of all the equity capital. The players provide the balls, bats, and gloves.

The players vary in skill and willingness to exert themselves in the team effort. These varying contributions must be recognized, measured and rewarded. Some players furnish more equipment than others, and they must be compensated for their disproportionate capital.

A baseball scorekeeper may be satisfied with keeping up with hits, runs and errors. Our partnership team must keep track of, allocate or distribute gross income, contributed property, other sources of capital, compensation, guaranteed payments and a host of other technical terms. We must know when we are dealing with ourselves as partners or as outsiders, and the tax consequences of each partnership decision.

Chapter Four discloses how a partnership draws up its game plan.

4.1 WHO MANAGES THE PARTNERSHIP?

The fact that every general partner has joint and several responsibility for every act of the partnership leads to the conclusion that every general partner has a responsibility for its management. This leads to the assertion that "If I'm going to be responsible for everything that's done around here, I'm going to have a say in how it's run." No one can fault this idea in theory, but in practice it just doesn't work. In the first place, a management style that resembles a town meeting and requires consent of all the partners for every management decision would slow down a two- or three-person partnership and would immobilize a larger firm. In the second place,

61

despite their assertions to the contrary, many (most?) partners really do not want to participate in management. It's more fun to build houses, or sell merchandise, or do tax research than it is to oversee the bookkeeping, interview job applicants, or supervise the purchase of office supplies. Despite the glamorous connotation of "management," management of a partnership is no fun! As a result, there is either no designated management (the problem existed in Biblical times; the book of Judges concludes its story of a chaotic period of history with the statement "In those days there was no king in Israel; every man did what was right in his own eyes"), or the job is dumped on an unfortunate person who has no taste for it and performs minimal duties as an unpleasant chore.

A variation on this theme is rotation of management. Rotating management has the advantage of acquainting more partners with the task, but that is one of its few virtues. It develops a short-term outlook and lacks continuity. It is a device that is usually forced to give way to a more permanent arrangement.

4.1.1 The Managing Partner

Management of a partnership isn't any fun, but it is essential. The firm must designate a partner as chief executive, and must give him authority and compensation commensurate with the task. The person selected as managing partner must be willing to undertake the job, must have a reasonable amount of organizational ability, and must have the confidence and support of his partners. Selection for a specific term is desirable and he should yield the job to someone else when he tires of it, when age affects his performance, or when new directions of leadership are needed. Although the managing partner must command the respect of his partners, he does not have to be the holder of the largest interest.

4.1.2 The Executive Committee

The large general partnership should consider having a managing partner who presides over an executive committee. This arrangement gives the partnership the operating advantages of centralized control usually found in corporations, with the executive committee being analogous to the corporate board of directors and the partners almost relegated to the role of stockholders.

The exposure to liability of a general partner is much greater than that of a stockholder and the powers and responsibilities of a partnership's executive committee are not as well delineated as those of a corporate director. Therefore, a partnership delegating management to a small group must be very careful to have clear policy statements for its guidance and control to be sure that the limits of its authority are not exceeded.

Partners are frequently reluctant to concede operating authority to central management. While fear of exposure to liability may be real, such reluctance is often based on a human temptation to reject any system under which anyone is deprived of the chance to "get his two cents worth in." These concerns can be countered with two answers. The first is "everybody's business is nobody's business"; when monitoring performance is left to a large, poorly organized group, many things never get done at all, and these omissions are sources of loss. The second is that the amount of time taken up in meeting and arriving at a consensus in a large assembly usually exceeds the value to be obtained from such broad input.

4.2   LIMITATION ON OUTSIDE ACTIVITIES

Outside activities can be both a boon and a bane to a partnership. Outside activities include everything that is not directly involved in carrying out the partnership's profit-making function. They range from activities through which such valuable contacts are made that they could be more important than inside activities, to activities (recreational, for instance) that are neutral in their business effects down to activities that are harmful to the partnership.

4.2.1 The Case for Outside Activities

Several points can be made for outside activities; clubs, fraternal organizations, churches and golf courses are inhabited by people whose good will you need to cultivate; the business that is supported by the community has at least a moral obligation to invest time in support of the community; hard-working partners need relaxation, a change of pace; some people don't want to put all their eggs in one basket and want to invest time or resources in businesses not related to the partnership function.

4.2.2 There Can Be Too Much of a Good Thing

Every partnership should have a strict prohibition against participating in competing business, and this should include other business ventures which, although they do not sell products or services in competition with the partnership, do compete for the time and attention of the partners.

Competition for the primary loyalty can come from churches, clubs, sports and politics. These are much harder to deal with than overt commercial competition. There are several ways that a partnership can deal with them, none totally satisfactorily. The first line of defense against competing nonpaid activities should be a clear policy statement as to what activities the firm condones and condemns. This should have the effect of allaying the fears of those partners who place the primary mission of the partnership at the top of their priorities. Over a period of time it will attract partners who share the firm's philosophy of the proper use of nonchargeable time, and discourage those whose views differ.

4.2.3 A Negative Defense

An effective, though negative, line of defense against overinvolvement in outside activities is a requirement that specified amounts of time be devoted to the direct activities of the partnership. Combined with a strong policy of discouraging activities that are harmful to the partnership, this approach assures the partnership that outside activities will not cause its business to be neglected.

4.2.4 A Positive Defense

A positive approach, particularly when added to a firm prohibition against negative activity and a commitment to reasonable participation in the stated business of the partnership, involves specifying participation in designated extracurricular activities, in the design of the partnership's compensation package, and in assignment of the work load.

4.2.5 Outside Activities Can Be an Embarrassment

Outside activities, although legal and honest, can be a source of embarrassment to the partnership. Partisan politics can offend important customers or clients; customers and clients resent finding their suppliers or professional counsel investing, albeit silently, in their competitors; some legal businesses convey an image not in keeping with the propriety of the partnership. Partners may invest in a business which becomes insolvent; having a partner in your firm sued because he is a partner or proprietor in a firm which is delinquent in its obligations to someone who is important to *your* firm is sure to promote strained relationships.

4.2.6 An Ounce of Prevention

A partnership provision giving the partnership reasonable control over each partner's investments and associations can be a valuable aid in preventing compromising situations or watered-down effort.

4.3   CAPITAL AND DRAWING ACCOUNTS

The partnership that tries to operate with inadequate capital will spend too much of its time and effort keeping the wolf from the door. The partnership that ties up too much capital prevents younger people, who are long on talent and short on treasure, from entering, or makes their participation an unnecessarily burdensome experience.

Partners' salaries can be guaranteed payments, earned whether the partnership has a profit or a loss. More frequently, partners' salaries are a draw against profits. If regular salaries are not provided for, regular draws will usually be required for a partner's sustenance. Both capital and drawing accounts will usually be needed to show the financial relationships between the partnership and its partners.

4.3.1 The Distinction Between Capital and Drawing Accounts

Surprisingly, considering the importance of the term, neither the Uniform Partnership Act nor the Internal Revenue Code define "partner's capital account." To draw the distinction, one must fall back on the usual definition of capital as the permanent investment by the owners in the business. A corporation maintains a capital stock account and a retained earnings account which together constitute the equity of the shareholders. Capital stock remains relatively stable. Retained earnings may take the form of permanent capital by a transfer to capital stock or to some form of contributed capital, but retained earnings take on such a nature only after a formal action by the stockholders. So it should be with the partnership. There should be a permanent capital account to which undrawn profits may be transferred, and there should be a drawing account for each partner to which distributive shares of income are credited and shares of losses or withdrawals are debited.

4.3.2 The Partnership Agreement Defines the Terms

Since there is no statutory basis for capital accounts, the partnership agreement should define the accounts, specifying what shall be charged and credited to each. To emphasize that the capital account is separate and distinct from the drawing accounts, the agreement might state that credit balances in drawing accounts are liabilities of the partnership and that a debit balance in a drawing account shall constitute an obligation of the partner to the partnership and shall not be considered as a reduction of his capital account.

4.3.3 How the Capital Account Is Created

Often, newer partners cannot immediately fund the full amount of capital required of them. If it is important that capital of a specified amount be maintained (its significance is discussed later in this chapter) then the partnership should require that the full amount be invested; if the partner can't get it any other way the partnership may endorse his note at the bank. If it is determined that it is not necessary for a partner to start off with an immediate substantial contribution to capital, the agreement could permit an installment buildup or require the contribution of a specified portion of his earnings until the desired capital account balance is obtained. Under such an arrangement the accounts might look like this:

<u>Allen Capital</u>

Balance, January 1, 19XX	$ 5,000.00	Cr.
December 31, 19XX		
10% of share of partnership earnings for year ended December 31, 19XX	4,000.00	
Balance, December 31, 19XX	$ 9,000.00	

<u>Allen Drawing</u>

Balance, January 1, 19XX	$ 337.27	Cr.
January 1, 19XX Distribution of opening balance	337.27	Dr.
January 31, 19XX monthly draw	2,000.00	Dr.
(similar entry for each month February - December)	22,000.00	Dr.
December 31, 19XX charges for Blue Cross for year	997.44	Dr.
December 31, 19XX 90% of share of partnership earnings for year ended December 31, 19XX	36,000.00	Cr.
Balance, December 31, 19XX (available to be drawn after year-end)	$11,002.56	

As the illustration shows, the capital account, particularly in a growing company or an inflationary economy, tends to remain constant or increase. A drawing account, however, fluctuates, and may, as in Allen's case, "zero out" once a year.

4.3.4 Shares of Capital and Shares of Profits

Whereas capital shares and shares of profits or losses are frequently proportional, they are not required to be proportional. The partnership agreement must specify each ratio.

U.S. Form 1065, Partnership Return of Income, asks questions about partnership "interests" and requires answers to questions about each partner's percentage of profit sharing, loss sharing, and ownership of capital.

The partner's share of capital is significant in applying several provisions of the Internal Revenue Code. It is the starting point for calculating the basis of a partner's interest (Section 705). An increase in a partner's capital (or an increase in his share of partnership liabilities) may permit him to deduct a share of a partnership loss which he could not deduct in the year in which the loss was sustained because he lacked basis (Section 704 (d)).

The relative shares of capital interests in the partnership are also significant in applying the Internal Revenue Code to partnership operations. Losses are disallowed between a partnership and a partner holding more than a 50 percent capital interest; gains on sale of other than Section 1221 capital assets between a partnership and a partner holding more than an 80 percent interest are taxed as ordinary income (Section 707).

4.3.5 Not All Capital Is on the Books

Capital of a partnership is the excess of assets over liabilities. For a partnership permitted to keep its books on the cash basis (which includes all professional partnerships) the capital on the books is very low compared to the real capital of the firm. Capital, or working capital, is those net liquid assets which will be used to fund current operations, whether on the books or not. An example shows the difference:

BALANCE SHEET OF ABC PARTNERSHIP
(CASH BASIS)
AS OF DECEMBER 31, 19XX

ASSETS

Cash		$10,000
Office equipment (at cost, less accumulated		
depreciation		5,000
Total Assets		$15,000

LIABILITIES AND CAPITAL

Payroll taxes withheld		$ 1,500
Capital - Partner A	$ 4,500	
Partner B	4,500	
Partner C	4,500	13,500
Total Liabilities and Capital		$15,000

BALANCE SHEET OF ABC PARTNERSHIP
(ACCRUAL BASIS)
AS OF DECEMBER 31, 19XX

ASSETS

Cash	$10,000
Accounts receivable	30,000
Work in process	25,000
Office equipment (at cost, less accumulated	
depreciation)	5,000
Total Assets	$70,000

LIABILITIES AND CAPITAL

Payroll taxes withheld		$ 1,500
Accounts payable		1,000
Capital - Partner A	$22,500	
Partner B	22,500	
Partner C	22,500	67,500
Total Liabilities and Capital		$70,000

In a professional practice, personnel costs represent most of the costs of doing business. If the next payroll can be met from conversion of the accounts receivable into cash and the cycle can be kept up, very little permanent capital is needed. The cash flow cycle looks like this:

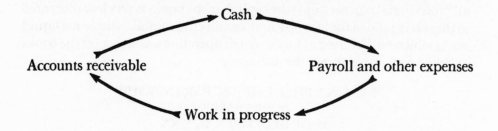

It should be clearly understood that "capital" as used in 4.3.5 and 4.3.6 is broader than the "partner's capital account" referred to in the Internal Revenue Code, and that the capital account referred to in 4.3.4 refers to the account maintained according to the method of accounting adopted for tax purposes.

4.3.6 "Off-Balance Sheet" Capital

The biggest asset that any business can have often does not appear on its balance sheet—its good name, its reputation. This asset can be converted into cash because a reputation supports credit standing, and can generate bank loans. Almost every business has peak periods when capital needs are greatest. It would be imprudent to maintain a capital balance year-round at the year's maximum level. Accordingly, each partnership should make and maintain a banking relationship adequate for its maximum anticipated needs, including a written commitment of a specified line of credit. Failure to do so may result in having to take time off when the work load is highest to scurry around rounding up cash for the payroll.

Business utilizes "off-balance sheet" financing in the form of leases. The statements of the Financial Accounting Standards Board have greatly narrowed the use of this device to improve the appearance of balance sheets of publicly held companies. Improving the appearance of the balance sheet is seldom important to partnerships, so partnerships are not much concerned as to whether they use facilities acquired under capital leases or operating leases. The important thing about a lease is that it may permit a capital-shy partnership to acquire the hardware or real estate that it needs with a minimum immediate outlay of cash.

4.4 INCREASES IN CAPITAL

The partnership agreement should provide a means for requiring additional capital to meet the needs of a growing business. If all of the partners have substantial resources, a provision specifying the vote required to call for a capital contribution and the time within which it must be paid may be sufficient. Many partnerships depend on infusions of capital from partners who can obtain it only by setting aside portions of their income. Considering the fact that such capital must come from after-tax income and that new partners are also facing demands related to family growth, this is a hard way to get capital.

4.4.1 Varying Ratios Offer a Solution to the Capital Problem

Partnerships on the cash basis can admit new partners with minimum capital contribution requirements by divorcing the profit sharing ratio from the capital ratio. Since income is recorded when collected, the new partner shares in collections from his first day as a partner, even though he did not share in the costs of earning the income. As the sample balance sheet in the preceding section shows, receivables and work in process of a service business usually greatly exceed its payables. Unquestionably, the partners who paid the costs of earning the income in which the new partner shares, have given him a break; it is more accurate to describe the "gift" as an exchange in which the new partner gets what he needs (income) in exchange for providing the vigor which the partnership needs.

4.4.2 Varying Ratios Present a Problem

To accomplish the result suggested above, the new partner needs to receive an income interest only. The partnership agreement should make it clear that repayment of the capital account upon the departure of a partner refers to the capital account maintained on the accrual basis. To do otherwise might permit the new partner to leave shortly after he came in, taking with him the fruits of his predecessors' efforts. If interest is to be paid on capital accounts, it should be based on accrual basis accounts.

Awarding a share of profits to an income partner is not a taxable event to anyone; awarding a capital share will usually trigger taxation of the new partner. This problem has been dealt with in paragraph 3.6.1.

4.4.3 Illustration of Accounting for Both the Cash Basis and Accrual Basis Capital Account

We shall illustrate the accounting for partnership capital for both methods with a case which assumes that A and B, equal partners, admit C on January 1, 19X1; that A and B remain equal while C's share of profits is 33-1/3 percent of A's or B's share for 19X1, increasing to 66-2/3 percent for 19X2 and equality in 19X3. Partners' salaries have been included in computing partnership profits. Net income increases $10,080 per year and since $5,040 is tied up in increased accounts receivable (which includes, for this example, unbilled services) each year, cash basis income increases $5,400 each year. In 19X0, A and B drew out all the profits as salaries. C is required to contribute all of his share of the profits to capital. A and B choose to contribute their entire shares of profit, and the partnership agreement permits this. The example assumes no cash basis capital just prior to C's admission. The books are kept and tax returns are filed on the cash basis.

Cash Basis Capital Accounts

	Total	A	B	C
Balance, Jan. 1, 19X1	$ -0-	$ -0-	$ -0-	$ -0-
Shares of profit for 19X1	5,040	2,160	2,160	720
Balances, Jan. 1, 19X2	5,040	2,160	2,160	720
Shares of profit for 19X2	10,080	3,780	3,780	2,520
Balances, Jan. 1, 19X3	15,120	5,940	5,940	3,240
Shares of profit for 19X3	15,120	5,040	5,040	5,040
Balances, Dec. 31, 19X3	$30,240	$10,980	$10,980	$ 8,280

Accrual Basis Capital Accounts

	Total	A	B	C
Balance, Jan. 1, 19X1	$20,000	$10,000	$10,000	$ -0-
Shares of profit for 19X1	10,080	4,320	4,320	1,440
Balances, Jan. 1, 19X2	30,080	14,320	14,320	1,440
Shares of profit for 19X2	20,160	7,560	7,560	5,040
Balances, Jan. 1, 19X3	50,240	21,880	21,880	6,480
Shares of profit for 19X3	30,240	10,080	10,080	10,080
Balances, Dec. 31, 19X3	$80,480	$31,960	$31,960	$16,560

Since profit sharing is 1/3 each for future years, the difference between C's balance and that of either A or B will remain constant, on either basis. If the partners should decide to equalize the accounts by payment of cash of $2,700 to A and $2,700 to B, the accrual basis capital accounts will have balances of $29,260, $29,260 and $16,560. Logically, a partner leaving the firm should be repaid his accrual basis capital account. See 4.4.2. Unless the arrangement is changed, the disparity in accrual basis capital accounts will remain constant forever.

4.4.4 Capital Accounts May Permanently Reflect an Opening Inequality

Invariably, partners in C's position look at these figures and yell "Foul!" They cannot see why a now equal partner will always have a lower balance. The explanation is simple; when one shares in net profits, one shares in gross receipts and expenses in the same proportion as he shares in net profits. For the years prior to 19X1, the services of A and B or expenses which they both shared produced the initial $20,000 of receivables. For the first and second years of the partnership, C bore a smaller share of the expenses than A or B bore. They have an investment that C does not have; they are entitled to a return on it and, eventually, to be repaid.

4.4.5 Changing Circumstances May Erase or Reverse an Inequality

Although C will have a mild flareup of his ulcers everytime he ponders the (to him) injustice of the situation, over a professional lifetime the situation may even out. As A and B grow older, they will probably accept lower salaries and/or a lower share of the profits, so that C's relative position will improve. It is not unusual to discount a departing partner's capital account for administrative costs, so that the amount actually realized by A or B will approach the value of C's account.

C's attitude may change when D is admitted under the same arrangement. By that time C will be high on the totem pole, and he will have no trouble seeing why D should occupy an inferior position. It is very easy for a person to see the capitalist point of view after he becomes one.

4.5 COMPENSATION FOR SERVICES

Partnerships occasionally start on the premise that each partner will contribute equally in capital and services and will share equally in the profits. The capital obligations and the profit sharing are easily quantifiable and present few problems. Unfortunately, different people seldom have equal capacities for work, or equal attitudes towards work. If they do, their services are not necessarily of equal value.

Even if the partners work equal schedules at the principal business, someone gets the responsibility of the administrative chores which eat up an alarming amount of time.

4.5.1 Partners' Salaries Are a "Must"

Partners should be compensated for services performed for the partnership, and the compensation should be reasonable. This "pay for services" should not bear a relationship to the amount of capital or to the seniority of the partner. There is no statute or tax law which demands this; it is simply good business. In fact, Section 18(F) of the Uniform Partnership Act denies remuneration to a partner unless the agreement specifically provides for it. Services to the partnership include both services to clients or customers and administrative duties, and may include promotional activities which only incidentally benefit the business.

4.5.2 Partners' Salaries and Payroll Taxes

Partners' salaries are not reportable on payroll tax forms such as Forms 940, 941 and W-2 and are not subject to income tax withholding. However, designation as salary can convert compensation for services, which otherwise would not be subject to the self-employment tax (Regulation 1.1402(a)-1(b)), into self-employment income. As an example, instructions for Form 1065 call for an adjustment to ordinary income from rentals of real estate which removes the income from the self-employment tax category. However, designation as part of the partnership's income as salary for services (managing partner, for instance), causes the recipient to report the salary on Form 1040SE. As in any area of taxes, the services must be real and the amount reasonable; to designate part of rental income as salary just to benefit a partner who needs a quarter or so of social security coverage would be held to be a sham.

4.6   INTEREST ON CAPITAL ACCOUNTS

Ideally, capital accounts (ratios) and profit sharing ratios should be identical. Because some partners must have time to build up capital, the capital and profit sharing ratios are often dissimilar. Since capital invested in a partnership is still capital, and since a purpose of investment of capital is to obtain a return on capital as such, the partnership agreement should provide for interest on capital accounts. If interest is to be paid, it must be specifically provided for in the agreement; otherwise, interest on capital accounts is prohibited by Section 18(d) of the Uniform Partnership Act.

4.6.1 The Tax Aspect of Interest on Capital Accounts

Instructions for Form 1065, U.S. Partnership Return of Income, state that payments or credits by a partnership to a partner for the use of capital should be entered as guaranteed payments to partners, not as interest expense, if the payments or credits are determined without regard to partnership income. Guaranteed payments are used to reduce income before the calculation of a partner's income under the profit sharing formula. If the interest payments or credit are an allocation of net profits (no profits, no interest) then the payments or credits are lumped along with the net profit subject to allocation.

This distinction was important to a partner in the over-50 percent tax bracket, as interest on his capital account, if not a guaranteed payment, was included in personal service income and was subject to maximum tax treatment under IRC Section 1348. By establishing a maximum rate of 50 percent, the Economic Recovery Tax Act of 1981 eliminated this distinction.

4.7 GUARANTEED PAYMENTS

"Guaranteed payments" are payments to a partner which are determined without regard to the income of the partnership, and may be for services or for the use of capital. The tax treatment of guaranteed payments is provided for in IRC Section 707(c) and a separate line is provided on U.S. Partnership Return of Income Form 1065, Page one and on Schedule K-1. An illustration could show compensation of $12,000 per year to A, managing partner of A-B-C, a partnership that has no partners' salaries and pays no interest on capital accounts. If the profit before any partners' compensation was $60,000, the division would be:

A, guaranteed payment	$12,000
A, share of profits	16,000
B, share of profits	16,000
C, share of profits	16,000
Total	$60,000

If, however, profits were only $6,000 before any partners' compensation, the division of profits would be:

A, guaranteed payment	$12,000
A, share of loss	(2,000)
B, share of loss	(2,000)
C, share of loss	(2,000)
Total	$ 6,000

If there had been a loss of $6,000 before any partner's compensation, the division of the loss would be:

A, guaranteed payment	$12,000
A, share of loss	(6,000)
B, share of loss	(6,000)
C, share of loss	(6,000)
Total	$(6,000)

All of the above illustrations assume that the agreement provides for profits and losses to be shared equally and that the guaranteed payment is to be treated as an expense. The above illustrations are appropriate when the purpose of the guaranteed payments is to compensate one (or more) partner for some special contribution, but not to insulate him against loss or against diminution of profits reflecting his compensation. A person may decline to join a partnership, or to remain a partner, unless he is guaranteed a minimum income. If A had such an arrangement when the loss before any compensation to partners was $6,000, the division would be:

A, guaranteed payment	$12,000
B, share of loss	(9,000)
C, share of loss	(9,000)
Total	$(6,000)

4.7.1 Receipt of Guaranteed Payments Does Not Make an Employee out of a Partner or Affect His Status as a Principal Partner

Section 707(c) says "payments to a partner for services or the use of capital shall be considered as made to one who is not a member of the partnership." To read those words, which are taken out of context, and to do so without comprehending the purpose of the provision, would lead a person to assume that A, in the last illustration above, is in fact to be treated as an employee. Certainly, there is very little practical difference between A and an employee participant in a nonqualified profit sharing plan. The Code and Regulations make several important distinctions between a partner receiving guaranteed payments and an employee. Regulation 1.707-1(c) provides that guaranteed payments are income to the partner for his taxable year within or with which ends the partnership taxable year in which the partnership deducted such payments as paid or accrued under its method of accounting; an employee would include similar payments in the year in which he received them. The recipient of guaranteed payments may not exclude wage continuation payments and his survivor is not eligible for exclusion of an employee death benefit. He may not be an employee for purposes such as tax withholding.

A guaranteed payment is not an interest in partnership profits for purposes of Section 706(b)(3) (defining a principal partner) or of Section 707(b) (covering losses disallowed between a partnership and a partner owning a 50 percent interest in capital or profits) or of Section 708(b) (relating to the reduction in interests required to terminate a partnership).

4.7.2 Guaranteed Payments and Capital Gains

There is an interesting interplay of Section 707(c) (defining guaranteed payments) and Section 702(a) (requiring a partner to take into account separately his share of capital gains). To illustrate this, we shall assume that

A has a 30 percent interest in profits and $10,000 guaranteed payment and that the partnership has "book" income of $20,000 consisting of $30,000 long-term capital gain and the $10,000 guaranteed payment. A's income for the partnership year is $10,000 guaranteed payment, $9,000 capital gain and $3,000 ordinary loss. The $3,000 is, of course, his share of the loss arising from his own "salary."

4.7.3 Guaranteed Payments Must Be Reasonable

Section 707(c), when it permits a partnership to take a deduction for guaranteed payments to a partner as if the payments were made to an outsider, limits the deduction to that permissible under Section 162(a). The latter limits a deduction for compensation to "a reasonable allowance for salaries or other compensation for personal services actually rendered."

4.7.4 Guaranteed Payments Are Deductible Only if They Are Expenses

Section 707(c) also invokes Section 263 to limit the deduction for guaranteed payments for services which do not result in a capital improvement. For example, an architectural partnership that built its own office building would have to capitalize guaranteed payments to a member of the firm who designed the building and supervised its construction.

The requirement for capitalization of a partner's service is not limited to those services for which compensation is set forth as guaranteed payments. In the above example, the architectural services still should be capitalized, even if the architect partner's share of partnership income could not be related to his services in designing and constructing the building. Your author believes that such an interpretation is justified by the language of Regulation 1.707-1(a).

4.7.5 Guaranteed Payments to Former Partners

Guaranteed payments to disabled or retired partners or to the estate or heirs of deceased partners will be covered in Chapter Five.

4.8   PROFIT AND LOSS SHARING RATIOS

Classic economic theory holds that wealth is created by an efficient combination of capital, labor, and management. Partners provide all three, though the bulk of the labor may be done by employees and much of the capital may be borrowed.

4.8.1 Profit Sharing Is Not a Substitute for Compensation

Partners must be compensated for their labor. In the author's opinion, this is best done through the mechanism of salaries or guaranteed payments. It is fairly easy to assign a value to routine services, even at the management level, by comparing the tasks to those performed by corporate employees. This is the amount that should be paid for partners' services; they will not be happy with less, and there is no good reason for paying a partner substantially more than you would pay an employee to do the same thing.

Partners must be compensated for the use of their capital. Interest should be paid on capital accounts, or allocation of profits to compensate for use of capital should be made. A high rate of return is appropriate; partners, like stockholders, are repaid last when the business is liquidated.

4.8.2 The Remaining Profit Is Shared

If capital, labor, and management can be compensated for adequately by salaries, guaranteed payments and interest on capital accounts, what function is left for a profit sharing ratio? The practical answer is: not much. Just as in a corporation, there is relatively little left for net income before taxes after all costs and expenses are covered.

There is no reason to believe that a partnership operating in competition with a corporation will bring any more down to the bottom line than a corporation will unless there is some inherent advantage in the partnership form of operation—and there is! It is this superiority of the partnership over the corporation that deserves reward, and the profit sharing ratio determines who gets the reward.

This partnership superiority is based on a partner's superior motivation. The motivation is partly negative. A partnership shares losses, too. A stockholder can lose only his investment; an employee can lose only his job. A general partner can lose his job and incur a lien against what he may accumulate in the future. The risks inherent in partnership tend to foster a closer interest in the business, and the opportunities for superior profits are the incentive for taking the risks. The partner who has a higher potential exposure should have a higher profit sharing ratio.

The motivation also is positive. Factors such as experience, reputation and contacts should enter into the determination of salaries or guaranteed payments. However, these unquantifiable assets can be rewarded best by allocating a higher share of the profits to those judged to possess them in greatest abundance.

To sum this up, the partnership that adequately compensates average people for their services and their capital will have only average profits to distribute and it doesn't matter much how you allocate them. Equality of sharing, or a ratio that reflects seniority or some other perceived reason for inequality can be justified.

However, even "average" encompasses a range, and if average people can be motivated to become "high average," the effect on distributable income can be spectacular. Therefore, the profit sharing ratio should be designed to provide the extra reward for those who have the capability of achieving outstanding results.

4.8.3 Losses Must Be Shared, Too

As a practical matter, some partners cannot afford to share significantly in losses. Although it would violate the principles on which partnerships are founded to completely insulate any partner from the risk of any loss, it is impractical to expect impecunious partners to pick up a share of a large deficit. The partnership should recognize this fact by adopting a two-tier ratio, under which losses up to a sustainable level are shared and beyond that point are allocated to other than all the partners. The effects of income taxes make such an apparently unfair arrangement more palatable; the greater losses are passed to those who are most likely to have income against which the losses can be offset.

Fairness demands that a two-tier profit sharing formula favor the same partners who have agreed to take the risks of large losses. Practicality demands it because no prudent investor assumes greater risks unless there is a chance of greater rewards.

4.8.4 Profit Sharing Ratios and Capital Ratios — Statutory Rules

Although there is much to be said for equal profit and loss sharing ratios and capital ratios, there is no requirement that they be equal or that they bear any relationship to each other. The Uniform Partnership Act disposes of the matter in Section 18 when it says "The rights and duties of the partners in relation to the partnership shall be determined, subject to any agreement between them (underlining supplied for emphasis), by the following rules:

(a) Each partner shall be repaid his contributions, whether by way of capital or advances to the partnership property and share equally in the profits and surplus remaining after all liabilities, including those to partners, are satisified; and must contribute towards the losses, whether of capital or otherwise, sustained by the partnership according to his share in the profits.

In other words, state law will permit any arrangement on which the partners agree. It follows that there is no required relationship of capital to profit sharing ratios and that profits and losses can be shared in tiers, or that capital gains may be shared differently from ordinary income.

4.8.5 The Internal Revenue Code Permits Income and Deductions to Be Allocated According to the Ratios Specified in the Agreement

In one of its most permissive utterances, the Internal Revenue Code gives a partnership amazing freedom to determine who shall bear the tax burden or receive the tax benefit of its operations. Section 704(a) says: "Effect of Partnership Agreement – A partner's distributive share of income, gain, loss, deduction, or credit shall, except as otherwise provided in this chapter, be determined by the partnership agreement."

Prior to the Tax Reform Act of 1976, the rules stopped there. Since Regulation 1.761-1(c) defined the agreement as the original agreement with modifications adopted up to the unextended date for filing the return, there were abundant opportunities for creative tax planning! Right up to April 15, when the year's results are all in, the agreement could be amended to allocate the capital gains to a partner who otherwise had capital losses, and to be fair to another partner who had an expiring net operating loss carryover by allocating to him a disproportionate part of the ordinary income. A partner could be admitted on the last day of the year and be allocated losses (incurred before his admission) that would produce a tax saving of up to 70 percent of his contribution. Alas! Congress killed Santa Claus by adding Section 704(b)(2) which requires that the allocation provisions of the partnership agreement must have substantial economic effect. "Substantial economic effect" can be loosely defined to mean that sooner or later the money must be divided in the same directions as the tax effect fell. The Tax Reform Act of 1976 also closed the door on retroactive allocations of income or losses.

4.8.6 The Tests for "Substantial Economic Effect"

There is a standing joke in large accounting firms to the effect that tax partners don't understand debits and credits, and don't have to. Section 704(b)(2) requires that an allocation of any item of income, gain, loss, deduction or credit other than simply in accordance with the general profit sharing ratio have substantial economic effect. Regulation 1.704-1(b)(2) describes "substantial economic effect" by saying "that is, whether the allocation may actually affect the dollar amount of the partner's shares of the total partnership income or loss independently of tax consequences." This seems to say that a special allocation, after running the gauntlet of proving that its principal purpose is not the avoidance or evasion of federal income taxes, must affect the dollars which go into or come out of a partner's pocket. This is where the understanding of debits and credits is critical to interpretation of the tax laws.

The issue is this: If a partner is allocated more or less than his general share of some item of income, gain, loss or deduction, must there be a compensating addition or reduction of some other item or of the bottom line?

Example 2 of Regulation 1.704-1(b)(2) states that it is permissible to allocate to a foreign partner "a percentage of the profits derived from operations conducted by him within such country which percentage is greater than his distributive share of partnership income generally." Example 4 of the same Regulation attributes to partners K and L all of the gain on the sale of securities arising from appreciation before M became an equal partner and says that has substantial economic effect. If the aforementioned tax partner can recall enough from Accounting 101 at dear old State U to set up "T" accounts (only the credit side is shown here), he will combine the two transactions like this:

	K	L	M
Drawing account balance Jan. 1, 19X0	$ -0-	$ -0-	$ -0-
Foreign income	5,000	5,000	11,000
Early appreciation on securities	15,000	15,000	-0-
Appreciation of securities after M became a partner	8,000	8,000	8,000
All other items of income and expense	10,000	10,000	10,000
Distributable income	$38,000	$38,000	$29,000

If the cash is distributed $38,000 to K, $38,000 to L and $29,000 to M, then the allocations do indeed have substantial economic effect. If however, the partners take the position that the allocations are for tax purposes only and that the total profit of $105,000 is to be distributed $35,000 each, then the allocations do not have substantial economic effect and risk reallocation by the IRS. It seems to your author that to meet the strict tests of Section 704(b)(2) the "all other items" should have been allocated $7,000 each to K and L and $16,000 to M.

4.8.7 Other Tax Effects of the Profit Sharing and Capital Ratios

Besides permitting allocations of income, deductions, and credits in accordance with the partnership agreement when the allocation has substantial economic effect, the Code lends significance to profit sharing and capital ratios in other provisions. Section 707 disallows losses between a partnership and a partner who owns more than 50 percent of the capital or profits interest. The same section denies capital gain treatment on a sale of assets other than capital assets as defined in Section 1221 between a partner and a partnership in which he owns more than an 80 percent interest in capital or profits. A partnership cannot elect a partnership year different from that of its principal partners, who are defined in Section 706(b)(3) as those who have an interest of 5 percent or more in profits or capital. A partnership is considered terminated for tax purposes when within a 12-month period there is a sale or exchange of 50 percent or more of the total interest in capital and profits. If a partner's share of profits is reduced by more than one-third before investment credit property is held for the useful life, his qualified investment is reduced proportionately.

It should be noted that Section 706 applies no rules of attribution to determine 5 percent ownership, whereas Section 707 specifically invokes the rules of constructive ownership to determine 50 percent or 80 percent ownership.

4.9 ALLOCATION OF TAX EFFECTS OF CONTRIBUTIONS OF PROPERTY

The partnership is unique in that it can decide who shall bear the burdens and receive the benefits when property with different tax basis and fair market value is placed in the partnership by the partners.

4.9.1 The Internal Revenue Code Permits Allocation

The authority that permits a partnership to allocate depreciation, depletion or gain or loss with respect to property contributed to the partnership by a partner is found in Internal Revenue Code Section 704(c). This section approaches the question in both a positive and a negative way. Positively, it provides that the partnership agreement may dictate how depreciation, depletion, gain or loss shall be shared among the partners so as to take account of the variation between the basis of the property to the partnership and its fair market value at the time of contribution.

4.9.2 The Internal Revenue Code Provides Automatic Allocation

Negatively, Section 704(c) provides that if the partnership agreement does not provide otherwise, depreciation, depletion, gain or loss with respect to undivided interests in property contributed to a partnership shall be determined as though such undivided interests had not been contributed to the partnership. For this rule to apply, all of the partners must have had undivided interests in the property prior to contribution and their interests in the capital and profits of the partnership must correspond with such undivided interests.

4.9.3 How and When the Undivided Interests Rule Applies

The undivided interests rule serves well in narrowly defined circumstances. In all other cases, the partner and his advisor must be alert so as to assure the adoption of a provision in the agreement to permit the desired allocation. The agreement must be adopted by the original (unextended) due date of the return.

If the partners had also had the same bases (or proportional bases, if shares are unequal) there would be no need for the undivided interests rule. There are many circumstances under which significantly different bases can be obtained for identical undivided interests. An undivided interest can be inherited when values have changed since other joint tenants obtained their interests; joint tenants may sell an undivided interest in appreciated (or depreciated) property and then form a partnership with the new owner; property can be obtained in a Section 333 liquidation of a corporation whose stockholders had different bases for their stock.

Let's assume that A and B have equal undivided interests in improved real estate with bases as follows:

A – land	$4,000
A – improvements	$6,000
B – land	$1,000
B – improvements	$5,000

The real estate is contributed to a partnership in which profits are to be divided equally and in which the partners have equal capital accounts. If the improvements are depreciated straight-line at 5 percent, allowable depreciation is $550, allocated $300 (5% of $6,000) to A and $250 (5% of $5,000) to B.

Now we assume that at the end of the first year the partnership sells the real estate for $20,000. Remember that Section 704(c)(3) provides that gain or loss as well as depreciation shall be determined as though the undivided interests had not been contributed to the partnership. The partners would have divided the proceeds equally if they had still been joint tenants. The basis, now reduced by one year's depreciation, is $9,700 for A and $5,750 for B. The gain is taxed $300 to A and $4,250 to B.

4.9.4 When the Undivided Interests Rule Doesn't Apply

The undivided interests rule works well as long as there is no change in the profit sharing or capital ratios and may serve for the entire life of a partnership set up to develop and manage real estate projects, such as the typical limited partnership. The Code recognizes that some partnerships can never qualify under the undivided interests rule and that some that did qualify must make changes in one ratio or the other to accommodate changing circumstances.

We shall use a simple case to show the effect of changes in either ratio. A and B own equal shares in unimproved land, which they contribute to the partnership. A's basis is $4,000 and B's basis is $6,000. Their interests in the property before contribution are the same as their capital and profit sharing ratios in the partnership. If the property is sold for $12,000, A reports a $2,000 gain and B reports no gain. This makes sense, because that is exactly how the transaction would have been taxed if there had been no partnership.

Now let's assume one small change. After formation of the partnership, but before sale of the property, A contributes some cash so that the capital ratio is amended to 60 percent for A and 40 percent for B, but, by agreement, the profit sharing remains equal. The undivided interests rule is no longer operative. Therefore, the $2,000 gain will be taxable half to each partner.

If the partners want the sale to be taxed as it would have been if the undivided interests rule were still in effect, or if the partnership never qualified for the undivided interests rule, the partnership can elect under Section 704(c)(2) to allocate the gain to the partner who contributed low-basis property. The entire $2,000 gain would be allocated to A.

4.9.5 Allowable Depreciation Is Limited to Total Depreciation

As another example, C and D form an equal partnership by the contribution of $10,000 cash by C and by the contribution of machinery with fair market value of $10,000, but tax basis of only $4,000, by D. Assuming an annual depreciation rate of 10 percent straight-line and no agreement to specially allocate deductions, depreciation of $400 will be allocated equally. If the partners choose to do so they may allocate the entire $400 to C. If C were to fall into the common trap of confusing tax law with logic, he might insist that depreciation of $1,000 would have been deductible if D had contributed property with a basis equal to its value, and that since only $400 was allowable, C should have had $500 allocated to him, with D reporting a minus allocation of $100. It doesn't work that way; partners can allocate the deductible depreciation as they choose, but they can't create a depreciation deduction where none exists.

4.9.6 Tax Treatment When the Contributed Asset Is Sold

Assume that the asset is sold on the first day of year two for $10,000. Since its basis has been reduced to $3,600, there is a taxable gain of $6,400.

The partners may agree to allocate $6,000 to D to compensate for his lack of basis in the contributed property, and the remaining $400 to C.

It is interesting to see what this series of transactions does to each partner's basis of his partnership interest. C's original basis of $10,000 is reduced by the prior year's depreciation of $400 and increased by the current year's gain of $400 to remain at $10,000. D's original basis of $4,000 is increased by the allocated gain of $6,000 to arrive at $10,000.

4.10 SIGNIFICANCE OF GROSS INCOME

Internal Revenue Code Section 702 lists the components of partnership income that the partner must show on his return separately. Perhaps surprisingly, this Section closes with "In any case where it is necessary to determine the gross income of a partner for purposes of this title, such amount shall include his distributive share of the gross income of the partnership."

The significance of this provision is that a partner must know how much his gross income is so that he can determine whether he is required to file a return. Under Section 6501(e), the statute of limitations on a return is extended to 6 years if there has been an omission of 25 percent of gross income. Soil and water conservation expenses are deductible under Section 175(b) up to 25 percent of the gross income from farming, and this includes a partner's share of gross income from farming carried on by a partnership. If at least two-thirds of a taxpayer's gross income is expected to be from farming or fishing, he may avail himself of the advantageous filing requirements of Section 6073. Section 931 uses gross income to compute the amount of income from sources within possessions of the United States.

4.10.1 How a Partner's Share of Partnership Gross Income Is Computed

A tax practitioner should be acutely aware of the significance of the six-year statute of limitations provision as it relates to partners, and the interesting way that the Regulations under Section 702 explain it. A partner is deemed to have reported in his return a share of gross income proportionate to his reporting of his distributive share of profits. If, for example, he has a one-fourth interest in a partnership that has gross income of $100,000, and his distributive share of profits of $20,000 was $5,000, by reporting $5,000 on his return he would have been regarded as having stated in his return that his share of gross income was $25,000. If he reported that his distributive share was only $3,000, then he is regarded as having reported only 60 percent (the ratio of $3,000 to $5,000) of his share of gross income, or $15,000 rather than $25,000. In many cases this under-reporting of $10,000 would amount to 25 percent of gross income shown on the return, so the six-year statute of limitations applies.

The Regulations, by defining share of gross income as pro rata to share of distributive share, make it easy to determine the amount of gross income allocable to each partner. Without such a simple formula, the task would be impossible in cases of two-tier profit sharing, for partners who were in the partnership for a fraction of a year, or for partners who share in only part of the partnership income.

4.11   SPECIAL TREATMENT ITEMS OF INCOME

Internal Revenue Code Section 702 specifies six items of income or deductions that each partner shall separately take into account in determining his income tax. They are:

1. Gains and losses from sales of capital assets held for not more than one year
2. Gains and losses from sales or exchanges of capital assets held for more than one year
3. Gains and losses from sales or exchanges of certain property used in a trade or business and involuntary conversions
4. Charitable contributions
5. Dividends or interest subject to exclusion under IRC Section 116 or 128 or deduction under Part VIII of Subchapter B
6. Taxes to foreign countries or U.S. possessions

The Code further specifies that other items of income, gain, loss, deductions, or credit, to the extent provided by Regulations, must be taken into account separately.

U.S. Partnership Return of Income, Form 1065, lists these items (in addition to those listed above):

1. Ordinary income
2. Guaranteed payments
3. Gain or loss from involuntary conversions due to casualty or theft
4. Payments for partner to an IRA
5. Payments for partner to a Keogh Plan
6. Payments for partner to a Simplified Employee Pension
7. Jobs credit
8. Credit for alcohol used as a fuel
9. Gross farming or fishing income

10. Net earnings (loss) from self-employment
11. Accelerated depreciation on real property
12. Accelerated depreciation on leased property
13. Reserves for losses on bad debts of financial institutions
14. Depletion (other than oil and gas)
15. Excess intangible drilling costs
16. Net income from oil, gas or geothermal wells
17. Investment interest expense
18. Net investment income
19. Excess expenses from "net lease property"
20. Excess of net long-term capital gain over net short-term capital loss from investment property
21. Property eligible for investment credit
22. Property subject to recapture of investment credit

While the above lists present a frighteningly long array of items to watch for, they do not include other items that may have to be separately stated for one reason or another, such as:

1. Recovery of bad debts, prior taxes, and delinquency amounts (Section 111)
2. Wagering gains and losses (Section 165)
3. Intangible drilling and development costs (Section 263(c))
4. Mining development expenditures (Section 616)
5. Soil and water conservation expenditures (Section 175)
6. Personal service income (Section 1348) (Repealed in 1981)
7. Section 1245 or 1250 recapture
8. Partially tax-exempt interest
9. Nonbusiness expenses as described in Section 212
10. Medical, dental, etc. expenses (Section 213)
11. Alimony payments (Section 215)
12. Amounts representing taxes and interest paid to cooperative housing corporations (Section 216)

The taxable income or loss of the partnership, exclusive of items requiring separate computation, must be stated separately for each partner, as must gain or loss to the partnership upon distribution of unrealized receivables or substantially appreciated inventory.

4.12 TIME FOR INCLUSION OF ITEMS OF INCOME

Section 706 provides that in computing the taxable income of a partner for a taxable year, the inclusions required by Section 702 (discussed in Paragraph 4.10) and guaranteed payments (Section 707 (c)) with respect to a partnership shall be based on the income, gain, loss, deduction or credit of the partnership for any taxable year of the partnership ending within or with the taxable year of the partner.

Since practically all partnerships and practically all individuals file their returns on the calendar year, there should be very few instances in which there is confusion as to time to report income for a partner who is a partner on the last day of the taxable year.

Some partnerships file their returns for a fiscal year ending on a date other than December 31. The partner should realize that the date on which he receives money from the partnership has nothing to do with when it is taxable. The date on which the partnership's year ends is the date on which all partnership income is "received."

The more likely area for confusion is in the receipt of guaranteed payments, which so closely resemble salaries, and partners' salaries. To illustrate how this works, we assume that Woody is a partner in a cash basis partnership with a November 30 year-end. He receives a guaranteed payment of $10,000 in December of each year. The payment he received in December 19X1 is included in his return for the year ending December 31, 19X2 because the $10,000 payment is taxable to him as of November 30, 19X2, the fiscal year in which the partnership reports the item.

4.13 ELECTIONS HAVING AN EFFECT ON COMPUTATION OF TAXABLE INCOME

If an election affects the computation of partnership income, it must be made by the partnership. Partners as individuals cannot rectify a partnership's failure to make an election. If an election is irrevocable, or if the election must be made on a timely filed partnership return, failure to recognize the partnership's responsibility can be costly.

Elective methods of calculating income or deductions are scattered throughout the length and breadth of the Internal Revenue Code. New elections are constantly being added. A logical approach to preparing such a list is to follow the arrangement of items on Form 1065, U.S. Partnership Return of Income. The list includes:

- Choice of the accounting year (Section 441 as limited by Section 706(b));
- Choice of the accounting method (Section 446);

- Last in, first out (LIFO) inventories (Section 472);
- Accrual of vacation pay (Section 463);
- Use of reserve method or direct charge-off of bad debts (Section 166);
- Method of depreciation or accelerated cost recovery (Section 167 or 168);
- Amortization. The instructions for this line of Form 1065 contain a handy list of potential amortization deductions and should be consulted for current items. Amortization elections may include: certain expenditures for research and experiment (Section 174); trademark and trade name (Section 177); mine or natural deposit development (Section 616); certified pollution control facilities (Section 169); child care facilities (Section 188); rehabilitation of historic structures (Section 191); organization and syndication expenses (Section 709); real property construction period interest and taxes (Section 189);
- Soil and water conservation expenses (Section 175) and farmland clearing expenditures (Section 182);
- Intangible drilling and development costs (Section 263(c));
- Expenditures in connection with certain railroad rolling stock (Section 263(d));
- Election of qualified progress expenditures' eligibility to be treated as investment credit property (Section 46(d)).

There are also elections peculiar to partnerships that will affect the total of taxable income (as contrasted with the allocation of that figure) such as the optional adjustment to basis of partnership property (Sections 734 and 743).

4.14 RETROACTIVE ALLOCATIONS AND VARYING INTERESTS

Retroactive allocations, under which a partner could be allocated a full share of partnership income or loss even though he became a partner late in the year, were prohibited by the Tax Reform Act of 1976. The purpose of such retroactive allocations was to give a high-bracket partner a share of loss which could equal all that he paid for the interest so that his income tax saving came close to offsetting his entire cost of becoming a partner.

Although the door was closed on retroactive allocations, the Committee Reports for the Tax Reform Act of 1976 said "The amendment amends

Section 706(c)(2)(B) to make it clear that the varying interests rule of this provision is to apply to _____ the incoming partner so as to take into account his varying interests during the year _____. These rules will permit a partnership to choose the easier method of prorating items according to the portion of the year for which a partner was a partner or the more precise method of an interim closing of books (as if the year had closed) which, in some instances, will be more advantageous where most of the deductible expenses were paid or incurred upon or subsequent to the entry of the new partners to the partnership."

4.14.1   A Superb Tax-Planning Opportunity Survived the Ban on Retroactive Allocations

Assume that X invests $50,000 in a cash basis calendar year partnership that owns unimproved land on December 1, 19X1, in exchange for a 50 percent interest in capital and profits and losses. On December 31, the partnership pays property taxes assessed for that calendar year in the amount of $100,000. The partnership follows the Committee's suggestion of an interim closing at November 30, so that the loss for the month of December is $100,000, of which X's share is $50,000. X appears to have achieved a deduction equal to his cash outlay.

4.15   DISTRIBUTIONS

Just as does any other investor of capital or effort, a partner expects to obtain a return. Whereas he may obtain his return by selling his interest in the partnership, he may take that route only once. In this chapter we shall address the return to a partner in the form of recurring distributions; liquidating distributions will be dealt with in a later chapter.

Internal Revenue Code Section 731 is the Code Section on distributions. You must remember that income is taxable to the partner when earned by the partnership, so that the distribution of income already earned is not a second taxable event. You must also remember that earnings increase the basis of the partner's interest in the partnership and that distributions reduce the basis of the interest.

4.15.1 Ordinarily, No Gain or Loss Is Recognized Upon a Distribution

Section 731 provides that gain is not recognized on a nonliquidating distribution (of money or of property) to a partner unless the money exceeds the basis of the partner's interest. The excess of basis over interest, no matter how small (including zero) becomes the basis of the property received.

Section 731 further provides that no loss is recognized upon a nonliquidating distribution.

4.15.2 The Exception to the General Rule

Section 751 contains an important exception, applicable when the distribution includes unrealized receivables and inventory items. Since those terms mean far more than the dictionary meaning of the terms, any partnership contemplating a distribution of property should consult the Regulations under Section 751 and the portion of Chapter Five of this book that covers "Appreciated Inventories and Unrealized Receivables."

4.15.3 How the Partnership Is Affected by Distributions

Section 731 further provides that no gain or loss is recognized to the partnership on a distribution to a partner, unless Section 751 has an effect.

4.15.4 The Nature of Gain Upon a Nonliquidating Distribution

In the event that a distribution to which Section 751 does not apply does result in a taxable gain, the gain is a capital gain.

4.15.5 Guaranteed Payments as Distributions

Guaranteed payments are not considered "distributions" for the purposes of these paragraphs.

4.15.6 Constructive Distributions

In determining when a distribution has been made, remember that a reduction of a partner's share of liabilities is considered to be a distribution of cash.

4.16   TAXATION OF DISTRIBUTIVE SHARES

There are at least three things one must know about taxation of distributive shares:

1. When are they taxed?
2. How are they taxed?
3. To whom are they taxed?

4.16.1 When a Distributive Share Is Taxed

Both distributive shares of income (Section 702) and guaranteed payments (Section 707) are taxed in the tax year of the partner with which or within which the taxable year of the partnership ends. Example: M, an individual filing his return for the calendar year 19X1 reports income from MN partnership whose tax year is also the calendar year 19X1. Example: O, an individual filing his return for the calendar year 19X0 reports income from OP partnership from its fiscal year that ended January 31, 19X0.

Partners sometimes think that guaranteed payments are so much like salaries that they should be taxed on the calendar year as salaries are; as pointed out above, this is not the case.

4.16.2 How a Distributive Share Is Taxed

A distributive share is taxed (or escapes taxation) just as if it had been received directly by the partner rather than through a partnership. Capital gains are taxed as capital gains; ordinary income is taxed as ordinary income; tax-exempt income does not lose its status by passing through a partnership.

4.16.3 To Whom A Distributive Share Is Taxed

A distributive share of income is taxed in accordance with the provisions of the partnership agreement, provided that the purpose of the allocation is not tax avoidance or evasion. See paragraphs 4.8.5 and 4.8.6 for a fuller discussion.

4.17   DEALINGS BETWEEN PARTNERSHIPS AND PARTNERS

A partner may deal with his partnership either as if he were an outsider or in his capacity as a partner. For instance, a partner who is engaged as a sole proprietor in the fuel oil business may sell fuel to his partnership, in which case he is dealing with the partnership as an outsider. The same person might provide the same partnership with fuel as property contributed to the partnership in exchange for an increase in his interest in the partnership. The question of the relationship in which dealings take place is one of fact.

4.17.1 Regulation 1.707.1 Defines Certain Transactions as Being Transactions Between Partnership and Partner as Outsider

A partner dealing with his partnership in the following transactions shall be treated as if he were not a member of the partnership:

1. Loan of money or property by the partnership to the partner or by the partner to the partnership
2. Sale of property by the partner to the partnership
3. Purchase of property by the partner from the partnership

4. The rendering of services by the partnership to the partner or by the partner to the partnership

5. Allowing the partnership to use personally owned property as security for its debt

4.17.2 Losses Between a Partner and a Controlled Partnership May Be Disallowed

Except for the sale of a partnership interest, no loss is allowed on a sale or exchange of property, directly or indirectly, between a partnership and a partner who owns, directly or indirectly, more than 50 percent of the capital interest or profits interest in the partnership.

4.17.3 Gains Between a Partner and Controlled Partnership Are Treated as Ordinary Income

Any gain recognized upon the sale or exchange of trade accounts receivable, inventory, stock in trade or depreciable or real property used in a trade or business is taxed as ordinary income if the transaction is between a partnership and a partner who owns more than 80 percent of the capital interest or profits interest in the partnership. This application of Section 707 applies to direct or indirect sales or exchanges, whether ownership is direct or indirect and the rules for constructive ownership of stock set forth in Code Section 267(c) apply as if the partnership interest were corporate stock.

A loss on a sale or exchange of property, directly or indirectly, between two partnerships in which the same persons, directly or indirectly, own more than 50 percent of the capital interest or profits interest in each partnership, is not allowed.

The loss that was disallowed under Section 707 may be used to reduce a future gain on the sale of the property involved in the loss. Section 707 says that Section 267(d) (which relates to gains where a loss previously was disallowed) shall apply as though the loss had been disallowed under Section 267(a)(1).

For the purposes of these paragraphs, a guaranteed payment is not an interest in partnership profits.

4.18 DISABILITY OF PARTNERS

Every partnership that requires the full-time services of its partners should have clear provision for disability. The provision should cover disability of such short duration that it is similar to the wage continuation plan provided for employees; that is, partners' salaries are not reduced for a period of a month or two. Disability insurance should cover the longer period. Since cases of severe disability will bring the disabled person under Social Security benefits within a year, a year or so should be enough disability coverage to be carried as a partnership responsibility. Each partner should consider his own needs and resources and take out his own insurance coverage to age 65.

Disability insurance premiums are not a tax deduction, whether booked as a partnership expense or charged to drawing accounts of individual partners. Disability insurance benefits are not taxable income if no deduction for the premium was allowable.

In determining the amount of disability insurance on partners and the duration of coverage, you should consider that group coverage is generally cheaper than individual policies, and partners who are individually uninsurable can obtain coverage under a group policy, or for greater amounts than could be obtained individually for partners with a poor medical history.

The partnership agreement should clearly specify the degree and duration of disability that causes mandatory retirement or withdrawal from the firm. This subject will be covered in Chapter Five.

4.19 SUMMATION OF CHAPTER FOUR

The preceding chapters should have helped you to understand partnerships, to select the partnership form on the basis of an informed opinion as to your choice of several forms, and to organize your partnership.

Those subjects constitute the design phase. Chapter Four has dealt with how you make the organization run smoothly; how you do the things that produce success.

The secret of profitable partnership operations can be summarized thus:

1. Get, keep and adequately compensate the people with whom you can most effectively work or invest.

2. Be sure that you have the management structure and techniques and the capital so that the organization can pull together and move toward its objectives with a minimum of lost motion or frustration.

3. Know the tax-wise methods of compensating, managing and financing the partnership.

CHAPTER FIVE

Transfers of Interest
In a Partnership

CONTENTS

INTRODUCTION 97

5.1 ADMISSION OF PARTNERS 97

    5.1.1   The Founding Partners – 97
    5.1.2   Admission of New Partners – 98
    5.1.3   Employees as a Source of New Partners – 98
    5.1.4   Relatives as a Source of New Partners – 98
    5.1.5   Be Thorough and Objective in Screening Applicants – 98
    5.1.6   What to Do When You Find the Right Person – 99
    5.1.7   The Partnership Agreement Spells Out the Terms for Admission of New Partners – 99

5.2 BUY-SELL AGREEMENTS 100

    5.2.1   Why a Written Agreement Is Needed – 101
    5.2.2   Essential Provisions of the Buy-Sell Agreement – 101

5.3 FUNDING THE BUY-SELL AGREEMENT WITH LIFE INSURANCE 101

    5.3.1   The Kind and Amount of Insurance Needed – 102

5.3.2   Cash Values Are a Resource and a Temptation – 102

5.3.3   Policies May Be Owned by a Partnership or by Partners – 102

5.3.4   Disposition of Policies for Which an Urgent Need No Longer Exists – 104

5.3.5   Insurance Proceeds Used to Fund a Deferred Payout – 105

5.4   PURCHASE AND SALE OF GOOD WILL   105

5.4.1   Guaranteed Payments Are the Normal Choice – 105

5.4.2   Guaranteed Payments May Not Be the Best Choice – 105

5.4.3   Good Will Does Not Include Unrealized Receivables and Inventory Items – 107

5.5   RETIREMENT OF A PARTNER   107

5.5.1   Retirement Can Be a Reward or Exile – 107

5.5.2   Retirement Should Be Scheduled – 107

5.5.3   Transition Should Be Controlled – 108

5.6   DISABILITY OF A PARTNER   108

5.6.1   Causes of Disability – 108

5.6.2   Defining Disability – 108

5.6.3   Disability Compensation – 109

5.6.4   The Tax Aspects of Disability Pay – 109

5.6.5   When Disability Invokes the Buy-Sell Agreement – 109

5.7   DEATH OF A PARTNER   110

5.7.1   Payments for a Deceased Partner's Interest – 110

5.7.2   Life Insurance as a Security Device – 111

5.8   DISAGREEMENT WITH OR EXPULSION OF A PARTNER   111

5.8.1   Contumacy Can Be a Weapon – 111

5.8.2   Submission of Disputes to Arbitration – 111

5.9   HOW AND WHEN THE DEPARTING PARTNER WILL BE PAID FOR HIS INTEREST   112

5.10   DETERMINATION OF THE PRICE TO BE PAID TO THE DEPARTING PARTNER   113

5.10.1   Determination of Fair Value – 113

5.10.2   Valuing Tangible Assets – 113
5.10.3   Valuing Intangible Assets – 114
5.10.4   Setting the Price – 114

5.11 GUARANTEED PAYMENTS TO RETIRED
      PARTNERS OR TO A DECEASED PARTNER'S
      SUCCESSOR IN INTEREST   115

5.11.1   Guaranteed Payments Defined – 115
5.11.2   The Good (Tax) News and the Bad (Tax)
          News About Guaranteed Payments – 115

5.12 INCOME IN RESPECT OF DECEDENT   115

5.13 CLOSING PARTNERSHIP YEAR UPON TRANSFER
      OF INTEREST   116

5.13.1   Death Does Not Necessarily Terminate a
          Partnership – 116
5.13.2   When the Partnership Year Closes for Tax
          Purposes – 116
5.13.3   Death Ordinarily Does Not Close the Part-
          nership Year – 117
5.13.4   Select the Estate's First Fiscal Year-End to
          Minimize Taxes – 117
5.13.5   A Deceased Partner Can Have Two Partner-
          ship Closings in His Final Year – 118

5.14 APPRECIATED INVENTORIES AND UNREALIZED
      RECEIVABLES   118

5.14.1   "Appreciated Inventories" Can Be a Mis-
          leading Term – 119
5.14.2   When the Sale of a Partnership Interest
          Produces Ordinary Income – 119
5.14.3   How Section 751 Is Applied – 119
5.14.4   The Paradoxical Definitions of Section 751
          – 120
5.14.5   Inventories Must be Substantially Appre-
          ciated to Invoke Section 751 – 120
5.14.6   Tax Effect to the Transferee Partner – 122
5.14.7   Tax Effect to the Transferor Partner – 123
5.14.8   Tax Effect to the Remaining Partners – 123
5.14.9   The Tax Effect to the Partners Giving Up
          an Interest in Property of a Character
          Different from the Property Received – 124
5.14.10   The Tax Effect to the Partnership of
          Giving Up an Interest in Property of a

Character Different from the Property Retained – 124

5.14.11   The Tax Effect When the Partners Do Not Specify What Will Be Exchanged – 125

5.14.12   Preplanning the Distribution Can Improve the Tax Consequences – 126

5.15   PARTNERSHIP ELECTIONS TO ADJUST BASIS OF PARTNERSHIP ASSETS   126

5.15.1   The Logic of Opportunity to Adjust Basis of Partnership Assets – 127

5.15.2   An Election Can Be Beneficial Whether Partners Are Coming or Going – 127

5.15.3   Elections to Adjust Basis of Partnership Assets Upon Transfer of Interests – 128

5.15.4   An Election, Once Made, Is Binding Upon Future Transfers – 129

5.15.5   Elections to Adjust Basis of Partnership Assets Upon a Distribution in Liquidation – 129

5.15.6   How an Election Under Section 754 Is Made – 131

5.15.7   Section 755 Provides for Designation of the Assets Whose Basis Is to Be Adjusted – 131

5.16   PARTNER'S ELECTION TO ADJUST BASIS OF DISTRIBUTED PROPERTY (SECTION 732)   132

5.16.1   The Partnership's Failure to Make a Section 754 Election Works Against the Withdrawing Partner – 132

5.16.2   Where the Tax Advantage to the Withdrawing Partner Lies – 132

5.16.3   How the Election Under Section 732 Is Made – 133

5.16.4   An Election Under Section 732(d) May Be Required – 133

5.17   THE MAIN POINTS OF CHAPTER FIVE   134

INTRODUCTION

An old farmer of my acquaintance was very proud of an axe which, he claimed, had been in his family for generations. He admitted that both head and handle had worn out and been replaced many times, but as far as he was concerned it was the same axe.

Many a successful partnership has replaced the founding partners, perhaps several times over. Any partnership that will be successful must plan to supplement and eventually replace its present partners or it will have only a limited life indeed. To maintain growth consistent with its desires, the partnership must plan for admission of new partners and must assure itself of a supply of new blood. Both to crown a successful career with pleasant retirement and to weed out those who have faded from full bloom, the partnership must offer and require a systematic turnover of responsibility.

Unless the sole reward for a lifetime of service to the partnership will be a gold watch (a Timex sprayed with gold paint?), funds must be set aside or other reliable sources of retirement pay must be assured. The person charged with retirement planning must understand that the same number of retirement dollars can cost substantially different amounts of taxes, depending on what you call those payments.

A partnership, like a marriage, is easier to get into than to get out of. Exit from a partnership is complicated by concepts like "appreciated inventories and unrealized receivables." The person who does not realize the problems exist will soon appreciate the seriousness of his tax problem.

Many areas of taxation depend on the basis of property, and both the existing partners and the partnership need to know not only the immediate tax effects of shifting interests but also the effect years down the road.

5.1 ADMISSION OF PARTNERS

5.1.1 The Founding Partners

Nothing is of more importance to the success of a partnership than the choice of partners. Two people (or other small number) may join together to form a partnership because they are very much alike. Examples of this are hobbyists who decide to "go professional," making money and pursuing their favorite activity simultaneously, or two people who split off from an existing business because they share a common philosophy which they cannot reconcile with that of the old firm. Sometimes, people pool their diverse talents because they recognize that each has something the other lacks and that together they will be stronger than they could be in sole proprietorships. Examples of this are the overburdened older man who will share his patients or clients with a young associate, or the construction business aspirants who recognize that different talents are needed in the office and in the field. It is not uncommon for such well thought out associations to remain viable until death or retirement part them.

5.1.2 Admission of New Partners

To grow beyond its founding stage, a partnership must add new partners. Ideally, a new partner is brought in because he (or she) fills a specific niche (a tax specialist in a general-practice law firm, for instance). A new partner may be needed because the present partners simply cannot carry the load and must spread the work around; in such a case, a "clone" of the existing partners may be the perfect choice.

5.1.3 Employees as a Source of New Partners

The poorest reason for admitting a partner is that a good employee may quit if partnership is not offered. Although it is obvious that a person who is not a good employee will not be a good partner, it does not follow that being a good employee is an infallible indicator that a person will be a good partner. Although proper management structure will reduce the need for each partner to be a skilled executive, both custom and law impose a management responsibility upon each partner. Rather than confer partnership status upon a potentially poor partner, you should "bite the bullet" and lose the employee.

5.1.4 Relatives as a Source of New Partners

In the author's opinion, an equally poor reason for admitting a partner to an operating partnership (as contrasted with a mere investment) is that the new partner is a relative, particularly a son (daughter), or in-law. Experience shows that the relationship is hard on both sides; if the younger person does well, there is a public conception that he (she) got to the higher echelons at least partly by nepotism. If the relationship turns sour, it is a traumatic experience for all concerned. There is also the problem that fathers and sons never seem to realize; good people will shy away from a firm in which nepotism is a policy or a potential because the "outsider" knows (or suspects, usually correctly) that when the plums fall, the "crown prince" is the most likely beneficiary.

5.1.5 Be Thorough and Objective in Screening Applicants

Regardless of the source from which new partners come, the question of whether the person will "wear well" as a partner should be carefully considered. If he (or she) has objectionable personal habits, they will become less tolerable with the passage of time. If there are differences of philosophy (particularly ethics) among partners, the dichotomy will eat into the organization like a cancer. If a workaholic teams up with an easygoing partner, conflict will come even sooner. An old saying, relating to matrimony, "marry in haste and repent at leisure" applies equally to selecting partners. Time spent in considering every conceivable reason why the prospect would not work out as a partner could be the most profitable hours of your business career.

5.1.6 What to Do When You Find the Right Person

Unless the firm has a record of frequent admissions of partners so that the transfer of burdens and benefits of new partner status follows a well-worn path, there will be misunderstandings on both sides. The normal situation in a professional firm is that established practitioners are seeking relief from a work schedule that permits too little time for anything else. Fearful that a promising candidate will escape, they make generous promises. The candidate, convinced that once he has a voice in management he can effect changes that will solve most, if not all, of the firm's problems, indulges in fantasies of future influence and affluence.

In the courtship days preceding admission of a new partner, there is a strong tendency to rationalize the lack of a thorough exploration of potential problem areas by saying "we know each other and we trust each other; we know what's good for us and what's good for the firm; why can't we just shake hands on it and get on with the business?" Perhaps you can, but without a written description of the terms and conditions there is a likelihood that you will find that there was never a meeting of the minds; that the expectations of the parties are irreconcilable.

5.1.7 The Partnership Agreement Spells Out the Terms for Admission of New Partners

Since this chapter concerns transfers of interests in existing partnerships, we shall assume that a partnership agreement is in existence. If it was tailor-made for the founders and doesn't provide for admission of others, it must be amended. If the agreement provides for admission of new partners, the pertinent sections, as well as those affecting intrapartnership relations, must be reviewed for timeliness.

The agreement must clearly cover these points:

- Capital required from the new partner
- Demands on the time of each partner, including a prohibition, if desirable, against other activities which, while not in competition with the partnership, are inimical to its best interests

- Sharing of profits, losses, and voting power (including any restriction on participation in management)

Illustrative Terms for Admission of a Partner

Peters, Powers and King, a professional partnership, consider their employee, Ball, to be good partnership material. The partners had income from the partnership for the last year of $80,000, $60,000, and $50,000, respectively. Ball's salary was $30,000 and the cost of his fringe benefits (including the employer's share of social security tax) was $5,000. Professional staff salaries are roughly 40 percent of charge-out rates and time chargeable to clients' accounts for about 80 percent of paid hours, with 20 percent consumed by holidays, vacations, sick pay, continuing education, and unassigned time. Ball, therefore, produced about $60,000 in billable time. As a partner, he might be able to justify a higher charge-out rate, but the additional time required to be a partner would offset that, so $60,000 is the projected billing for his first year as a partner. What compensation arrangement will seem attractive to Ball without unduly taking net income away from the partnership?

With the exuberance frequently encountered in prospective partners with visions of sugar plums dancing in their heads, Ball suggests that since he earns $60,000 for the firm, $60,000 should be about right for his compensation as a partner. King protests, testily pointing out that that is more than he makes, and Powers doesn't like the idea of a junior partner sharing his level of earnings. They explain to Ball that there are costs incurred in having a partner on board, such as his share of rent, utilities, supplies, insurance and administrative personnel costs. They offer him $40,000, based on two-thirds of production, which he accepts. Since he cannot come up with his share of capital in cash, they will permit him to pay in 10 percent of his annual income from the partnership until he reaches the required level. How does Ball fare? From his $40,000 comes $4,000 as his capital contribution, and his former fringe benefits of $5,000 are now a deduction from his draw. His spendable income (before income and social security taxes) has gone up from an employee's $30,000 to a partner's $31,000. Though this may seem like little incentive to become a partner, it is typical of how the finances actually work out.

How did the partnership fare? Its gross profit on employee Ball was $25,000 ($60,000 minus $30,000 minus $5,000). Its gross profit on partner Ball is $20,000 ($60,000 minus $40,000).

5.2   BUY-SELL AGREEMENTS

In its formative stage, or at the time the partnership agreement is written, provision should be made for an agreement requiring the purchase and sale of a partner's interests under described conditions.

5.2.1 Why a Written Agreement Is Needed

A partner may wish to leave, or be forced to leave, the partnership under any of these conditions:

1. Disagreement
2. Expulsion
3. Disability
4. Death
5. Retirement

Any of these events may happen in any partnership. Although retirement may be anticipated, aging partners seldom look forward to a complete cessation of activity and usually want considerable flexibility as to the age of mandatory retirement. There may be insistence upon a tapering-off period preceding retirement. There are also degrees of disability, so that a partner in declining health may want to continue part-time participation for an extended period of time.

When the time for consummation of a buy-sell agreement comes, there is almost certain to be disagreement about implementation, and this is true no matter how carefully the provision is worded or how sincere the partners were at the time the agreement was reached. If the provision is worded too rigidly, arbitration or litigation is likely. If the provision is worded too loosely, each side will interpret as it wishes, and it may destroy any value the provision might have been intended to have. The odds are against the draftsman of a buy-sell agreement, but an honest attempt must be made.

5.2.2 Essential Provisions of the Buy-Sell Agreement

The buy-sell agreement must encompass these principles:

1. What will trigger implementation of the provision?
2. What price will be paid for the departing partner's interest?
3. When will payments be made, and what will be the source of funds for payment?
4. Will the tax implications favor the departing or surviving partners?
5. What restrictions will be placed upon the departing partner?

5.3 FUNDING THE BUY-SELL AGREEMENT WITH LIFE INSURANCE

When it comes to retiring a partner, a partnership is at a distinct disadvantage compared to a corporation retiring an employee. Partners' qualified retirement plans are limited to Individual Retirement Accounts and Keogh Plans, none of which is adequate for a substantial retirement fund.

5.3.1 The Kind and Amount of Insurance Needed

The only practical way to pre-fund purchase of a partner's interest upon retirement or death is through life insurance. If the partnership can afford the premiums, ordinary life insurance can fund the buy-out upon death, or cash values can provide money to purchase the interest of a retiring partner. During the years between issuance of the policy and the death or retirement of the insured partner, its existence gives all the partners a sense of security about their ability to meet the obligation when it is due.

There is, of course, a problem in determining how much life insurance to carry, considering that the purchase value may be based upon a formula whose details will not be determined until well in the future. An obvious answer is to acquire a maximum amount of insurance commensurate with probable need and availability of premium money. Another answer is to acquire policies on younger partners in minimal amounts with the right to increase coverage in the future with guaranteed insurability.

5.3.2 Cash Values Are a Resource and a Temptation

When interest rates soar, there is a temptation to borrow against policies to use the money for normal partnership operations. Obviously, borrowing thwarts the opportunity to use the cash value or an equivalent amount of death proceeds for the intended purpose. Partnership policy should discourage borrowing for any reason other than to invest at rates better than the policy loan interest, and borrowing should be absolutely prohibited without the consent of the insured.

5.3.3 Policies May Be Owned by a Partnership or by Partners

Two ways of owning partnership policies are ownership by the partnership or cross-ownership, an arrangement under which all the other partners own the policy on any partner's life.

Under either arrangement, cash values should be recorded as a partnership asset, with an offsetting credit to the various partners' capital accounts. It is logical to credit increases in cash values to partners' accounts pro rata to the amount of premiums, policy by policy, that were charged to partners' accounts. If interest is paid on partners' capital accounts, capital accounts arising from recording increases in cash values probably should not earn interest.

The partnership agreement should specify how the above matters will be handled and should specify how death proceeds will be credited. The author recommends that death proceeds be credited in proportion to how the total premiums paid on that policy were charged to partners' accounts.

To understand the logic of the suggestions above, you must remember that insurance premiums on the lives of partners are not tax deductible and the death proceeds are not taxable income.

Illustration of Allocation of Premiums and Proceeds

When A and B formed their partnership, it took out $100,000 ordinary life policies on each partner, providing that premiums would be allocated to the partner (partners) other than the insured, and the proceeds would be allocated in the same proportion as premiums had been allocated over the life of the policy. The annual premium was $3,000. For three years A and B were the only partners. In the fourth year, C was admitted as a 30 percent partner. In the fifth year, D was admitted as a 20 percent partner and this arrangement continued through the 10th year when A died.

Premiums were charged to partners:

	B	C	D
Year 1	$ 3,000		
Year 2	3,000		
Year 3	3,000		
Year 4	1,616	$ 1,384	
Year 5	1,167	1,000	$ 833
Year 6	1,167	1,000	833
Year 7	1,166	1,000	834
Year 8	1,167	1,000	833
Year 9	1,167	1,000	833
Year 10	1,166	1,000	834
	$17,616	$ 7,384	$ 5,000

The proceeds of the $100,000 would be allocated $58,720 to B, $24,613 to C, and $16,667 to D.

Illustration of Computation of Payout to a Retiring Partner

This illustration is based on the provisions of Articles 9 and 14 of the sample partnership agreement shown in Appendix B.

A has had an income from his cash basis partnership of $80,000 in each of the last four years. Net fees of the partnership were $1,000,000 for the year prior to A's retirement. A's cash basis capital account has a balance of $50,000. The combined accounts receivable and work in process of the firm (all considered collectible at face amount) are $300,000 at the moment of A's retirement. How much money does he get and when does he get it?

Under Article 9 of the sample partnership agreement, A's $50,000 capital account will be paid to him in 36 equal monthly installments of $1,389 per month beginning in the first month after his retirement.

Under Article 14, he will receive guaranteed payments which are the lesser of the sum of his earnings from the partnership for the three years preceding his retirement ($240,000, being 3 times $80,000) or 150 percent of $1,000,000 times 20 percent, which is $300,000. Monthly guaranteed payments of $2,000 will commence in the first month after his retirement.

A is also entitled to 20 percent of the collections on accounts receivable and work in process, which will be received:

1st month after retirement	$ 90,000
2nd month after retirement	75,000
3rd month after retirement	60,000
4th month after retirement	45,000
5th month after retirement	30,000
	$300,000

A will receive payments from his partnership as follows:

	Guaranteed Payments	Capital Account	Work in Process and Accounts Receivable	Total
Month 1	$2,000	$1,389	$18,000	$21,389
Month 2	2,000	1,389	15,000	18,389
Month 3	2,000	1,389	12,000	15,389
Month 4	2,000	1,389	9,000	12,389
Month 5	2,000	1,389	6,000	9,389
Each of next 31 months	2,000	1,389	none	3,389
Each of next 84 months	2,000	none	none	2,000

Since the payments for his capital account are a return of capital, they are nontaxable to A. Each payment on work in process and accounts receivable is taxable to him as ordinary income and is subject to self-employment tax.

5.3.4 Disposition of Policies for Which an Urgent Need no Longer Exists

Other problems concerning life insurance premiums should be covered in the partnership agreement. The first covers policies on the life of a partner who leaves the firm. The author suggests that the departing partner have the right to purchase the policy for its cash value. The proceeds would be credited to the partners under the formula applicable to death proceeds. The second problem relates to the equity which a withdrawing, retiring, or deceased partner has in the policies on the lives of other partners. The author suggests that the partnership be required to purchase them for their cash values, with the purchase price charged to partners as if it were a premium.

Another question to be dealt with is whether a policy must be kept in force after the retirement or disability of a partner. The partnership should have the right to cash in the policy, with proceeds placed in escrow for future payments to the departed partner, if appropriate.

5.3.5 Insurance Proceeds Used to Fund a Deferred Payout

Another section of this chapter deals with guaranteed payments to retired partners and with payments to the heirs of a deceased partner as income in respect of a decedent. There may be an advantage to the recipients to spread the receipt of this money, which is ordinary income, over several years. If it is desirable to protect this tax advantage, then there should be provision for life insurance money to be held in escrow and doled out according to the original terms. Obviously, there should be sufficient restriction placed upon the escrow account so that the tax authorities cannot claim constructive receipt by the retired partner or the heirs of the deceased partner, and so that the partnership cannot, in a moment of crisis or fiscal irresponsibility, divert the money from its intended purpose.

5.4   PURCHASE AND SALE OF GOOD WILL

A partnership has the right to determine, by agreement among the partners, whether the payments to a retiring partner or to the heirs of a deceased partner are for good will (taxed as the sale of a capital asset) or are distributive shares or guaranteed payments (taxed as ordinary income). Internal Revenue Code Section 736 covers these options.

5.4.1 Guaranteed Payments Are the Normal Choice

The normal reaction of the tax advisor to the partnership is to recommend that the payments to the departing partner or his heirs be designated as guaranteed payments under Code Section 736(a)(2). The logic of this recommendation is that the surviving partners get an income tax deduction and are assumed to be in a higher bracket than the retired partner or the heirs, who must pick up guaranteed payments as ordinary income. In most situations, this view will prevail, especially since the partners who look forward to the tax deduction probably have the votes to get it. An illustration of how a formula for guaranteed payments can be developed is found in Chapter Nine, following 9.10.

5.4.2   Guaranteed Payments May Not Be the Best Choice

The logic on which the selection of the guaranteed payments approach is based is not always sound. A retiring partner may have accumulated sufficient investments during a long and successful career to provide a post-retirement income high enough to put him or his heirs into a tax bracket as high as the 50 percent bracket at which the surviving partners may pay their taxes. In such a case, the fact that as high as 60 percent of what he receives as good will payments will be excluded from taxable income may encourage him to negotiate payments for good will. The tax on good will payments to heirs might be eliminated completely because the estate valuation may equal the amount to be received. A well-to-do senior partner would be well advised to negotiate with his partners to obtain a sale of good will, and should consider taking a substantially reduced price. The partners, recognizing that they can get no tax deduction for amortizing good will, should consider their probable tax bracket in these negotiations.

The partner facing retirement should include in his calculations the fact that ordinary income inuring to him is subject to self-employment tax, and the receipt of guaranteed payments may affect his eligibility for social security benefits. Imposition of social security taxes on guaranteed payments received by a retired partner is based upon Internal Revenue Code Section 1402(a) (10), which excludes only those payments made to a retired partner who has been paid in full for his capital interest, and will continue to receive payments for life. Some authorities contend that a retired partner whose payments will not continue for life does not need Section 1402(a) (10) to save him from self-employment taxes, because he does not meet the requirements to be taxed covered in ʼSection 1402(a). This includes only distributive shares of partnership income, the logic being that a person who has neither a capital nor a profit interest does not have a distributive share of partnership income. Affected persons should seek the latest possible information on this point, as several influential organizations, including the American Institute of CPAs, have urged Congress to redress this inequity. He should also consider that guaranteed payments to his heirs are taxed as income in respect of a decedent, involving what approaches double taxation.

A particularly affluent senior partner should recognize that the combination of income taxes and self-employment taxes, and the possibility of estate taxes plus income taxes on income in respect of a decedent are very high. Considering the fact that estate tax is payable within nine months of death on partnership remittances due possibly years in the future, and considering the time value of money, the effective tax take rises even closer to the confiscatory level.

In summary, it may be to the advantage of all parties to give serious consideration to designating the proceeds of a buy-sell agreement as payments for good will, except as limited by Code Section 751.

5.4.3 Good Will Does Not Include Unrealized Receivables and Inventory Items

Payments may not be designated as good will and ordinary income taxation avoided to the extent that payments are for "unrealized receivables and inventory items" as defined in Internal Revenue Code Section 751. These terms are discussed in paragraph 5.14 of this chapter. Since the payments will be taxed as ordinary income to the recipient, the value of Section 751 items should be specifically covered by guaranteed payments.

5.5   RETIREMENT OF A PARTNER

An agreement to buy and sell a partnership interest upon the long-scheduled retirement of a partner is most susceptible to orderly planning.

5.5.1 Retirement Can Be Reward or Exile

Ideally, a partner should retire before age or infirmity causes his value to the partnership, and therefore the value of his interest, to decrease materially. The idea of retirement evokes opposite reactions from different people. To many, retirement is the aim in life, and working is a necessary evil to be endured only until retirement can commence at the earliest possible date. To others, for whom the working career was a source of greater satisfaction, retirement is approached with equanimity; retirement provides the opportunity to pursue different interests. With either of these types, negotiating a retirement clause is relatively easy.

There is a third type of partner. To him, the business is his life. He dreads the loss of status or purpose that working affords him; he sees retirement as endless days of puttering, of activities engaged in only as an antidote to utter boredom. He may even dread the possibility that the business may discover that it can get along without him. Writing and enforcing a retirement provision for him will challenge the skill of the most adroit negotiator and wordsmith.

5.5.2 Retirement Should Be Scheduled

Unless you intend to negotiate a retirement clause when one or all parties are under duress, you must write a clause of general application. Special arrangements set dangerous precedents and are a source of resentment and jealousy. A retirement clause should provide for flexible retirement dates. If the mandatory retirement age extends beyond the traditional retirement age of 65, there should be a reduction of price at dates beyond that point to encourage retirement before the problems of aging become acute.

5.5.3 Transition Should Be Controlled

For the good of the retiring partner and of the partnership, consideration should be given to gradual phasing out. A reasonable transition period affords the business the opportunity to transfer functions and responsibilities in an orderly manner. The transition avoids the trauma that afflicts people who work at full speed until the day on which the gold watch is presented, only to discover that there is no longer any need to know what time it is because there is no activity that needs scheduling.

Transition can be a good thing, but it can extend too long. Full-time workers are inconvenienced when they must share tasks or responsibilities with a person who works part-time, particularly if the part-timer does not have a regular schedule. A problem can develop if a partner who is not enthusiastic about retiring, or cannot reconcile himself to giving up authority, is reluctant to cooperate in the transition. Such a situation creates resentment in the partner assuming responsibility, and confusion for everyone.

5.6 DISABILITY

The prudent partnership will recognize that disability is a threat to the partnership as well as to the partner. The threat to the partner is obvious; forced inactivity and loss or impairment of earning power. The threat to the partnership includes not only its humane concern for the predicament of the unfortunate member, but a broad spectrum of problems, many of which are unexpected by the unwarned.

5.6.1 Causes of Disability

The partnership that enforces a reasonable mandatory retirement age protects itself against disability from the most obvious cause—aging; ranging from the creakiness and loss of vigor that afflicts all of us sooner or later, to outright senility.

Disability, unfortunately, is not limited to the elderly. Heart conditions, accidents, serious disease, loss of sight or hearing strike people in the prime of life. To add to the problem of coping with disability, the extent, the progression, or the duration of disability can seldom be predicted. The same degree of disability will encumber different people to different degrees because of their adaptability and the demands of the job.

5.6.2 Defining Disability

The first problem in making provision for disability is in how to define it and measure it. The highly motivated partner will resist acceptance of the diagnosis "Disabled." Economic pressures, real or perceived, as well as reluctance to admit that he cannot contribute a full share, drive a person to deny (to others) the obvious deterioration of his condition. He may insist that the problem is temporary and should not be dealt with in any permanent way.

The best way to define disability in the partnership agreement is by specifying the duties and responsibilities of a partner in such a way that failure to meet the specifications establishes disability. Such a mechanical provision absolves the other partners of the responsibility of invoking the charge of disability in many cases. It does very little to reassure the partners (or clients or patients) of a person who meets a physical presence test but who is in much less than satisfactory mental or emotional health. In such cases, if persuasion fails, a requirement that any partner submit to physical, mental or emotional examinations is the only protection that the firm can have.

5.6.3 Disability Compensation

The most strenuous objection to retirement or extended furlough for disability usually has an economic basis. It follows, then, that the best inducement to acceptance of inactivity is the removal of the financial penalty for not working. For short-term disability, a simple, unfunded uninsured plan similar to an employee's sick leave should suffice. For protection in the longer term, the partnership must obtain a group disability policy or require partners to maintain individual policies adequate to maintain an appropriate standard of living.

Besides giving the disabled partner the economic independence conducive to accepting disability status, insurance removes a psychological barrier to enforcing the disability provisions. Other partners, employees, clients or customers, motivated by sympathy, will conspire to cover up shortcomings if they can thus salve their consciences by lending assistance. Removing the financial detriment to disability reduces their temptation to serve as "crutches."

5.6.4 The Tax Aspects of Disability Pay

Disability insurance premium payments for partners are not deductible expenses and benefits received under such policies are not taxable income.

5.6.5 When Disability Invokes the Buy-Sell Agreement

Clearly, short-term disability is not a cause for invoking the buy-sell agreement. However, dragged-out uncertainty has a deleterious effect on the entire organization, and there must be a stopping point.

Especially in a small partnership, an extended temporary disability, or the stages of a permanent disability prior to the time at which its permanency is determined, will have weakened the partnership. The business has suffered, both from the financial drain of continued compensation to the disabled partner, and from the loss of his services. It is, therefore, less able to live up to a price for the partnership interest that would invoke less hardship in case of death (with life insurance) or retirement for age (when orderly planning would have been done). The disabled partner has already received substantial benefits, and should recognize that he has less to sell than he would have had when he was a full partner in every sense of the word.

The buy-sell agreement should be invoked when there is a mechanical or medical determination of long-term disability, or when an indefinite state of disability is posing a real threat to the financial or operating stability of the partnership, or when disability benefits have reached a specified percentage of the buy-sell price. As the last phrase suggests, consideration should be given to reducing the price by part or all of the disability benefits received prior to retirement or death.

5.7 DEATH OF A PARTNER

The drafter of the partnership agreement should be mindful that statute law ordinarily terminates a partnership upon the death of a general partner. However, Internal Revenue Code Section 706(c) provides that the death of a partner will not cause the partnership year to close unless the partnership is terminated. A partnership agreement can be written to permit the partnership to continue after the death of a partner, so a buy-sell agreement to take effect at death is an appropriate part of any partnership agreement.

5.7.1 Payments for a Deceased Partner's Interest

Death may affect the purchase of a partnership agreement in two ways; death of an active partner triggers the transaction, or death of a retired partner may terminate or affect the status of payments under a plan already in operation.

An interest in a partnership has an ascertainable value. The payment of the price should not be affected by the partner's mortality. It is not uncommon for an agreement to stipulate that payments to a retired partner should cease upon his death. Such an arrangement is analagous to a pension with no provision for survivor's benefits. If the agreement should provide for payment for life, it should provide for payment for a number of years certain; preferably, at a specified price, with the possibility or even the likelihood that payments will stop before the retired partner dies.

It may seem heartless to advocate a plan under which payments may terminate while support needs still exist. Nonetheless, it is a fact that a partnership interest is worth only so much, and the partner who negotiates payment for life will probably get smaller payments than he could have gotten had he opted for a specific amount or number of payments.

5.7.2 Life Insurance as a Security Device

In an inflationary economy, payments due far in the future have a present value that diminishes to almost nothing. Funding the agreement with life insurance is the subject of a separate section of this book, but it is appropriate to mention here that life insurance gives a sense of security to all parties to the negotiations. Clearly, it is in the interests of each partner to urge the partnership or his partners to carry as much life insurance as is feasible, both to enhance security and to speed up payments.

Paragraphs 5.12 and 5.13 and subheadings under 5.13 discuss income in respect of a decedent, the effect of death on the partnership's year, and the timing of partnership income for the decedent's return and for the fiduciary return for his estate.

5.8   DISAGREEMENT WITH OR EXPULSION OF A PARTNER

There is no effective way to provide for a price to be paid to a partner who leaves after disagreement or is expelled, except when expulsion is for loss of a professional license or for some act that prevents or impairs the offending partner's continued participation; for example, conviction of a felony, bankruptcy, or financial condition so bad that he cannot fulfill his obligations. Common sense should tell you that partners who are forced to separate because of the seriousness of their disagreement will not reach agreement on the final issue, the most basic bread-and-butter issue of them all, that of who gets what and who pays what.

5.8.1 Contumacy Can Be a Weapon

A disagreeable partner can use his cantankerousness to force a separation on his terms. Disagreement does not have to be violent or continuous to render a partnership ineffective; the attrition of repeatedly resolving differences of opinion by arriving at compromises satisfying no one will destroy the partnership just as surely.

5.8.2 Submission of Disputes to Arbitration

The only workable solution to the problem of buying and selling the interest of a partner or partners without whom the partnership is significantly better off, is submission of the matter to impartial arbitration. Your attorney can provide the wording, or the American Arbitration Association, 140 West 51 Street, New York, NY 10020, can make suggestions. Obviously, submission to mandatory arbitration should require a majority vote, and that every attempt to resolve differences through internal negotiation will have been made.

Care must be exercised in determining just what will be submitted to arbitration. For example, the agreement may provide that the value of the assets will be determined by arbitration, or that the value of the departing partner's interest will be determined by arbitration. In such a case, all assets must be valued by the arbitrators. Though an arbitrator is sworn to "faithfully and fully hear and examine the matters in controversy between the parties, in accordance with their arbitration agreement, and make a just award according to the best of his understanding," he cannot possibly know as much about your business as you do. He will be very conservative in placing a value on past-due receivables or on good will when there has been well-publicized tension in the partnership. When you insert an arbitration clause you have the right to limit the assets that go into the arbitration "basket," and should provide that reasonable efforts at negotiation, on an item-by-item basis, be required before submission of any issue to arbitration.

Lest these reservations appear to contradict a recommendation for an arbitration clause, be assured that any properly selected arbitrator or panel of arbitrators is infinitely superior to any jury to whose lack of business acumen you might fall victim.

5.9 HOW AND WHEN THE DEPARTING PARTNER WILL BE PAID FOR HIS INTEREST

Generally, the terms of payment will depend upon available funds and upon the tax emphases of the partners. Seldom is cash available for a one-shot buy-out. If the partnership expects to continue operations and must replace the services and the capital of the departing partner, an ideal solution is to find an acceptable person who will buy the interest directly from the departing partner. A variation on this is to have the partnership buy the interest and simultaneously sell it to a new partner under substantially the same terms under which the interest was bought. Under such an arrangement, the partnership might buy the entire interest of the departing partner and sell part of it to a new partner and retain part for future sale; or divide the unsold part among the surviving partners; or even hold it until the newly admitted partner's circumstances improve so that he can acquire the remainder. There is no requirement that the partnership sell at the price at which it bought the interest.

If the departing partner's share of the work load can be carried by the surviving organization, the partnership might simply buy out the departing partner's interest. In the case of a substantial interest, this can be very difficult if the buy-out must be made with after-tax funds. The partnership has considerable latitude in deciding whether to use before- or after-tax money to buy the interest, a subject that is covered in paragraph 5.11.3.

The partner who approaches retirement age in a partnership that has no plans to accumulate funds beforehand is taking a great risk that comfortable retirement will have the same substance as the pot of gold at the end of the rainbow. Funds for the purchase of his interest may be accumulated by a gradual increase in the capital account of each partner. The partner facing retirement should participate in the capital accumulation, as death or disability of a younger partner can thwart his plans. As a minimum funding device, life insurance dedicated solely to redemption of partnership interests should be carried on each partner with a material interest.

5.10   DETERMINATION OF THE PRICE TO BE PAID TO THE DEPARTING PARTNER

Property is a partnership interest, and any property has an ascertainable value if it can be valued under the classic definition of fair market value, which is the price a willing buyer and willing seller would probably reach after negotiation when neither is acting under compulsion. The estate of the deceased partner and a disabled partner are under strong compulsion; an aging partner is under strong compulsion, though the pressure may be less immediate.

5.10.1 Determination of Fair Value

The price to be sought is based on fair value. A partnership interest consists of many things. It includes tangible assets that may be assumed to be worth more as part of a going concern than they would bring if disposed. of under the auctioneer's hammer. It includes those things that give a going concern its value; experienced workers, an organization in place and functioning, systems and procedures, location, and lines of credit. It includes other intangibles usually lumped under "good will," including clients or customers, an image in the community, a logo.

5.10.2 Valuing Tangible Assets

Tangible assets present very little problem. The price of a partnership interest that included the pro rata share of the fair market value of investments and real estate, plus the book value of personal property, all reduced by the liabilities of the partnership, would in most cases be eminently fair with respect to tangible assets.

5.10.3 Valuing Intangible Assets

Intangibles add value to the partnership because they augur a future stream of income. They can be valued according to the value generally placed in the profession on a dollar of annual gross billings. Intangibles such as insurance renewals are regularly bought and sold, and a price can be determined by finding out what an outsider would pay for them. The future stream of income itself can be valued by reducing the gross receipts by predicted expenses, including replacement of the services of the departing (or departed) partner, and reducing that remainder to its present value.

A highly subjective way to value intangibles would be to calculate the difference in income accruing to the interest over the income that would be earned by an entity starting from scratch until it reached the level of the interest being valued. Although this is subject to much guesswork, it follows the same procedures that a prospective partner must follow—a calculation of how much it is worth to him to step into a going concern rather than starting from "ground zero"—and sets a cap on the value of an interest in a successful business.

5.10.4 Setting the Price

The above procedures are useful in determining the *value* of a partnership interest. If the partnership is buying the interest, the price should be very close to the value, especially if there is in existence a provision requiring the purchase and sale at certain times or under certain conditions.

If, however, no such requirement exists or is loosely worded, and a partner wants to get out or his partners want to get him out, considerable compulsion exists. If a departing general partner wants to sell to an outsider, he may have to make a price adjustment to attract a person who is acceptable to the other partners. If he is under a time constraint such as advancing age or failing health, he may have to accept a lesser price to avoid negotiations that will go on so long that he has nothing to sell, or no time to enjoy the proceeds of the sale.

The best solution to the problem of setting a price for a partnership interest is to place in the agreement a specified price or a formula by which the price will be calculated. Because of changes affecting the partnership specifically, or affecting the economy in general, a stated price or a formula should be updated frequently.

5.11 GUARANTEED PAYMENTS TO RETIRED PARTNERS OR TO DECEASED PARTNERS' SUCCESSORS IN INTEREST

Internal Revenue Code Section 736 provides that payments for a partnership interest may be designated as distributive shares of income, as guaranteed payments, or as payments for good will.

5.11.1 Guaranteed Payments Defined

Section 707(c) and the Regulations thereunder define guaranteed payments as payments made to a partner for services or for the use of capital when the payments are determined without regard to the income of the partnership. Section 736 permits payments to a retired partner or to a deceased partner's successor in interest in liquidation of his partnership interest. Only a partnership may make guaranteed payments; a partner may not sell his interest to someone else and have the payments designated as guaranteed payments.

5.11.2 The Good (Tax) News and the Bad (Tax) News About Guaranteed Payments

Guaranteed payments are taxable to the recipient as ordinary income, and are deductible by the partnership. For this reason, they are a very attractive way, from the continuing partners' point of view, to buy out a retiring or deceased partner. For the same reason, they are less attractive to the recipient. The fact that guaranteed payments may be self-employment income to the retiree and income in respect of a decedent to his heirs make them even less attractive to the recipient.

A fuller discussion of the "pros and cons" of guaranteed payments versus sale of good will will be found in paragraph 5.4.2 of this book.

5.12 INCOME IN RESPECT OF DECEDENT

Payments to the estate or heirs of a deceased partner, when paid as distributive shares or guaranteed payments under Section 736(a), are taxed as income in respect of a decedent (Section 61(a)(14)). This means that they are taxed just as if the decedent had received them, except that a deduction for estate tax on income in respect of a decedent is allowed as a deduction and the payments are not self-employment income (Regulations 1.1402(f)(1)).

Since the estate tax proportionate to the income in respect of decedent is allowed as a deduction (Section 691(c)) rather than as a credit, there is an element of double taxation of payments made after the death of a partner.

This realization is an added inducement to a senior partner to seek a faster payment schedule to permit him to receive maximum payment during his lifetime and thereby have some chance to avoid tax on income in respect of a decedent and to take some action to minimize estate taxes.

A retiring partner with charitable inclination should consider bequeathing future income payments to a charity, in whose hands they are worth 100 cents on the dollar because they escape estate and income taxation.

5.13   CLOSING PARTNERSHIP YEAR UPON TRANSFER OF INTEREST

Partners may come or go at any time during the partnership year. Such changes in the makeup of the partnership may terminate the partnership, and if they don't, they raise the question of how income is divided between partners who stayed for the entire year and those who came or went during the year.

5.13.1   Death Does Not Necessarily Terminate a Partnership

Section 29 of the Uniform Partnership Act provides that a partner leaving the business causes the partnership to be dissolved. This can be refuted by the terms of the partnership agreement, so the agreement must specify the division of profits and losses in a year when there is a change of partners. The Uniform Limited Partnership Act, Sections 2(a)X and 2(a)XI, indicates that it is normal for partners to shift and requires the agreement to cover this point, if transferability is desired.

5.13.2   When the Partnership Year Closes for Tax Purposes

The Internal Revenue Code addresses itself to closing the partnership year upon a transfer of interest in two sections. The first is Section 706, which says that, with certain exceptions, the taxable year of a partnership shall not close because of partners entering or leaving the partnership. The second is Section 708, which says that a partnership shall continue unless there is a sale or exchange of 50 percent or more of the total interest in the partnership capital and profits within a 12-month period.

Once the Code sets the general rule, we must turn to the Regulations to find out how to implement the Code. Regulation 1.706 says that the partnership taxable year shall close with respect to a partner who disposes of his entire interest. In order to avoid a closing of the partnership's books, a departing partner's share of distributive income and credits may be estimated by taking his pro rata part of the amount of the items that he would have included in this taxable income had he remained a partner until the end of the taxable year. The proration may be based on the portion of the taxable year that has elapsed prior to the date of his withdrawal, or may be determined under any other method that is reasonable. The partner who acquires his interest may include in his taxable income the pro rata part of the items that he would have included if he had been a partner from the beginning of the taxable year of the partnership. Transferor and transferee partners must use the same method of proration.

We can illustrate how this would work if Shaw, the senior partner of Shaw and Rowell, sells his 40 percent capital interest and 50 percent profit interest to Rollins on June 30. Profit for the year turns out to be $60,000, so that a half interest would receive a $30,000 share. Since the transfer took place on June 30, Shaw would report $15,000, Rowell would report $30,000, and Rollins would report $15,000 from this calendar year partnership.

5.13.3 Death Ordinarily Does Not Close the Partnership Year

When a partner dies, the partnership tax year shall not close as to him or as to the partnership, unless the death causes the partnership to terminate. If the decedent partner's estate or other successor disposes of its entire interest in the partnership, the partnership taxable year shall close for it as of the date of disposition of the interest. The last return of a decedent partner shall include only his share of partnership income for any partnership taxable year (years) ending within or with the year ending with the date of his death. The distributive share of partnership taxable income for a partnership taxable year ending after the decedent's last taxable year is includible in the return of his estate or other successor in interest.

An example will show how this works. Gone, a partner in Going, Going, Gone and Co., a partnership filing its return on the June 30 fiscal year, dies on July 31. The final return for the decedent includes Gone's share of income for the year that ended June 30. The distributive share of taxable income for the partnership year ending on the June 30 following Gone's death will be included in the estate's return for its years which includes June 30. Assuming that the estate elects the fiscal year August 1 - July 31, the income for the partnership year which included the date of Gone's death will be included in the first estate fiduciary income tax return. The income from the partnership for the year of Gone's death will be taxed as income in respect of a decedent.

5.13.4 Select the Estate's First Fiscal Year-End to Minimize Taxes

The tendency to select a first fiscal year of maximum length for a new estate can cause unnecessary taxation. Let's assume that Gone had died on May 31 and that June is a slack month for prosperous Going, Going, Gone and Co. so that its taxable income for the 11 months that ended May 31 is equal to its income for the full year. If Gone's executor selects the May 31 fiscal year and distributes all income to Gone's widow, their final joint return will show no taxable partnership income and her first year return filing as a single person will include the last partnership income of her late husband. To avoid this situation of no income on a joint return and high income at single rates, the executor should end the first taxable year of the estate not later than December 31 of the year of death and be sure that income of sufficient amount is distributed or is distributable to the widow. This is one problem area in which Treasury rules can be helpful; Section 441 permits a new estate to elect any taxable year it chooses, but failure to make such an election by filing a timely fiscal year return forces the estate to use the calendar year. Along about April 15, or until June 15, with an automatic extension, the preparer of Gone's final return might discover that there is no partnership income to report. Since at that time no timely return for a year ending May 31 has been filed, the executor may file a calendar year return for the estate (delinquent, perhaps) and pass the income through to Mrs. Gone so that the final year's partnership income does receive favorable married-filing-jointly rates, assuming that the estate's income was distributed or distributable.

Persons filing returns for partnerships with a deceased partner or for the deceased partner should remember that the above rules apply even if the decedent partner had drawn his entire share of profit before his death.

5.13.5 A Deceased Partner Can Have Two Partnership Closings in His Final Year

We have gone into considerable detail to describe a situation in which a deceased partner (and/or his widow) might have no taxable income from a partnership in a year in which the decedent earned a sizeable amount. It is possible to have two years' income in one. If Gone had died on November 30 with an agreement that someone would buy his partnership interest upon his death, then the partnership year which began on July 1 would close as to Gone on November 30. His share of distributable income for the years ended June 30 and November 30 would be included on his form 1040 for the year of his death. Both would be income of the decedent, not income in respect of decedent.

5.14   APPRECIATED INVENTORIES AND UNREALIZED RECEIVABLES

Internal Revenue Code Section 741 provides that in the case of a sale or exchange of a partnership interest, gain or loss shall be recognized to the transferor partner. Such gain or loss shall be considered as gain or loss from the sale or exchange of a capital asset, except as otherwise provided in

Section 751, relating to unrealized receivables and inventory items that have appreciated substantially in value.

5.14.1 "Appreciated Inventories" Can Be a Misleading Term

The term "appreciated inventories" has a meaning that is not apparent at a casual reading. As you would expect, it includes stock in trade of the partnership; or other property of a kind that would properly be includible in the inventory of the partnership if on hand at the close of the taxable year; or property held by the partnership primarily for sale to customers in the ordinary course of its trade or business.

5.14.2 When the Sale of a Partnership Interest Produces Ordinary Income

You have now been put on notice that a selling partner can't prepare his return by simply saying that the selling price of the entire partnership interest reduced by basis of partnership interest is capital gain. His selling price must be expressed as a proportionate part of the value of each partnership asset; then each part must be reduced by the appropriate part of his basis. The net gain or loss on the sale of items identified by Section 751 is ordinary gain or loss; what's left is capital gain or loss.

5.14.3 How Section 751 Is Applied

Though the verbiage of Section 751 and the Regulations can be as impenetrable as any in the tax field, the application is reasonably simple. A tabular comparison of adjusted basis (book) asset figures with fair market value figures, with a corresponding restatement of capital balances, tells you what you need to know. In the following example, Skarns pays $30,000 for Gandy's 50 percent share of Ryan and Gandy, a cash basis personal service partnership. The balance sheet shows:

ASSETS	Adjusted Basis Per Books	Market Value
Cash	$ 6,000	$ 6,000
Unrealized receivables	0	24,000
Other assets	34,000	34,000
Total	$ 40,000	$ 64,000
LIABILITIES AND CAPITAL		
Liabilities	$ 4,000	$ 4,000
Capital:		
Ryan	18,000	30,000
Gandy	18,000	30,000
Total	$ 40,000	$ 64,000

Section 751 applies to this sale. Ryan actually received $32,000 for his partnership interest, because Skarns paid $30,000 cash and assumed $2,000 of the liabilities allocable to Ryan. When we allocate the selling price to the assets sold, we find that Ryan was paid $12,000 for unrealized receivables with a zero tax basis. Therefore, Ryan has $12,000 ordinary income. He sold his half-share in the remaining assets (1/2 of $6,000 plus 1/2 of $34,000) for $20,000 and applied against it his remaining basis (capital account $18,000 plus his share of liabilities, $2,000 less basis applied to unrealized receivables, zero) $20,000. He has no capital gain or loss.

Just in case we oversimplified the example by making the fair market value of other assets equal to tax basis, let's assume that Ryan's basis in cash and other assets had been only $18,000, as it would have been if the basis of other assets had been only $30,000 and his capital account had been $16,000. In such a case, he would have a capital gain of $2,000 (1/2 of $3,000 plus 1/2 of $34,000 less basis of $18,000). If his basis in cash and other assets had been $22,000, he would have had a $2,000 capital loss.

"Appreciated inventories" encompasses any other property of the partnership which, on sale or exchange by the partnership, would be considered property other than a capital asset and other than land or depreciable property used in a trade or business. Thus, accounts receivable arising from the sale of services or merchandise are inventory items, as are any unrealized receivables.

5.14.4 The Paradoxical Definitions of Section 751

The language of Section 751 is paradoxical when it tells us that "inventories," usually thought of as tangible, include receivables, which are intangible. The Section and the Regulations cause Section 1245 property, such as machinery, elevators and some real property, which are about as tangible as anything can get, to be legally defined as "unrealized receivables." Section 751 includes some other unlikely fish which are caught in the "unrealized receivables" net, including mining property, stock in a DISC (Domestic International Sales Corporation), stock in certain foreign corporations described in Section 1248, real estate that has depreciated at faster than straight-line rates, some farm property, franchises, trademarks, trade names, and some oil and gas properties.

5.14.5 Inventories Must Be Substantially Appreciated to Invoke Section 751

Whereas any "unrealized receivables" are scooped up in the Section 751 net and set aside for treatment as ordinary income items upon sale of a partnership interest, only "substantially appreciated" "inventory items" are seined in. The Code gives this test of "substantially appreciated"; the "inventory items" must have fair market values greater than 120 percent of the adjusted basis to the partnership of the property and their fair market value must exceed 10 percent of the fair market value of all partnership property other than money.

A partnership reporting on the accrual basis is less likely to have unrealized receivables consisting of uncollected fees or work in process. The balance sheet of a partnership filing its tax return on the accrual basis illustrates how you can detect the existence of substantially appreciated inventory.

	Adjusted Basis Per Books	Market Value
ASSETS		
Cash	$ 15,000	$ 15,000
Accounts receivable	9,000	9,000
Inventory	21,000	30,000
Depreciable property	42,000	48,000
Land	9,000	9,000
Total	$ 96,000	$ 111,000
LIABILITIES AND CAPITAL		
Liabilities	$ 36,000	$ 36,000
Capital:		
Eeeny	20,000	25,000
Meeny	20,000	25,000
Miny	20,000	25,000
Total	$ 96,000	$ 111,000

East, Mason, Miny and Co. makes a distribution in liquidation to Miny of $25,000, consisting of $10,000 cash and depreciable property with fair market value of $15,000 and adjusted basis to the partnership of $15,000. The 120 percent and the 10 percent tests must be applied to partnership assets to determine the applicability of Section 751. The "inventory" items are accounts receivable and inventory, with combined fair market value of $39,000 and adjusted basis of $30,000; $39,000 is more than 120 percent of $30,000. The $39,000 also exceeds 10 percent of total fair market value of $111,000 less money of $15,000.

The fact that Miny's entire interest is to be liquidated brings the distribution under Section 736. Since the distribution is not a distributive share of partnership income nor a guaranteed payment, it falls under Section 736(b), which invokes Section 751. Note that he received a share of only two assets. This requires us to compare what he got with his pro rata share of each asset:

	He Received	His Share
Cash	$ 10,000	$ 5,000
Accounts receivable		3,000
Inventory		10,000
Depreciable property	15,000	16,000
Land		3,000
		37,000
Less: liabilities		12,000
	$ 25,000	$ 25,000

Miny received his share of cash and received all but $1,000 of his share of depreciable property. He received an extra $5,000 of cash plus a $12,000 reduction of liabilities, counted as receipt of cash, in exchange for the $1,000 share of depreciable property; a $3,000 share of accounts receivable; $10,000 share of inventory; and $3,000 share of land. Each set of figures adds up to $17,000. He received $13,000 ($10,000 and $3,000) for "inventory" items, accounts receivable and inventory.

We calculate the tax consequences to Miny by treating the distribution in lieu of inventory items as if he had received $13,000 for items in which he had a basis of $10,000 (1/3 of $9,000 plus $21,000). Therefore, he has ordinary income of $3,000. He received his share of depreciable property so there is no Section 751 gain or loss attributable to that part of the liquidation.

5.14.6 Tax Effect to the Transferee Partner

At this point, we must remember that Section 731 says that:

> In the case of a distribution by a partnership to a partner, gain shall not be recognized to such partner, except to the extent that any money distributed exceeds the adjusted basis of such partner's interest in the partnership immediately before the distribution.

We recognize that the total distribution to Miny was $22,000 in cash and liabilities assumed and $15,000 in depreciable property. Miny had a basis of $32,000 ($20,000 capital account and $12,000 share of liabilities) immediately before the distribution. When we reduce his basis by the $10,000 assigned to the "inventory" items, we have $22,000 left as basis for everything else. Since Miny received more than his share of money, the $13,000 received for "inventory" items is considered to be cash, so $9,000 is left to be considered as a money distribution for items other than "inventory" items. This $9,000 does not exceed the remaining basis, so there is no taxable gain on the non-Section 751 part of the liquidating distribution. Subtracting $9,000 from $22,000, we find that Miny has $13,000 basis left, and that this becomes the basis of his depreciable property with fair value of

$15,000. If you aren't sure that all this came out right look at it the simple way; he put in $20,000 and got back $25,000, so he is ahead $5,000, taxable sooner or later; he is taxed on $3,000 now (sooner) and the receipt of $15,000 value of depreciable property with a basis of $13,000 assures him of $2,000 taxable income later.

5.14.7 Tax Effect to the Transferor Partnership

Having found out the tax consequences of the liquidating distribution to departed partner Miny, we turn to the question of what is the tax effect to the partnership. The first question to answer is: did the partnership give up any Section 751 assets in the sale? The answer is "no" because it gave up money (cash and assumption of liabilities) to *acquire* $13,000 of "inventory" items ($10,000 for inventory and $3,000 for receivables). Since it paid $13,000 in money for these items, it acquires a basis of $13,000 in them. The partnership had a basis of $30,000 in accounts receivable and inventory before the distribution, which was reduced by Miny's $10,000 basis in them and is now increased by $13,000. Since the basis and value of receivables was the same, the net $3,000 increase in basis is applied to inventory increasing its basis from $21,000 to $24,000.

In the remainder of the distribution, Miny received $15,000 in depreciable property (basis $15,000) and $9,000 in money. This part of the distribution is not governed by Section 751. Sections 731 through 736 dealing with distributions by a partnership, apply. Section 731(b) plainly states that no gain or loss shall be recognized to a partnership on a distribution to a partner of property, including money. Since no election under Section 754 (see paragraph 5.15.1) is in effect, the partnership makes no adjustment to the basis of remaining depreciable property. The basis of the depreciable property before the election was $42,000, which is reduced by the basis of the property distributed to Miny of $15,000, or $27,000. If an election under Section 754 had been in effect, the partnership would have increased the basis of depreciable property to $29,000, picking up the $2,000 basis which Miny lost.

5.14.8 Tax Effect to the Remaining Partners

We have considered the effect of the liquidating distribution on Miny and on the partnership, and now we must consider the effect on the remaining partners, East and Mason. Each had a basis of $32,000, consisting of a capital account of $20,000 and a $12,000 share of debt; since Miny's $12,000 share of liabilities remained with the partnership, each remaining partner increased his share of liabilities by $6,000, increasing the basis of his partnership interest by $6,000, to $38,000.

5.14.9 The Tax Effect to the Partner of Giving Up an Interest in Property of a Character Different from the Property Received

Receipt of property of a different character but of the same total value produces different results for the withdrawing partner. Using the same predistribution trial balance, Miny could have received $5,000 in cash and $20,000 of partnership inventory with a basis of $14,000. He would have received his share of partnership cash of $5,000 and his share of appreciated inventory items of $13,000 and additional appreciated inventory items with fair market value of $7,000, but basis of $4,900. Miny has relinquished his interest in $16,000 of depreciable property, $3,000 of land and $3,000 of accounts receivable. The accounts receivable are "inventory" items, so that part of the deal was not an exchange of Section 751 assets for other property. Therefore, the exchange with which we are concerned here is based on the assumption that the $7,000 of inventory was received by Miny in exchange for $7,000 of depreciable property. Miny is treated as if he had received his 7/16 share of the depreciable property in a current distribution. His basis for that share is 42,000/48,000 times $7,000, or $6,125. Miny is considered to have sold his 7/16 share of depreciable property to the partnership for $7,000 and to have received a gain of $875.

When we reduce Miny's original basis of $32,000 by the $6,125 basis for inventory, he has $25,875 basis left. Of the $37,000 total received by Miny, his proportionate share of inventory (($13,000) and his cash ($17,000) are excluded from the grip of Section 751(b). When we further reduce his basis by the amount of cash received, he has basis of $8,875, which becomes his basis for $13,000 fair value of inventory, which had a partnership basis of $9,100. His total basis in inventory is now $7,000 plus $8,875 or $15,875 for inventory which had a basis of $14,000 to the partnership.

5.14.10 The Tax Effect to the Partnership of Giving Up an Interest in Property of a Character Different from the Property Retained

Looking at this transaction from the partnership angle, we find that the partnership has $2,100 ordinary income from the sale of inventory with basis of $4,900 to Miny for $7,000. As we said in connection with Miny's situation, the partnership is assumed to have received depreciable property of a value of $7,000, and now has a basis of $7,000 for it. Its basis in depreciable property is now $42,875 ($42,000 less the $6,125, the basis of the 7/16th share considered as distributed to Miny, plus $7,000 purchase price from Miny). On the remainder of the transaction, the part which was not under Section 751(b), the partnership realizes no gain or loss since no Section 754 election is in effect; the inventory of the partnership is not adjusted for the $225 basis ($9,100 minus $8,875) which Miny "lost." Now the basis of each partner's interest is $39,050, made up of:

Original contribution	$ 20,000
Original share of liabilities	12,000
Liabilities assumed from Miny	6,000
1/2 of recognized gain	1,050
New basis	$ 39.050

5.14.11 The Tax Effect When the Partners Do Not Specify What Will Be Exchanged

The above example assumes that the partnership and Miny had entered into an agreement to the effect that $7,000 of inventory was received by Miny in exchange for $7,000 of depreciable property. If no such agreement had been reached, we would have gotten a different result, because Miny will have been presumed to have sold a proportionate amount of each property in which he relinquished an interest. Thus, Miny has received $7,000 of inventory in exchange for his release of 7/19ths of the depreciable property and 7/19th of the land. The arithmetic fraction derives from the $7,000 fair market value of property released over $19,000, which is the sum of the fair market values of Miny's interests in the land and in the depreciable property.

We look first at how Miny fares tax-wise. He is treated as if he had received his 7/19ths shares of the depreciable property and land in a current distribution. His basis for those shares is $6,263, which is obtained by taking 51,000/57,000 of $7,000, their fair market value. Miny is considered to have sold his 7/19th shares of depreciable property and land to the partnership for $7,000, realizing a gain of $737.

The balance of the distribution is not subject to Section 751(b). Miny's original basis of $32,000 is reduced by $6,263, so he has a basis of $25,737 for the remainder of his partnership interest. When we subtract the $17,000 in money distributed, we find a basis of $8,737 for Miny's inventory, which had a fair market value of $13,000 and a basis to the partnership of $9,100. Thus, Miny has a basis of $15,737 ($7,000 plus $8,737) in the inventory.

As in the previous examples, there are tax consequences to the partnership. Once again, the partnership has $2,100 ordinary gain on the sale of $7,000 of inventory which had a basis of $4,900. The basis of this segment of the inventory increases to $7,000. The basis of the land remains at its original basis of $9,000. The basis of the depreciable property goes through the following steps to become $42,737:

Original basis to the partnership	$ 42,000
Increased by the part of the purchase price allocated to the depreciable property (16,000/19,000 of $7,000)	5,895

Reduced by the basis for Miny's 7/19 interest constructively distributed (42,000/48,000 of $5,895)	(5,158)
	$ 42,737

Although the basis of the land remains at $9,000, it too goes through a similar calculation:

Original basis to the partnership	$ 9,000
Increased by the portion of the purchase price allocated to the land (3,000/19,000 of $7,000)	1,105
Reduced by the basis for Miny's interest constructively distributed (9,000/9,000 of $1,105)	(1,105)
	$ 9,000

Once, again, the partnership realizes no gain or loss on the part of the distribution which is not under Section 751. Each partner's basis for his interest becomes $39,050, computed as follows:

Original contribution	$ 20,000
Original share of liabilities	12,000
Share of Miny's liabilities assumed	6,000
1/2 of recognized gain	1,050
	$ 39,050

5.14.12 Preplanning the Distribution Can Improve the Tax Consequences

The reader who has followed us in this recitation of the complications injected into tax law by Section 751 of the Internal Revenue Code knows by now that a sale of a partnership interest or a distribution in complete liquidation of a partnership interest is anything but simple. As in other areas of partnership tax practice, preplanning the transaction and prior agreement by the partners can minimize the tax bite or at least put it where it is least objectionable. The practitioner who must advise on a Section 751 problem must carefully study Regulation 1.751.

5.15 PARTNERSHIP ELECTIONS TO ADJUST BASIS OF PARTNERSHIP ASSETS

When a partnership is formed by infusions of cash and property, the basis of all partnership property and of all partners' interests in the partnership is identical. Increases in partnership assets, resulting from investment of additional property as contributions to capital by partners, maintains this identity of basis because basis to the partnership is the former basis of the property in the hands of the partner. Partnership profits and losses and acquisition of property with borrowed funds do nothing to disturb the relationship of basis of partnership assets to basis of partnership interests.

Trouble creeps into this Eden of equality of bases when there is a transfer of partnership interests. The problem can arise when a new partner is admitted or when a current partner increases his partnership interest and he (the transferee partner) pays a price that is more or less than the basis of a proportionate share of partnership assets. The problem can arise when the partnership liquidates the interest of a partner, paying more or less than the basis of a proportionate share of partnership assets. By "paying" we mean transferring an amount composed of property expressed in terms of its basis and/or money.

5.15.1 The Logic of Opportunity to Adjust Basis of Partnership Assets

Logic and common sense (two qualities seldom encountered in the tax field) tell us that if a person pays a certain amount for an asset and places it in a partnership, and the partnership thereby obtains a basis equal to what he paid for the asset, then when another person pays the same amount to acquire an interest in the partnership representing the same amount of assets, the partnership assets should obtain the same basis they would have had if newly contributed.

Logic and common sense tell us that if a partnership gives a withdrawing partner assets with fair market value proportionate to his share in the partnership, and does it by distributing to him assets with a share of basis disproportionate to his interest in the partnership, then the partnership should have a chance to recover the "lost" basis. This is particularly true since the basis of the assets in the hands of the distributee partner is the basis of his partnership interest, which may be less than the basis which attached to the assets when they were partnership property.

Logic and common sense prevail because Congress put Section 754 into the Internal Revenue Code to permit a partnership to adjust the basis of partnership assets in the case of the distribution of property to a withdrawing partner or in the case of a transfer of a partnership interest. This right to adjust the basis of partnership property is one of the advantages that gives the partnership form of operation superiority over the corporate form.

5.15.2 An Election Can Be Beneficial Whether Partners Are Coming or Going

To illustrate this, we look at a simple balance sheet:

ASSETS

Land held for investment $ 60,000

<u>CAPITAL</u>

Tom	$ 20,000
Dick	20,000
Harry	20,000
Total capital	$ 60,000

The tax basis of the land is $60,000 and its fair market value is $90,000. If this were a corporation and Tom sold his stock with $20,000 basis and par value to another individual, Bill, for $30,000, the basis of the land for future sale by the corporation would remain at $60,000 and neither the new stockholder nor anyone else could get a tax benefit from the new stockholder's higher basis until he disposes of his stock, even though Tom has paid tax on a $10,000 capital gain.

The preceding paragraph illustrates how a corporate shareholder is deprived of immediate benefit of the price he paid, and depicts a problem that the partnership would face if the Internal Revenue Code did not contain Sections 754 and 743.

We shall now look at a situation in which assets have appreciated in value so that the fair value of a distribution in liquidation of a partner's interest exceeds either the basis of his interest or the share of basis of partnership assets which is proportionate to his interest. This entity owns inventory with basis of $20,000 and fair market value of $21,000 and depreciable assets with adjusted basis of $20,000 and fair market value of $40,000. This $21,000 excess of market value over basis gives each partner's interest a value that is $7,000 greater than its tax basis of $15,000. A withdrawing stockholder or partner would expect to receive $22,000 in cash or market value of assets in liquidation of his interest in the business. If he were a stockholder, he would have a taxable gain of $7,000. Assuming the buy-out was for cash, the corporation has in effect bought a greater share in the appreciated assets which remain; all it adds to its balance sheet is treasury stock, and the basis of the assets remains the same. This is true even though the withdrawing stockholder is taxed on his $7,000 gain. A partnership with identical facts would face the same problem if the Internal Revenue Code did not contain Sections 754 and 734.

5.15.3 Elections to Adjust Basis of Partnership Assets Upon a Transfer of Interests

Sections 734, 743 and 754 of the Code provide relief. Section 754 titled "Manner of Electing Optional Adjustment to Basis of Partnership Property" provides that in the case of the transfer of a partnership interest, the partnership may file an election of adjust the basis of its property. Section 743 says that a partnership may elect to:

> 1. Increase the adjusted basis of the partnership property by the excess of the basis to the transferee partner of his interest in the partnership over his proportionate share of the adjusted basis of the partnership property, or
> 2. Decrease the adjusted basis of the partnership property by the excess of the transferee partner's proportionate share of the adjusted basis of the partnership property over the basis of his interest in the partnership.

The Section goes on to say that the adjustment will be with respect only to the transferee partner (Bill in our illustration). The Section tells how to make the election by using the well-worn phrase "under Regulations prescribed by the Secretary." The Secretary of the Treasury took the Congressional hint and issued Regulation 1.743-1. The Regulation says that assets covered by a proper election will have a "special basis," and the regulation writers indulge their penchant for stating the obvious by defining special basis as the partner's share of common basis of partnership assets plus or minus his special basis adjustments.

5.15.4 An Election, Once Made, Is Binding Upon Future Transfers

The word "minus" has significance. A Section 754 election, once made, is binding on future transactions unless the Commissioner of Internal Revenue agrees to revoke the election, and it works both ways; an election made to take advantage of an increase in basis could, under opposite circumstances, reduce basis. Accordingly, an election should not be made unless there is significant advantage to be gained by making the election.

5.15.5 Elections to Adjust Basis of Partnership Assets Upon a Distribution in Liquidation

Section 754 also permits a partnership to adjust the basis of retained assets in the case of a distribution of property, and provides that the adjustment shall be made in the manner provided in Section 734. Unlike a Section 743 adjustment, which is allocated only to a transferee partner, a Section 734 adjustment will be allocated to the remaining property held by the partnership and will affect the remaining partners only. A Section 734 adjustment may:

> 1. Increase the adjusted basis of partnership property by the amount of any gain recognized to the distributee partner or by the amount of basis that the distributee partner "loses" when the basis of the

distributed property to him is limited by the basis of his partnership interest.

2. Decrease the adjusted basis of partnership property by the amount of any loss recognized to the distributee partner or by the amount of basis that the distributee partner "gains" when the basis of the distributed property to him is set by his having a basis in his partnership interest greater than the basis of the property immediately before the distribution.

A few simple illustrations show how the basis adjustment works. A has a basis of $10,000 for a one-third interest in a partnership. The partnership assets consist of cash of $11,000, and property with a basis of $19,000 and value of $22,000. There are no liabilities. When A receives $11,000 cash in liquidation of his partnership, he has a recognized gain of $1,000. Since the partnership has a Section 754 election in effect, the basis of its property increases from $19,000 to $20,000.

If, however, A had received property with a partnership basis of $11,000 in liquidation of his entire interest in the partnership, he would have had no gain or loss but his basis in the distributed property would be only $10,000. Since the partnership has a Section 754 election in effect, $1,000 is added to the basis of its remaining property.

By changing the figures slightly, we can illustrate the adverse effect that a Section 754 election can have. Partner B has a basis of $11,000 for his one-third interest in a partnership, the assets of which are cash of $10,000, and property with basis of $23,000 and value of $20,000. There are no partnership liabilities. B receives the $10,000 cash in liquidation of his entire interest in the partnership, thereby sustaining a loss of $1,000. Since the partnership has a Section 754 election in effect, the basis of its property drops from $23,000 to $22,000.

A final illustration of the effect of a Section 754 adjustment under the Section 734 method of adjustment has partner C receiving property with a partnership basis of $10,000 in liquidation of his entire interest, which has a basis of $11,000. Since the partnership has a Section 754 election in effect, the partnership must adjust the basis of the remaining property downward by $1,000.

Perhaps the partnership that distributed property in two of the above illustrations had property the basis of which to the partnership was determined in favor of the departed partner and the special basis property was retained by the partnership. If so, Section 734 permits the partnership to adjust the basis of its remaining property to take advantage of the special basis adjustment which formerly worked only in favor of the now-withdrawn partner.

5.15.6 How an Election Under Section 754 Is Made

Regulation 1.754-1(b) provides that an election under Section 743 or 734 is made by filing a written statement with a timely filed partnership return. Even though a Section 743 adjustment affects only the transferee partner, he cannot make the necessary election; it must be made by the partnership. Persons drafting partnership agreements should consider a requirement that an election under Section 754 shall be made under specified circumstances. Advisors must be alert to the need for a Section 754 election.

5.15.7 Section 755 Provides for Designation of the Assets Whose Basis Is to Be Adjusted

In our example of Tom, Dick and Harry partnership, we would readily understand that an election under Sections 754 and 743 would increase the partnership's interest in land by $10,000 and that the adjustment would be effective only to Bill. The business world is seldom that simple, so the draftsman of a Section 743 special basis adjustment finds himself asking "which assets are to be adjusted and how much shall each be adjusted?" The ever-helpful Congress and its rule writer, the Secretary, provide the answer in Section 755 and Regulation 1.755-1, lest the eager adjuster put the adjustment where it will produce the greatest tax benefit. Section 755 provides that the adjustment to basis under Sections 734 and 743 shall be allocated so as to reduce the difference between the fair market value and the adjusted basis of partnership properties and that adjustment shall be made to partnership capital assets, land and depreciable property when the adjustment is occasioned by distribution of that kind of property, and to other property when the adjustment is occasioned by distributions of property other than capital assets or land and depreciable property used in the trade or business. The Code helpfully tells you not to adjust the basis of either class of property below zero; the unusable adjustment is carried over to be applied to later-acquired property.

An example assumes that, among other balance sheet items, Allis, Bee and Carter partnership has inventory with basis of $20,000 and fair value of $21,000 and depreciable assets with adjusted basis of $20,000 and value of $40,000. This $21,000 spread gives each partner's interest a value $7,000 greater than its tax basis of $15,000. The partnership buys Allis' interest for $22,000. To keep things simple, this partnership has no liabilities; if it did, both Allis' selling price and his basis would include his share of liabilities. The difference between basis and market value of depreciable assets is 20 times the difference with respect to inventory. Therefore, 1/21 of the adjustment is applied to inventory and 20/21 to depreciable assets, or $333 and $6,667.

5.16   PARTNER'S ELECTION TO ADJUST BASIS OF DISTRIBUTED PROPERTY (SECTION 732)

For various reasons, a partnership may fail to make an election under Section 754 to adjust the basis of partnership assets in accordance with Section 743, upon a transfer of an interest in the partnership by sale or exchange or upon the death of a partner. If such an election had been in effect, the basis of partnership assets would have been adjusted, but only with respect to the transferee partner.

5.16.1 The Partnership's Failure to Make a Section 754 Election Works Against the Withdrawing Partner

Consider the plight of the transferee partner who withdraws within two years from a partnership that had not given him the benefit of an adjusted basis for his share of the partnership assets. Section 732(b) says that the basis of property (other than money) distributed by a partnership to a partner in liquidation of the partner's interest shall be an amount equal to the adjusted basis of such partner's interest in the partnership reduced by any money distributed in the same transaction. Section 732(c) goes on to say that the basis of the distributed properties shall be allocated first to any unrealized receivables in an amount equal to the adjusted basis of each such property to the partnership and that any remaining basis shall be allocated among the other distributed properties in proportion to their adjusted bases to the partnership. In other words, a partner whose basis of his partnership interest exceeds the basis of the distributed property to the partnership is stuck with the partnership's basis for unrealized receivables and inventory and must spread his excess basis over other property.

5.16.2 Where the Tax Advantage to the Withdrawing Partner Lies

The tax advantage lies with allocating basis to items likely to be sold first, such as inventory, and to avoiding basis to properties promising no immediate tax benefit, such as undeveloped land. We shall illustrate how the election available under Section 732(d) to a withdrawing partner can be advantageous. Kurly buys a one-fourth interest in a partnership for $17,000 at a time when no election under Section 754 was in effect, and when the partnership inventory had a basis to the partnership of $14,000 and a value of $16,000. Kurly, then, paid $4,000 for an interest in inventory worth $4,000 but with a basis of only $3,500. Within two years of becoming a partner, Kurly withdrew and received inventory with a basis of $3,500, cash of $1,500 and a capital asset with an adjusted basis to the partnership of $2,000 and a depreciable asset with an adjusted basis to the partnership of $4,000, for total partnership basis of $11,000. Kurly's $17,000 basis less $1,500 cash leaves him with $15,500 to be allocated to properties.

If an election under Section 743 had been in effect when Kurly joined the partnership, he would have enjoyed a $500 step-up in basis of inventory then. Since Kurly wants to allocate $500 to the basis of the inventory received in liquidation of his partnership interest, he makes a Section 732(d) election to assign a basis of $4,000 to the inventory, leaving $11,500 to be allocated to the remaining properties. Since the capital asset has a partnership basis of one-half of the partnership basis of the depreciable asset, the $11,500 is allocated one-third ($3,833) to the capital asset and two-thirds to the depreciable asset ($7,667).

5.16.3 How the Election Under Section 732(d) Is Made

A transferee partner who wishes to elect under Section 732(d) shall make the election with his tax return—

> "(i) For the year of the distribution, if the distribution includes any property subject to the allowance for depreciation, depletion, or amortization, or
>
> (ii) For any taxable year no later than the first taxable year in which the basis of any of the distributed property is pertinent in determining his income tax, if the distribution does not include any such property subject to the allowance for depreciation, depletion or amortization."

A taxpayer making an election under Section 732(d) shall submit with the return in which the election is made a schedule setting forth the following:

> "(i) That under Section 732(d) he elects to adjust the basis of property received in a distribution; and
>
> (ii) The computation of the special basis adjustment for the property distributed and the properties to which the adjustment has been allocated. For rules of allocation, see Section 755."

5.16.4 An Election Under Section 732(d) May Be Required

A partner who acquired any part of his partnership interest in a transfer to which the election provided in Section 754 was not in effect, is required to apply the special basis rule contained in Section 732(d) to a distribution to him, whether or not made within two years after the transfer, if at the time of his acquisition of the transferred interest—

> "(i) The fair market value of all partnership property (other than money) exceeded 110 percent of its adjusted basis to the partnership.
>
> (ii) An allocation of basis under Section 732(c) upon a liquidation of his interest immediately after the transfer of the interest would have resulted in a shift of basis from property not subject to an allowance for depreciation, depletion, or amortization, to property subject to such an allowance, and
>
> (iii) A special basis adjustment under Section 743(b) would

change the basis to the transferee partner of the property actually distributed."

5.17   THE MAIN POINTS OF CHAPTER FIVE

The partnership, to grow or even to endure, must admit new partners from time to time. Unless new partners are selected from good scions and skillfully grafted into the stock of the partnership and unless partners who have become old, tired, or simply incompatible are removed, the partnership begins to resemble a ragged weed and eventually succumbs to decay and dies. Not luck or chance, but planning and careful selection made Luther Burbank the preeminent name in horticulture; the same qualities of selection and ingrafting can determine that your partnership will be a prize specimen instead of a wilted stem in the trash can of business.

If partners are to leave without acrimony, advance plans must be made to purchase their interests, and such plans must call for a fair price and must consider the need for funds with which to buy. Life insurance is a logical source of funds to meet an unexpected need as well as a way to accumulate funds systematically and at least partially free of taxes on growth of the funds. The plans to purchase the interest of a retiring partner should be financially responsible as well as tax-efficient. The partners have considerable leeway in determining the tax burdens and benefits of payments to a departing partner.

The departure of a partner calls up some of the most complicated and easily overlooked provisions of partnership taxation. When departures cause the entity to lose its status as a partnership, and when there must be a closing of the books, must be determined. The effect of a transfer of interest upon transferee and transferor must be understood, including possible changes in basis of property, both that retained by the partnership and that which is distributed.

Although a partnership interest is property, gain on its sale is not always capital. Section 751 of the Internal Revenue Code introduces "unrealized receivables" and "appreciated inventory" and gives those words meanings that Noah Webster had never even heard of, much less contemplated.

Chapter Five emphasizes over and over again the need for planning the partnership's affairs. Some of the planning needs to be done when the partnership is formed; some is to be done at or just prior to major changes; and some can be done after the fact. All of the planning is important and most of it requires an understanding of human psychology as well as tax law; and all of it is moderated by the laws of economic reality, which will set awry any plans that exceed the resources with which the partners will attempt to carry them out.

CHAPTER SIX

Bases of Partnership Assets
And of Partnership Interests

←——————————————————→

CONTENTS

INTRODUCTION   137

6.1   DISTINCTION BETWEEN BASIS OF PARTNERSHIP
      ASSETS AND BASIS OF PARTNERSHIP INTERESTS   137

      6.1.1   How a Partnership Asset's Basis Is Deter-
              mined – 138
      6.1.2   How the Basis of a Partnership Interest Is
              Determined – 138
      6.1.3   The Significance of Basis of a Partnership
              Interest – 139
      6.1.4   The Sums of the Partnership Asset Bases
              and Partnership Interest Bases Frequently
              Are Identical – 140

6.2   SOURCES OF BASIS OF PARTNERSHIP INTEREST   141

6.3   EFFECTS OF LIABILITIES ON BASIS OF
      PARTNERSHIP INTEREST   141

      6.3.1   Increases in Liabilities Increase Basis of
              Partnership Interests – 142
      6.3.2   Decreases in Liabilities Decrease Basis of
              Partnership Interests – 142
      6.3.3   Special Rule for Nonrecourse Liabilities –
              142

6.4   OTHER CAUSES OF CHANGES IN BASIS OF
        PARTNERSHIP INTEREST   143

6.5   ALTERNATE RULE FOR DETERMINING BASIS OF
        PARTNERSHIP INTEREST   143

6.6   BASIS OF PARTNERSHIP ASSETS AND BASIS OF
        PARTNERSHIP INTERESTS FREQUENTLY RUN
        "IN SYNC"   144

6.7   DATES ON WHICH BASIS OF PARTNERSHIP
        INTEREST MUST BE DETERMINED   146

6.8   LOST BASIS OF PARTNERSHIP INTEREST UPON
        DISTRIBUTION   146

6.9   CHAPTER SIX IN RETROSPECT   147

INTRODUCTION

Partnerships may sell or depreciate assets. In either case, the tax basis of the asset must be known. If the asset came into the partnership by a tax-free contribution to capital from a partner, its basis to the partnership is its basis in the hands of the contributing partner. If the asset was purchased by the partnership, basis is cost. If the asset was obtained by trade-in, basis is basis of traded asset plus "boot" given. These rules are reasonably familiar to all tax practitioners.

If a partner obtains his interest in a partnership by contribution of cash, the basis of his partnership interest is equal to the amount of his contribution. If he contributes only property, the basis of his partnership interest is the basis of the contributed property. The basis of his partnership interest is increased by additional contributions or by his share of profits and decreased by withdrawals and by his share of losses. This, too, is forthright and presents little problem of understanding.

When partners sell their interests to others, the purchaser may pay more or less than the basis of the seller's interest in the partnership. The new partner has a basis for his interest equal to what he paid for it. The partnership may have the right to adjust the tax basis of its assets to reflect the premiums paid by its new partner.

A partner may receive property from the partnership, in which case he needs to know the basis of his property.

Answers to all the questions are found in the Internal Revenue Code and in the Regulations issued thereunder. Chapter Six alerts you to these problems and tells you how to find answers.

6.1 DISTINCTION BETWEEN BASIS OF PARTNERSHIP ASSETS AND BASIS OF PARTNERSHIP INTERESTS

Any asset used in any trade or business has a "basis." IRC Section 1012 defines the basis of property as its cost, except when basis is determined by reference to the basis in the hands of a transferor, donor or grantor or is determined by reference to other property held at any time by the person for whom the basis is to be determined. "Adjusted basis" is basis increased by expenditures properly capitalizable or decreased by losses, depreciation, amortization, obsolescence or other appropriate credits to the capital account. For example, the original cost of a business machine, reduced by depreciation allowed or allowable, is its "adjusted basis."

6.1.1 How a Partnership Asset's Basis (or Adjusted Basis) Is Determined

Several examples show ways in which basis of partnership assets may be determined:

Partnership A buys a building and land for $10,000; the basis of the property is $10,000. At the end of one year, depreciation of $500 is allowable, so that adjusted basis becomes $9,500.

Partner B buys an interest in newly formed partnership AB by investing inventory which was included on his final return as a sole proprietor at a value of $7,000; the basis of the inventory to AB is $7,000.

Law partnership CD receives an automobile from a client who is short of cash, in full payment for services, correctly valued at $5,000; the basis of the automobile to CD is $5,000 and CD has received $5,000 in taxable income.

The city, under threat of condemnation, requires partnership EF to grant it an easement across a piece of farmland for a deeply buried sewer line, and pays $5,000 for the easement. EF paid $10,000 for the land and is permitted to continue to farm it but may place no structure over the property subject to easement and must grant access for maintenance; the $5,000 received is not income to EF, but the adjusted basis of the land is reduced to $5,000.

Partnership GH owns a parking lot that was purchased for $1,000. GH swaps the lot for another parking lot and gives $1,000 additional consideration, and pays a lawyer $100 to prepare the deeds. The basis of the new lot is $2,100.

6.1.2 How the Basis of a Partnership Interest Is Determined

Generally, the basis of the combined interests in a partnership is equal to the basis of all of the assets of the partnership. The simplest possible illustration shows the opening trial balance when two persons put cash into a newly formed partnership:

ASSET	
Cash	$10,000

PARTNERSHIP EQUITY	
Partner I	$ 5,000
Partner J	5,000
Total Partnership Equity	$10,000

If they had invested, instead of cash, raw land which they had pur-chased for $10,000, the equity figures would be the same. If they had inherited the property, shown on the estate tax return at a value of $10,000, the equity figures would be the same. If they had contributed machinery with an original cost of $12,000, on which depreciation of $2,000 was allowable before the partnership acquired it, the equity figures would be the same.

The rule is that the opening basis of all interests in the partnership is equal to the sum of cash plus the bases of all property invested in the partnership.

If partnership operated that simply, we could end this chapter by saying that there is no distinction between basis of partnership assets and basis of partnership interests. Partnerships usually don't operate simply, and the basis of partnership assets and of partnership interests do vary.

6.1.3 The Significance of Basis of a Partnership Interest

A partner is typically unconcerned about the basis of his partnership interest. He reasons that, like his basis in corporate stock, basis of his partnership interest is important only when he disposes of his interest.

His reasoning is incomplete because basis of the partner's interest is important in determining whether the partner can deduct his full share of a partnership loss. To illustrate this point, we assume that partners A, B, and C each invested $12,000 cash in a partnership. Expecting profits, the partners authorized a monthly draw of $1,000 for each partner and for six months each partner drew his $1,000. At midyear, they realized that things were not going well and that cash was getting short. A and B decided to forego further monthly draws, but C's obligations and lack of any other source of income required him to continue drawing, so that by the end of the year he had withdrawn his entire capital, which was the source of basis of his partnership interest. The partnership's net loss for the year is $12,000, allocated $4,000 to each partner. A and B, with bases of $6,000 each for their partnership interests may deduct $4,000 of loss from the partnership; C, with no basis, may deduct no loss from the partnership for his year which includes the year-end of the partnership. If C restores his basis in a subse-quent year, he may deduct the loss in that subsequent year.

In such a simple illustration, where C has no taxable income from any source, inability to claim the partnership loss would be no detriment. As a matter of fact, the ability to claim the loss in a future year, perhaps even a year of his own choosing, may be an advantage. However, to the partner who has substantial income from sources other than the partnership, inability to claim the loss for lack of basis may be both frustrating and expensive. Considering that such a simple act as paying in enough capital to bring basis of partnership interest high enough to cover the loss will preserve the deductibility of the loss, the importance of understanding the principles and of having accurate and timely accounting cannot be stressed too much.

Another illustration of the importance of basis of partnership interest is found in IRC Section 731(a) (1), which says that gain shall be recognized to the extent that a distribution of cash exceeds the adjusted basis of the partner's interest in the partnership immediately before the distribution. Thus, if a partner receives a cash distribution of $11,000 when his adjusted basis is $10,000, he reports a capital gain of $1,000.

6.1.4 The Sums of the Partnership Asset Bases and Partnership Interest Bases Frequently Are Identical

A partnership may have a variety of assets, each of which has a basis acquired in any of a variety of ways. The sum of all the bases of individual assets (including adjusted bases) may be described as the "basis of partnership assets." Despite the fact that basis of partnership assets and basis of partnership interests are not necessarily identical, the sum of the bases of partnership assets and the sum of the bases of partnership interests are frequently identical. This is true despite the number and variety of business transactions. A consideration of the accounting effect of various transactions will show why this is true.

1. Some transactions, such as drawing a check to buy a machine, or collecting a receivable, merely reduce one asset and increase another, with no effect on total assets.
2. Borrowing money or financing a purchase increases an asset, while the offsetting increase in liability increases basis of partnership interests.
3. Using money to pay debt decreases an asset, and by decreasing the liability, decreases basis of partnership interests.
4. Recording an expense decreases cash if it is by disbursement, or decreases a fixed asset or prepaid expense if it is by depreciation or amortization; the effect is to reduce partnership income by the same amount, thereby reducing basis of partnership interests. Accrual of an expense increases basis of partnership interests by increasing debt, and reduces basis of partnership interests by decreasing income.
5. Recording income increases an asset (cash, receivable) and in-

creases basis of partnership interests by increasing partnership income.

6.2 SOURCES OF BASIS OF PARTNERSHIP INTEREST

A partner may acquire his interest in a variety of ways. He may be a founding partner contributing cash or tangible or intangible assets with a tax basis. In this case, the basis of his interest is the cash plus the basis of the property contributed in a tax-free exchange. He may purchase an interest in an existing partnership, in which case the basis of his interest is what he paid for it.

Sometimes a person receives a partnership interest as a gift; his basis is the donor's basis increased by the portion of the gift tax attributable to the net appreciation on the gift. The increase is computed by multiplying the gift tax paid by a fraction, the numerator of which is the gift's fair market value less the adjusted basis, and the denominator of which is the fair market value. The basis so obtained may not exceed the fair market value of the gifted interest at the time of the gift.

A partnership interest may be acquired by inheritance, in which case the basis is the estate tax valuation, usually the fair market value at the time of the testator's death.

The same principles apply to the basis of an increased interest in a partnership, acquired by a person who is already a partner.

6.3 EFFECTS OF LIABILITIES ON BASIS OF PARTNERSHIP INTEREST

Seldom does a partnership or any other business entity operate without incurring debt. In the previous section, I and J put $10,000 cash into their partnership and recorded partnership interests with the bases of $5,000 each. We shall expand the illustration to show the trial balance when they have used the cash as down payment on a machine and for inventory of raw material.

ASSETS	
Inventory (at cost)	$ 5,000
Machinery (at cost)	50,000
Total Assets	$55,000
LIABILITY	
Note payable	$45,000

PARTNERSHIP EQUITY

Partner I	5,000
Partner J	5,000
Total partnership equity	10,000
Total Liabilities and Partnership Equity	$55,000

A person more familiar with corporate accounting than partnership accounting would conclude that after the very first transaction, the general rule that basis of partnership assets equals basis of partnership interests has already been discarded, because, whereas basis of partnership assets has risen to $55,000, partnership capital accounts remain at $10,000. The following paragraph shows the fallacy of such a conclusion.

6.3.1 Increases in Liabilities Increase Basis of Partnership Interests

The general rule prevails because Internal Revenue Code Section 752 says that an increase in a partner's share of the liabilities of the partnership is considered as a contribution of money by the partner to the partnership. To paraphrase that, partner I is considered to have contributed $22,500 to the partnership, so the basis of his interest rises to $27,500, though his capital account remains at $5,000. Since the same principle applies to partner J, their combined basis of partnership interests rises to $55,000, the same as the basis of the partnership assets.

6.3.2 Decreases in Liabilities Decrease Basis of Partnership Interests

Not surprisingly, Section 752 goes on to say that any decrease in a partner's share of the liabilities of the partnership is considered as a distribution of money by the partnership.

6.3.3 Special Rule for Nonrecourse Liabilities

Occasionally, a partnership is able to obtain financing on terms under which the lender looks only to the mortgaged property for repayment of his loan. The lender has no recourse to the borrower if the value of the property turns out to be less than the amount of the debt.

The rationale of allowing a partner to increase his basis by his share of partnership debt is that the partner has, in effect, borrowed the money and contributed it to the partnership. Carrying this analogy one step further, we would conclude that when the partnership retires debt, it has, in effect, paid the money to the partner who uses it to retire his debt.

This logic fails when we attempt to apply it to a limited partnership. The chief advantage of being a limited partner is that the partner's liability is limited to the amount of his capital contribution. If a limited partnership has debt on which there is recourse to the partners, only the general partner (partners) obtains a step-up in basis of partnership interest when debt is incurred because only he (they) has incurred liability.

Perhaps the chief attraction of a limited partnership is the leverage obtained by borrowings that are substantial in relation to equity, permitting depreciation deductions that may quickly exceed the limited partner's investment. IRC Section 704(d) permits increase in basis from increased partnership liabilities to be allocated to all partners, including limited partners, in proportion to their interests, only when no partner has any personal liability and only when the partnership is an investor in real estate or engages in one of the "deductions limited to amount at risk" activities specified in IRC Section 465. Also, increase in basis attributable to share of nonrecourse liabilities is available only for purposes of determining a partner's allowable loss deduction.

6.4   OTHER CAUSES OF CHANGES IN BASIS OF PARTNERSHIP INTEREST

In addition to contributions of capital (in cash or in property with tax basis), or increases in share of partnership liabilities, a partner's basis for his partnership interest is increased by:

1. His distributive share of partnership income
2. His distributive share of tax-exempt income
3. His share of capital gains and Section 1231 gains
4. His share of the excess of depletion deductions over his share of the basis of the property subject to depletion

In addition to withdrawals of capital or decreases in share of partnership liabilities, his basis for his interest in the partnership is decreased by:

1. His distributive share of partnership losses
2. His share of capital losses and Section 1231 losses
3. His share of partnership expenditures which are nondeductible and may not be capitalized

In the case of withdrawals in the form of property, the amount chargeable to a partner's basis is the adjusted basis of the property to the partnership. The basis of the property to the partnership will become the basis of the property to the distributee partner.

6.5   ALTERNATIVE RULE FOR DETERMINING BASIS OF PARTNERSHIP INTEREST

Although the general rule for determining basis of a partnership may be applied easily if all the needed information is available, there are times when the information cannot be obtained. Section 705(b) comes to the rescue by providing an alternative method, by which the adjusted basis of a partner's interest in a partnership may be determined by reference to his proportionate share of the adjusted basis of partnership property, which would be distributable upon termination of the partnership.

A simple illustration assumes that a three-partner partnership has property with an adjusted basis of $1,500, $1,500 cash and has no other assets and no liabilities. The adjusted basis of each partner's interest is $1,000.

Since basis and fair market value are seldom identical, it would not surprise us to find that a partnership's property with an adjusted basis of $1,500 is worth $3,000. An incoming partner is willing to pay $1,000 for a third interest, and receives a $1,000 basis for his interest, though his share of the basis of partnership property is only $500. The new partner has an "adjustment" of $500 in determining the basis of his interest, which means that henceforth the basis of his partnership interest is his share of the adjusted basis of partnership assets plus $500. Presumably, if he fails to maintain a record of his adjustment and has to fall back on the alternative rule, his basis is his share of the adjusted basis of partnership assets; $500 less than the basis to which he is entitled.

6.6 BASIS OF PARTNERSHIP ASSETS AND BASIS OF PARTNERSHIP INTERESTS FREQUENTLY RUN "IN SYNC"

Accountants are accustomed to think of the basis of a partnership interest as being related to the partner's capital account (which it is) and as being the same as the capital account (which it isn't). Since capital accounts represent the excess of assets over liabilities, accountants have difficulty seeing how fluctuations in liabilities can simultaneously and equally affect both the liability accounts and the basis of the partnership interests.

To show how neatly the total assets and total partnership interests move as if synchronized, we shall prepare a worksheet accounting for these typical partnership transactions (page 145).

1. A and B open the partnership with $10,000 cash each.
2. Depreciable assets are acquired for $50,000 with 10 percent down and the balance in 45 payments of principal of $1,000 plus interest.
3. Six payments on the note are made.
4. Expenses, including interest, totaling $100,000 are incurred, of which $15,000 remain unpaid at year-end.
5. Depreciation of $6,000 is allowable.

A AND B PARTNERSHIP
ANALYSIS OF TRANSACTIONS
FOR THE FIRST YEAR OF OPERATION

	Opening Trial Balance		Transactions				Income Accounts		Ending Balance Sheet	
	Dr.	Cr.	Dr.		Cr.		Dr.	Cr.	Dr.	Cr.
Cash	$20,000		(6) $125,000	(2)	$ 5,000				$35,000	
				(3)	6,000					
				(4)	85,000					
				(7)	14,000					
Accounts receivable			(6) 25,000						25,000	
Depreciable assets			(2) 50,000						50,000	
Accumulated depreciation				(5)	6,000				(6,000)	
Accounts payable				(4)	15,000					$ 15,000
Notes payable			(3) 6,000	(2)	45,000					39,000
Depreciation			(5) 6,000				$ 6,000			
Other expenses			(4) 100,000				$100,000			
Income				(6)	150,000			$150,000		
Close income accounts			(8) 44,000				$ 44,000			
Capital – A		$10,000	(7) $ 7,000	(8)	$ 22,000					25,000
Capital – B		10,000	(7) $ 7,000	(8)	$ 22,000					25,000
	$20,000	$20,000	$370,000		$370,000		$150,000	$150,000	$104,000	$104,000

145

6. Income of $150,000 is recorded, of which $25,000 is receivable at year-end.

7. Each partner draws out $7,000.

8. Net income is closed into partnership capital accounts.

You will notice that basis of total assets at inception ($20,000) equals basis of partnership interests at inception ($20,000).

Applying the rules for basis of partnership interests, we develop these figures:

Beginning basis of partnership interests	$ 20,000
Add: Increase in partnership liabilities	60,000
Net income	44,000
Less: Decrease in partnership liabilities	(6,000)
Withdrawals of cash	(14,000)
Ending basis of partnership interests	$104,000

The ending basis of partnership interests ($104,000) is equal to the adjusted basis of all partnership assets ($104,000).

6.7 DATES ON WHICH BASIS OF PARTNERSHIP INTEREST MUST BE DETERMINED

Partners making reasonable withdrawals from a well-financed and profitable partnership have no need to be constantly concerned about the basis of their partnership interests. In many cases, if not in most, the partner who maintains a positive balance in his capital account need not be concerned as to what the basis of his partnership interest is.

A partner who withdraws cash in an amount that exceeds the adjusted basis of his interest in the partnership, will be taxed on the gain as if the distribution had been made on the last day of the partnership taxable year (Regulations 1.731-1(a)(ii)).

For a partner who retires or whose entire interest is sold, gain or loss is determined by comparing what is to be received to basis of partnership interest as of the date of the sale, exchange, or liquidation.

6.8 LOST BASIS OF PARTNERSHIP INTEREST UPON DISTRIBUTION

The general rule of basis in partnership taxation is that someone, partner or partnership, gets the tax benefit of basis. Various elections are available to prevent loss of basis when assets are distributed to partners. In paragraph 5.15.5 we discussed how a partnership may make an election under Section 754 and Section 734 to increase the adjusted basis of remaining partnership properties by the amount of basis which the distributee partner loses when the basis of the distributed property to him is limited by the basis of his partnership interest. Sometimes, a partnership is not aware of the existence of the opportunity to make the election, or neglects to make it. To illustrate the unfortunate result, we look at the plight of AbBaCadabra partnership which liquidated Ab's interest (basis $9,000) by distributing to him cash of $6,000, inventory items having an adjusted basis to the partnership of $6,000 and real property having a basis to the partnership of $4,000. The cash payment reduces Ab's basis to $3,000, which is allocated to the inventory items. The remaining partnership basis of $3,000 in the inventory items and the partnership basis of $4,000 in the real estate is "lost" in the sense that Ab can't use it and the partnership can't reallocate it to its remaining properties because no election under Section 754 was in effect.

6.9   CHAPTER SIX IN RETROSPECT

Basis of property owned is seldom uppermost in the minds of investors. Typically, the investor in real estate or corporate stock gives no thought to the basis of his acquisition until (or usually, after) the time to sell it arrives. He is usually safe in his unconcerned state because basis seldom enters into an operating decision concerning passive investments.

Partnerships are not passive investments. Basis of a partnership interest is changing constantly, and affects decisions on borrowing or repayment of debt as well as decisions on withdrawal or investment of funds.

The partner and his advisor should have a clear understanding of the significance of bases, and, at least annually, they should be sure that they have a correct figure as to the basis of a partnership interest and a correct understanding of the possible effect of basis, or lack of it, on the decisions and operations of the future.

CHAPTER SEVEN

Termination of a Partnership

CONTENTS

	INTRODUCTION	151
7.1	STATUTORY PROVISIONS FOR TERMINATION	151
7.2	CONTINUATION OF A PARTNERSHIP UNDER THE INTERNAL REVENUE CODE	152
7.3	INCORPORATION OF A PARTNERSHIP	153

7.3.1   Tax Implications of Incorporation – 153
7.3.2   Arranging for Tax-Free Incorporation – 153
7.3.3   Importance of Competent Legal Counsel for Incorporation – 154
7.3.4   Methods of Transferring Assets in Incorporation of a Partnership – 154

7.4	DISPOSITION OF ASSETS AND LIABILITIES	154

7.4.1   Dividing the Partnership's Business So That Former Partners Continue the Business as Sole Proprietors – 155
7.4.2   Dividing the Partnership's Business So That One Partner May Retire and the Other Partner May Continue the Business – 157
7.4.3   Dividing the Partnership's Business by Selling All or Part of the Assets – 158

7.5	AVOIDING UNWANTED TERMINATION OF A PARTNERSHIP	159

7.6   TAX HAZARDS OF TERMINATION OF A
        PARTNERSHIP   160

        7.6.1   Recapture of Investment Credit Upon Ter-
                  mination of a Partnership – 161

7.7   CHAPTER SEVEN SUMMARIZED   162

INTRODUCTION

We have often alluded to the superiority of the partnership over the corporation when it comes to flexibility in tax-planning. In the area of termination, particularly unwanted or unexpected termination, the partnership has dangers and complexities that the corporation does not have.

Corporate stockholders come and go as they please and the corporate existence is unaffected. Even a 100 percent turnover in stockholdings does not cause a corporate termination, and no percentage of change in stockholdings affects tax elections made by the corporation.

An unwanted, or technical, termination of a partnership may trigger many unfortunate events. These are discussed in paragraph 7.6.

Partners and their advisors are well advised to know the circumstances under which a partnership will be terminated, both under the Uniform Partnership Act and under the Internal Revenue Code.

There are far fewer causes for termination of a limited partnership. Since a limited partnership agreement must specify the term for which it will exist, obviously the expiration of the term terminates the partnership. The retirement, death or insanity of a sole general partner will terminate the partnership. If there is more than one general partner, the retirement, death, or insanity of a general partner will not terminate the partnership if the business is continued by the remaining general partners under a right to do so stated in the certificate or with the consent of all partners. A limited partnership is terminated when all limited partners withdraw or lose their status as limited partners.

7.1 STATUTORY PROVISIONS FOR TERMINATION

The Uniform Partnership Act covers termination in Sections 31 and 32, saying:

SECTION 31: Causes of dissolution. Dissolution is caused:
(1) Without violation of the agreement between the partners,
   (a) By the termination of the definite term or particular undertaking specified in the agreement,
   (b) By the express will of any partner when no definite term or particular undertaking is specified,
   (c) By the express will of all the partners who have not assigned their interests or suffered them to be charged for their separate debts, either before or after the termination of any specified term or particular undertaking,
   (d) By the expulsion of any partner from the business bona fide in accordance with such a power conferred by the agreement between the partners;

151

(2) In contravention of the agreement between the partners, where the circumstances do not permit a dissolution under any other provision of this section, by the express will of any partner at any time;

(3) By any event which makes it unlawful for the business of the partnership to be carried on or for the members to carry it on in partnership;

(4) By the death of any partner;

(5) By the bankruptcy of any partner or the partnership;

(6) By decree of court under Section 32.

SECTION 32. Dissolution by decree of court:

(1) On application by or for a partner the court shall decree a dissolution whenever:

   (a) A partner has been declared a lunatic in any judicial proceeding or is shown to be of unsound mind,

   (b) A partner becomes in any other way incapable of performing his part of the partnership contract,

   (c) A partner has been guilty of such conduct as tends to affect prejudicially the carrying on of the business,

   (d) A partner wilfully or persistently commits a breach of the partnership agreement, or otherwise so conducts himself in matters relating to the partnership business that it is not reasonably practicable to carry on the business in partnership with him,

   (e) The business of the partnership can only be carried on at a loss,

   (f) Other circumstances render a dissolution equitable.

(2) On the application of the purchaser of a partner's interest under Sections 27 or 28:

   (a) After the termination of the specified term or particular undertaking,

   (b) At any time if the partnership was a partnership at will when the interest was assigned or when the charging order was issued.

7.2 CONTINUATION OF A PARTNERSHIP UNDER THE INTERNAL REVENUE CODE

Internal Revenue Code Section 708, entitled "Continuation of Partnership," specifies only two general rules for termination:

(1) No part of any business, financial operation, or venture of the partnership is carried on by any of its partners in a partnership, or

(2) Within a 12-month period there is a sale or exchange of 50 percent or more of the total interest in partnership capital and profits.

Disposition of a partnership interest by gift, bequest, inheritance, or liquidation is not a sale or exchange for termination purposes. Thus, over 50 percent of a firm's assets may be distributed to liquidate a partner's interest without ending the firm.

At first impression, one might think that the death of one partner in a two-partner firm would terminate the partnership for tax purposes. If the estate or other successor in interest acquires the partnership interest, the partnership is unaffected. If, however, the surviving partner acquires the estate's partnership interest, the partnership terminates after a reasonable period for effectuating the transfer.

7.3   INCORPORATION OF A PARTNERSHIP

Although the partnership form is well-suited to the operation of many businesses, there may come a time when a business must change to the corporate form. Reasons may include:

(1) Recognition of need for the corporate shield against personal liability;

(2) Need to tap capital resources that will not or cannot participate in a partnership;

(3) Franchise or other contractual mandates, or regulatory rules;

(4) Estate planning needs, including use of devices such as preferred stock to freeze present estate values;

(5) Opportunity to build up capital at lower corporate tax rates;

(6) Opportunity to obtain more generous employee benefits under corporate plans.

7.3.1   Tax Implications of Incorporation

A partnership that decides to incorporate must decide whether it wants to effect a taxable or a nontaxable incorporation. Occasionally, there are sufficient reasons to justify planning a taxable incorporation. One of the more common reasons is to get, at the cost of a capital gains tax, a stepped-up basis in land about to be subdivided. There may be cases where obtaining a higher basis for depreciation will justify taxable incorporation; in most cases, the present value of benefits of tax-saving from larger ordinary deductions for depreciation in the future will not equal the immediate capital gains tax needed to get stepped-up basis for depreciation.

7.3.2   Arranging for Tax-Free Incorporation

A partnership that is about to incorporate can avoid the recognition of gain or loss by availing itself of the provisions of Internal Revenue Code Section 351. Without the protection of Section 351, the excess of value of the stock received, over the tax basis of the property placed in the corporation in exchange for stock, would be taxed as capital gain at the time of the transfer. No gain or loss is recognized if property is transferred to a corporation solely in exchange for stock or securities in the corporation, and immediately after the exchange the transferors are in control of the corporation. Since "securities" and "control" are technical terms as used here, the reader is referred to the Regulations under Sections 351 and 368(c).

7.3.3 Importance of Competent Legal Counsel for Incorporation

The partnership that is contemplating incorporation must have the services of an attorney. Although the services of an attorney specializing in taxation may not be required, incorporators should make sure that the attorney selected is reasonably well-versed in the tax aspect of incorporation.

7.3.4 Methods of Transferring Assets in Incorporation of a Partnership

At least three techniques are available to incorporate a partnership without recognition of taxable gain to the partners or partnership:

(1) The partners transfer their partnership interests to the newly formed corporation solely in exchange for all of the stock or securities of the corporation.

(2) The partnership transfers all of its assets to a newly formed corporation in exchange for all of its stock and securities.

(3) The partnership distributes all of its assets to the partners, who then transfer their assets to the newly formed corporation in exchange for all of its stock and securities.

In each case, the partnership terminates and the corporation takes as its basis the partnership's basis in assets and each partner's basis for his stock is the adjusted basis of his interest in the former partnership.

Since the basis of assets to the corporation is the basis to the partnership, it is important that elections under Section 754 be made, if appropriate, so that the partnership's basis will reflect a basis of a partner's interest higher than the basis of a proportionate share of assets. Elections under Section 754 are discussed in paragraph 5.15 *et seq*.

7.4   DISPOSITION OF ASSETS AND LIABILITIES

The relationships in a partnership can be almost as sensitive as they are in a marriage, and the division of assets and liabilities can be as difficult, even as sentimental and emotional, as a property settlement incident to a divorce or the division of an estate.

When a parting of the ways becomes inevitable, several ways to divide the business may be considered. They include the following:

(1) Divide the clients, patients or customers, the furniture and the staff in some agreeable and equitable manner, so that the former partners continue the business as sole proprietors.

(2) Divide the business so that partners who intend to continue in the business retain staff and clients, patients or customers; and other partner(s) take(s) cash, investments, real estate, or even a disproportionate part of unrealized receivables.

(3) Sell the whole business, or parts of it so that some or all partners can leave that line of work and thereafter receive investment income to replace their partnership earnings.

We shall illustrate how a partnership might handle each of these approaches.

7.4.1 Dividing the Partnership's Business so That Former Partners Continue the Business as Sole Proprietors

In our first illustration, the calendar year, accrual basis partnership of Butler and Propst operates a combined retail and industrial bottled gas business, which has this balance sheet at the moment of dissolution:

ASSETS

Cash	$ 4,000
Inventory (at cost)	10,000
Accounts receivable (good)	30,000
Office equipment (at tax basis)	6,000
Delivery equipment (at tax basis)	40,000
Bulk plant (at tax basis)	50,000
Total Assets	$140,000

LIABILITIES

Accounts payable	$ 10,000
Long term debt	30,000
Total liabilities	40,000

PARTNERS' EQUITY

Butler	50,000
Propst	50,000
Total partners' equity	100,000
Total Liabilities and Partners' Equity	$140,000

Butler and Propst agree to sign a covenant not to compete in the fields taken over and agree that Butler will sell to Propst so that Propst can limit his activity to selling, delivering and collecting. They will share office space, personnel and the vehicle parking area on an equitable basis. They have equal access to the retail customer list.

For simplicity, we have arranged for an equal distribution of assets. Had it not come out so neatly, the partners could have juggled cash or payables, or even have used notes to equalize the distribution. The question is: does this distribution involve any tax problems?

Since the partnership is on the accrual basis, there are no unrealized receivables and since fair market values and tax bases of tangible assets are the same, there are no problems under Section 751.

The retail business consists of serving hundreds of residences and small businesses and is seasonal. The industrial business consists of serving a much smaller number of accounts who buy in large quantities.

Although the relationship between the partners is good, they cannot agree on which line of business to promote most aggressively; in fact, Butler seriously questions that the retail business is worth the problems of frequent small deliveries, collection problems, and the seasonal aspect. They agree to terminate the partnership and to divide the business this way:

	Retail	Wholesale
Cash	$ 4,000	
Inventory		$ 10,000
Accounts receivable	11,000	19,000
Office equipment	6,000	
Delivery equipment	30,000	10,000
Bulk plant		50,000
Accounts payable	(1,000)	(9,000)
Long term debt		(30,000)
Net Assets	$ 50,000	$ 50,000

We can determine whether there are any other tax problems by analyzing the basis of each partner's partnership interest and the effect thereon of the distribution:

	Propst	Butler
Capital account	$50,000	$50,000
Share of liabilities	20,000	20,000
Basis	70,000	70,000
Reduced by:		
Distribution of cash	4,000	
Reduction of share of liabilities	19,000	
Increased by:		
Increase in share of liabilities		19,000
Remaining Basis	$47,000	$89,000

To be applied to:

Inventory		$10,000
Accounts receivable	$11,000	19,000
Office equipment	6,000	
Delivery equipment	30,000	10,000
Bulk plant		.50,000
	$47,000	$89,000

Since there was no distribution of cash (including reduction of share of liabilities treated as a distribution of cash) in excess of basis, there is no taxable gain to either partner resulting from the liquidating distribution. The adjusted basis of each partnership interest is then allocated to the property received.

7.4.2 Dividing the Partnership's Business so That One Partner May Retire and the Other Partner May Continue the Business

Considering the limitations on retirement plans available to partnerships, termination of the partnership by retirement of a partner through a disproportionate distribution may be necessary.

In our second illustration, the calendar year equal partnership Debit and Credit, CPAs, has this situation at the moment of dissolution:

1. A lease on the office space at prevailing rates
2. Cash of $10,000
3. Receivables and work in process of $100,000
4. Furniture and library with book and fair market values of $10,000
5. A client list worth $100,000
6. Staff adequate to handle the present work load and some growth

Since Debit and Credit keep their books for tax purposes on the cash method, there is no basis for the receivables and work in process nor for the client list. Debit and Credit readily agree that since Debit wants to continue the business as a sole proprietor, and credit wants to retire and live on his social security and investment income, Debit will keep the clients, the lease, the furniture and the staff, and Credit will get the cash and the proceeds from collecting the receivables. All work not yet paid for can be reduced to cash within six months and July 1 has been set for the date of Credit's withdrawal.

Under Section 708(b)(1)(B), the partnership will be terminated because after the departure of Credit, no part of the partnership's business will be carried on by any of its partners in a partnership. Regulations 1.736-1(a)(1)(ii) covers the timing in this case by saying:

"A partner retires when he ceases to be a partner under local law. However, for purposes of Subchapter K, Chapter 1 of the Code, a retired partner or a deceased partner's successor will be treated as a partner until his interest in the partnership has been completely liquidated."

From July 1 to the end of the year, Debit and Credit, CPAs, continues in business only to collect for work done prior to July 1, so that net income for the period July 1 through December 31 will be $100,000.

Debit and Credit could amend the partnership agreement to provide that 100 percent of taxable income after July 1 would be allocated and paid to Credit. Such an arrangement would serve their purposes. Would the arrangement bear tax scrutiny? IRC Section 704 and the regulations thereunder provide that any item or class of income may be allocated by the partnership agreement and that the agreement will be honored unless the principal purpose is avoidance or evasion of income taxation. A presumption of avoidance or evasion of income tax can be rebutted by establishing that the allocation has a business purpose and that the allocation has substantial economic effect, meaning that the allocation affects the dollars going to the partners. In this case, no tax is avoided since Credit reports the $100,000 ordinary income; orderly liquidation of the business is a business purpose; the dollars distributed to Credit exactly equal the tax effect of the special allocation.

Credit and the Internal Revenue Service would have preferred an agreement under which the partners would have divided the final $100,000 equally and Debit would have paid Credit $50,000 for good will. Credit would have had $50,000 ordinary income and $50,000 capital gain on the sale of good will; Debit would have had $50,000 ordinary income and would have purchased a nonamortizable asset, good will. Partners have the right and the obligation to use their negotiating strengths to serve their individual purposes at minimum tax cost.

If Debit and Credit, CPAs, had owned its office building with market value substantially in excess of mortgage, the figures might have worked out so that Credit could receive the real estate and a smaller part, or even none, of the receivables. In such case, particularly if the fair market value of the real estate exceeded its tax basis, the complicated rules of Section 751 would have come into play.

7.4.3 Dividing the Partnership's Business by Selling All or Part of the Assets

It is possible to terminate a partnership by selling the entire business and dividing the proceeds among the partners. Though this seldom happens to an operating partnership, sale of the principal asset frequently terminates a real estate or equipment leasing venture. Assets may be transferred subject to the liabilities which they secure, and cash proceeds used to settle other liabilities so that the remaining cash may be distributed to liquidate all partnership interests.

Assets sold may include depreciable property, gain on which is subject to recapture of depreciation under Sections 1245 or 1250, farm property, gain on which is subject to tax as ordinary income under Sections 1251 or 1252, or oil and gas property, gain on sale of which is subject to tax as ordinary income under Section 1254. Proceeds of the sale of unrealized receivables or substantially appreciated inventory (as defined in Section 751) are subject to tax as ordinary income.

There may be a sale of the principal asset of a partnership, followed by a distribution of cash and miscellaneous other property. The point to remember in the sale of all or only some assets is that the sale is reported on the partnership's return, with allocation of taxability governed by the terms of the partnership agreement, and the taxability of the gain is controlled by Section 731 and the basis of property received is determined under Section 732. Due regard must be given to the nature of taxability as affected by Sections 751, 1245, 1250, 1251, 1252, 1253 and 1254.

7.5   AVOIDING UNWANTED TERMINATION OF A PARTNERSHIP

Under Section 708 of the Internal Revenue Code, a partnership shall be considered as terminated only if no part of its business is carried on by any of its partners in a partnership, or if, within a consecutive 12-month period, there is a sale or exchange of 50 percent or more of the total interest in partnership capital and profits.

It is unlikely that a cessation of business can come as a surprise or be an unintended action. However, some partnerships have very restrictive rules as to when a person must leave the partnership or as to who may be a successor in interest. Such a partnership may find itself terminated at a time and in a manner definitely not of its choosing.

We illustrate this by describing the plight of a medical practice established by two doctors in 1952, who selected a fiscal year ending January 31 (back then partnerships had as much flexibility as corporations have now in selecting a fiscal year). Four other doctors have been admitted since then, and these four have capital and profits interests totaling 48 percent. The partnership has no qualified retirement plan, but does carry enough life insurance to require a cash buy-out of the interest of a deceased partner within three months of death. The partnership has avoided the possible strain of supporting a sick partner for a long time by providing for only two months continuation of a partner's salary (or draw), mandatory retirement upon proof of 50 percent disability, and has attempted to avoid financial strain to a sick partner by carrying a disability policy providing generous benefits commencing sixty days after the onset of disability.

The partners have been enjoying an eleven-month deferral of taxability because income reported to them on Form 1065, Schedule K-1, earned in a year ending January 31, does not find its way onto a Form 1040 until the following December 31.

In February, a partner who has a 26 percent interest dies. According to plan, the life insurance is collected and the deceased partner's interest is liquidated. Almost before those arrangements are complete, the other 26 percent partner suffers a paralytic stroke which results in permanent disablement. Before December 31st, the disabled partner exceeds the two months for which he is paid as a partner and his interest is liquidated.

The four remaining partners rearrange their schedule so as to carry on the practice. The partners realize that if the partnership is terminated, they face an almost doubling of taxable income, because they will report income from Form 1065, Schedule K-1 for the fiscal year ended January 31 and for their new year ending December 31. There may be recapture of investment credit, and elections such as accelerated depreciation are voided.

Regulations 1.708-1(b)(1)(i)(b)(ii) come to their rescue by making it clear that a liquidation of a partnership interest is not a sale or exchange.

If one of the younger doctors had been a potential heir of one of the older doctors and had received a 26 percent interest by inheritance or gift, there would have been no "sale or exchange." A sale or exchange is required. In our illustration, if other doctors (present partners or outsiders) had bought the interests of the deceased and disabled doctors, the partnership would have been terminated. It follows, then, that the writers of a partnership agreement should be very careful to anticipate departures and provide for transfers of interest in such a manner that inadvertent termination cannot come to pass.

The reader must realize that the twelve consecutive months do not have to be one taxable year of the partnership; sale of more than 50 percent of partners' interests in both capital and profits in two transactions on July 1, 19X1 and on June 30, 19X2 will terminate a partnership.

7.6 TAX HAZARDS OF TERMINATION OF A PARTNERSHIP

Serious tax consequences can arise from the termination of a partnership. Perhaps the most serious effect occurs when a partnership filing a return on a fiscal year is deemed to be terminated. Since the business is continued without apparent interruption by the remaining partners, a new partnership is deemed to have been formed, and it does not have the right to elect a taxable year which does not coincide with the taxable year of its principal partners. Since most partners are individuals filing their returns on the calendar year, the "new" partnership is forced to adopt the calendar year. This causes the partners to have two closings in one of their taxable years, bunching perhaps as much as 23 months income into one partner's tax year.

The right to use 200 percent declining balance or sum-of-the-years digits depreciation will be lost upon the termination of a partnership. However, since depreciation computed under the Economic Recovery Tax Act of 1981 is more liberal than even former accelerated methods, this may not be a disadvantage.

In many cases, termination of a partnership will trigger recapture of all unearned investment credit (discussed in paragraph 7.6.1). The basis of distributed property is determined by reference to the basis of the partner's interest in the partnership; his basis for the property may be less favorable than the basis attached to the same items when they were partnership property.

A partner may find that reduction of his share of liabilities, considered a constructive distribution of cash, may result in recognition of taxable gain upon termination of a partnership.

7.6.1 Recapture of Investment Credit Upon Termination of a Partnership

The general rule is that credit will be recaptured when a partner disposes of his partnership interest prior to the end of the useful life of the asset for which investment credit was claimed. In some cases, Section 47(b) provides an escape from recapture when the property is transferred in connection with a "mere change in the form of conducting the trade or business so long as the property is retained in such trade or business as Section 38 property and the taxpayer retains a substantial interest in such trade or business."

The Regulations add two conditions that make retention of the credit more difficult. The first is that the basis of the property in the hands of the transferee must be measured by the transferor's basis for it. The second is that substantially all of the operating assets must be transferred, so that the same business is carried on with the same assets. "Substantially all of the assets" means transfer of not only the Section 38 assets but also the non-Section 38 assets such as land and buildings.

The law and the regulations throw up formidable obstacles to retention of investment credit when a partnership terminates. The first hurdle is that the basis of assets in the hands of the transferor partner is not determined by the basis in the hands of the partnership, but is determined by the basis of his partnership interests. Another hurdle is that it would be difficult to terminate a partnership, including paying off a retiring or deceased partner, and still retain substantially all of the assets.

If a partnership incorporates, transfers all assets to the new corporation in a tax-free exchange, and the shareholders' interests in the corporation are identical to their former interests as partners expressed in percentages, then the investment credit will not be recaptured. If some partners receive greater interests in the corporation than they had in the partnership, they should avoid recapture; obviously, some partners will receive decreased percentages of interest and they will suffer recapture.

It appears that any termination of a partnership other than by incorporation would cause recapture of all unearned investment credit. However, a partner who acquires substantially all of the assets upon termination and continues the business as a sole proprietor may be able to present a convincing case for avoidance of recapture.

7.7 CHAPTER SEVEN SUMMARIZED

The alleged advantage of a corporation over a partnership, that the corporation enjoys unlimited life whereas a partnership's life is always limited, may be less of an advantage than it seems. In the first place, proper drafting of a partnership agreement can provide for alternatives to termination so that a partnership can theoretically exist in perpetuity. In the second place, the average partnership (excluding intentionally short-term joint ventures) probably lasts longer than the average corporation. Some accounting and law partnerships antedate General Motors or U.S. Steel, and are absolutely Methuselahs compared to IBM, Litton Industries or Polaroid.

Nonetheless, planners of a partnership should recognize that they should include an exit as well as an entrance. Partners should be permitted to depart with grace and equity; the tax effects of going out of business or of changing the form of doing business should be no more unfavorable than necessary. At the risk of being morbid and likening a partnership termination to death, or, worse yet, introducing poetic philosophy into the prosaic fields of law and management, the recommendation is made that you approach the inevitability of termination with the philosophy of William Cullen Bryant, expressed in *Thanatopsis*:

> So live, that when thy summons comes to join
> The innumerable caravan, which moves
> To that mysterious realm, where each shall take
> His chamber in the silent halls of death,
> Thou go not, like the quarry-slave at night,
> Scourged to his dungeon, but, sustained and soothed

> By an unfaltering trust, approach thy grave,
> Like one who wraps the drapery of his couch
> About him, and lies down to pleasant dreams.

Planning for termination should encompass these concepts:

1. What event (or events) should cause the partnership to terminate?

2. What shall be the financial terms upon which termination will be based?

3. Are there unduly restrictive provisions that may result in unwanted termination?

4. Have plans for termination been formulated to insure the optimum tax treatment for the greatest number of participants, or for those who have the most at stake?

In the language of literature, will the survivors of a termination feel that they can lie down to pleasant dreams, or will they feel that they have been sent through the gates of hell as described by Dante in his *Inferno*?

CHAPTER EIGHT

Branch Offices
Of Professional Partnerships

$$\longleftrightarrow$$

CONTENTS

INTRODUCTION   167

8.1   HOW BRANCH OFFICES ARE ACQUIRED   167

8.2   STAFFING BRANCH OFFICES   168

    8.2.1   Staffing Branch Offices of Large Firms – 168
    8.2.2   Staffing Branch Offices of Small Firms – 169
    8.2.3   Staffing with Recruits or Transferees – 169
    8.2.4   The Pros and Cons of Rotation of Personnel – 170
    8.2.5   Potential Personnel Problems of the Branch Office – 171
        A Case Study in Opening A Branch Office – 172

8.3   DEFECTIONS BY BRANCH OFFICE PERSONNEL   174

    8.3.1   Prevention of Defection – 174
        A Case Study on Branch Partner Defection – 175

8.4   COMMUNICATION BETWEEN MAIN AND BRANCH OFFICES   176

    8.4.1   The Vices of Written Communication – 176

8.4.2   Verbal Communication Must Supplement
          Written Communication – 177
8.4.3   The Engagement as a Communication Me-
          dium – 177
8.4.4   Illustration of the Engagement as a Mixer –
          177
8.4.5   Seminars to Build Business and Cement Re-
          lations – 178
8.4.6   Introductions Are a Two-Way Street – 178

8.5   CONTROL OVER IMAGE AND QUALITY   179

8.5.1   Constant Vigilance Is Required – 179
8.5.2   Specific Controls Are Needed – 179

8.6   THE BRANCH OFFICE SYNDROME   180

8.6.1   Estrangement Strains Loyalty – 181
8.6.2   Prevention of Estrangement and Disloyalty
          – 181

8.7   DUPLICATION OF EXPENSES IN BRANCH OFFICES 182
8.8   CHAPTER EIGHT IN REVIEW   183

INTRODUCTION

Some professional partnerships acquire branch offices because they want to grow, and see branch offices as a medium for growth; others acquire branch offices not because they are interested in them as a means for growth, but because branch offices permit them to serve existing clients better, or with less travel.

Whatever your reasons for keeping or acquiring branch offices might be, you should realize that they present problems as well as opportunities. There are problems of staffing, of managing, and of maintaining communications. Without constant monitoring, different standards of performance will prevail in different locations. Finally, the procedures necessary to keep a multioffice organization working as a unified team will be costly in money, time, and the patience of all concerned. Hours spent considering the pros and cons of opening a new office (and, sometimes, of continuing one) can be counted among your most productive. Finally, make the decision based on facts, or on well-reasoned estimates; expansion for the excitement of it, or to keep up with the Price Waterhouses, can be an expensive mistake.

Opening a new office involves cooperation between home office management and the person(s) who will be in charge of the branch. It can be assumed that arrangements for space and furnishings, telephone and a basic library will have been made before operations begin. An initial stock of forms and supplies will be on hand. There will, however, for a long time, be a series of minicrises as the lack of some small item impedes smooth operation. There will be repeated conflicts between the branch office manager and the home office watchdogs over the cost and scope of library facilities, over the cost and capabilities of copiers, of word or data processors. The typical result is a compromise in which the branch executive has less than he thinks he needs but has gotten far more than the firm originally intended to supply.

8.1   HOW BRANCH OFFICES ARE ACQUIRED

Branch offices are acquired in several ways. They may result from:

1. A decision to enter a new market, or a market in which the partnership has a toehold that would become more secure with a presence in the locality.

2. A merger. Occasionally, two sole proprietorships or small partnerships combine their practices but continue to operate from both

former locations. If a party or parties to the merger already were multioffice operations, there may be several offices. If acquired offices are in close proximity to each other, decisions to close or merge offices may be made.

3. Branch offices may be opened to follow expanding or relocating clients or patients. Examples include:

   A. Law or CPA firms in established industrial areas whose clients move to or open new facilities in the Sun Belt.

   B. Law, CPA or brokerage firms with wealthy clients who are retiring and moving to warmer climes and who want to continue to be served by professionals with whom they are familiar and comfortable.

   C. An established surgical practice quartered near older hospitals may, for the convenience of the doctors or to meet the needs or preferences of their patients, open an office near a new hospital.

4. Law firms in particular may open offices for better contact with centers of political of financial power or influence, such as New York or Washington, D.C. The same logic could justify opening an office in a regional center.

8.2   STAFFING BRANCH OFFICES

Pitfalls abound in the staffing of branch offices. In theory, staffing would be in accordance with a carefully developed analysis of the needs of the offices and the personalities and capabilities of the available people. In many cases, when existing offices are retained, everyone essentially stays where he was, goes on doing what he was doing, and there is a merger in name only. The opening of a branch office by an existing firm is frequently inspired by the ambitions of one or a small group of partners who, seemingly logically, go out to colonize this new frontier of their dreams. The firm may find, to its quick sorrow, that the dream has become a nightmare.

8.2.1 Staffing Branch Offices of Large Firms

The very large CPA and law firms apparently have the discipline to select and send appropriate people to branch offices, either new or established offices. Professionals in such environments have been conditioned, as have corporate management types on the way up, to understand that (thinking positively) a variety of assignments and a loyalty demonstrated by willingness to go where the company needs them are essential to climb up the ladder of success. Negative thinking is an equally strong persuader when it forces an aspirant to realize that declining reassignment may be interpreted as selfishness and indifference to the firm's goals.

8.2.2 Staffing Branch Offices of Smaller Firms

In smaller firms, partners are sent out as "missionaries" to new branch offices either because the partners to be reassigned were strong advocates of the creation of the office in the first place and see opportunities for personal advancement, or because partners are induced to volunteer by being offered better compensation arrangements and/or an increase in perquisites. In some cases, employees are promoted to partner status as a condition of transfer to the branch. Unless the branch is a nearby satellite and is a very small operation, placing a person with little or no demonstrated management skills in the position of branch office manager or resident partner is an invitation to disaster. The plight of the unprepared branch office partner is reminiscent of the adolescent complaint "Mother said there would be days like this, but she didn't tell me there would be so many."

8.2.3 Staffing With Recruits or Transferees

Although home office people, such as the personnel director, the managing partner or the director of clerical staff, may assist in recruiting and orienting new employees, the principal burden falls on the resident partner. Even if the office is adequately staffed, the established procedures with which he was familiar are not in place. The ease with which people get the job done when they have worked together for a while is missing. The home office can be of significant help if it can lend experienced help, releasing them from the branch as the new staff is broken in. Despite the obvious advantage to such a transition, the newly designated manager, following a "Mother, I'd rather do it myself" attitude is likely to want everything crisply new and fresh out of the wrapper on opening day, including everything from file cabinets to people.

When a new office is to be opened or a newly merged office is to be enlarged, the question of hiring locally or of relocating veteran employees must be considered. The advantages of bringing in a staff already acquainted with the firm's policies and procedures has been pointed out. Relocation carries its own problems. An obvious problem is the direct cost of moving people and their possessions. It is also readily apparent that any uprooting of people creates personal problems. Inflation of housing prices and values will cause a transferee to shop for a house priced well above what he paid for his former residence; with a little luck his equity has risen to about the level of the down payment now required of him; provisions of the Internal Revenue Code and similar provisions of state laws allow for nonrecognition of gains on sale of residences.

More subtle questions should be asked and answered in connection with relocation. Among these are:

    1. Is the transferee properly prepared for the reassignment?

While no one can anticipate all the problems that may or will arise, management should insist that all foreseeable problems are discussed and that the transferee be willing and able to cope with them. The emphasis, of course, should not be entirely negative. The transferee should be as acquainted with the advantages as with the disadvantages, and should have made his decision based on an intelligent weighing of the pros and cons. Management must not permit the entire burden of making the decision to accept a transfer to fall on him; when the alligators start to bite, morale sags and management has a problem that will not be exorcised by any amount of ex post facto assertion that he should have thought of the problem sooner.

2. Has the transferee been oversold? Top management of professional partnerships attained their positions by being good persuaders. Having decided to acquire a branch office, an easy next step for management is to use hard sell on those staff members who can most likely make a success of the venture, thereby proving that management was right in its original decision.

Management needs to resist the tendency to use hard sell for two reasons. The first is that truly excellent people will do well anywhere; the up-and-coming employee who was sold on what accepting relocation will do for him could have done well back at the old stand, and without taking on a whole new set of problems. The second reason becomes apparent when the impetus for the new office comes from management. Having conceived the idea, management is reluctant to abandon it just because the lower echelons do not rush to volunteer. The best people, realizing that they do not need to jump at transfers to reach career goals, are not available; management drops its standards and begins to see virtues in lesser people. The oversell may move people around, but it may also result in mediocrity in the new venture.

3. Does the person seek relocation for the wrong reason? Is he running away from problems at his old job site? Are his expectations for his new job wildly unrealistic? If he has peer problems, or client relation problems now, he certainly will not shed them when he faces them in the new office at the same time that he is also trying to adjust to unfamiliar surroundings and unfamiliar procedures.

8.2.4 The Pros and Cons of Rotation of Personnel

Another staffing problem for branch offices is setting and enforcing a policy for tenure. A policy of rotation on a regular schedule, with at least the executive levels coming and going between branch offices and the home office, tends to maintain uniformity of procedures throughout the organization. If people at a policy-making or policy-enforcing level remain in a branch location for an extended period, they will adjust policies to suit their management style so that policies supposedly in effect throughout the organization are subverted. However, there is much to be gained by having professionals stay in one place long enough to become well-known in the community, and family disruptions are lessened by longer tours of duty.

Professional firms are not alone in wrestling with the dilemma of frequent rotation versus long (even permanent) tours of duty. Some bank officers move frequently while others stay so long that they not only put down roots, they grow moss. Chain stores and stock brokerage houses have an uneven policy of rotation. Methodist preachers are routinely transferred every few years; other clergymen serve all, or almost all, of their professional lifetimes in one parish, or move at random intervals. Apparently, there is no single right answer. The answer must be determined in each case based on the perceived facts in each case. The only certainty is that if there is not a consistently enforced policy of rotation, in time there will be no policy of rotation.

8.2.5 Potential Personnel Problems of the Branch Office

Personnel problems in the newly acquired branch office fall into three categories, depending on how the office became part of the organization:

1. An existing office is merged in toto, in which case it will continue as before. Assuming that adequate care was taken to assure that quality controls in the now-a-branch office were satisfactory, this arrangement can work very well in providing a field office to serve clients who are at a distance from other offices of the firm. Minimal changes in personnel practices and office procedures may suffice to be sure that uniformity in essentials is achieved. A fair amount of good will assures success of the merger. If, however, branch office people were not adequately prepared for the merger, or even actively opposed it, clashes will come quickly and frequently. Unless such conflicts are resolved, personnel defections will come quickly. This completely defeats the purpose of merger if obtaining additional competent staff was a principal consideration.

2. A weak office, or one in which retirement of key people is imminent, requires a transfusion of people from other offices. Except in the case of the tired or sick practitioner who is anxious to shed responsibility as quickly as possible, the newcomers will be greeted with suspicion. Even in this case, and in all other cases, resentment against the newcomer is very likely. The new manager will require the wisdom of Solomon and the patience of Job to overcome resistance to any change, however obviously needed. The new manager's faith in his own wisdom will be questioned as he wonders what form of

insanity caused him to leave the old site, where he was obviously performing well, to inherit this bottomless bucket of snakes. The reptilian analogy continues when one tries to summon up an extra measure of patience with recalcitrant staff when up to the waistline in the alligators of new clients in unfamiliar surroundings. When the snapping 'gators include an uprooted family and the problems of moving into a new home, the problems may be, and sometimes are, more than the transferee can bear.

3. A very different challenge awaits people transferred into an area where the partnership had no or very little business. If they had been traveling to this location frequently, the opportunity to cut travel time and inconvenience is a tremendous motivator to overcome the problems encountered when the new doors are opened. At best, a small cadre of people with experience in the firm will be transferred in. In many cases, the new resident partner comes alone.

A Case Study on Opening a Branch Office

In many parts of America, land that was recently field or forest is being covered with homes, shopping centers and industrial facilities. Sometimes this is a sudden development, as when a new resort area or retirement community springs up; a new industrial park attracts a variety of new businesses as well as branches of established manufacturers; a theme park sparks a new town.

Juster and Price, an established general practice law firm in a nearby metropolitan area, looks at its booming new neighbor. It sees its clients extending their services to the new town. It sees substantial real estate work as newcomers buy homes and business sites. It sees executives or well-heeled retirees moving in, needing estate and tax services. The bankers in the new community, themselves executives of state-wide banks, are familiar with the firm's reputation and are expected to recommend the firm to their new customers.

Very little further analysis is needed to show that opportunity exists. A young partner, Rister, is amenable to transfer; his wife, active in Junior League when she isn't chauffeuring their two small children to their myriad activities, is reluctant to pull up roots, but after some urging, agrees to go.

Office space was obtained, a supply closet was stocked and a basic library was placed on the new shelves. It soon became apparent that all experienced secretaries were married to men with jobs in Home City or were unwilling to move. An offer of a substantial salary increase persuaded one paralegal that a transfer made sense.

Finding a secretary was a problem. A new community has no pool of people who can be persuaded to change jobs. Since the community didn't exist a few years ago, there is no pool of native sons and daughters finishing school and returning home to begin careers. Some husbands transferred in or coming on their own initiative, had wives with work experience, and a young lady with some law office experience was found.

Even though his home in Home City was only five years old, Rister soon found that house prices in his new community were much higher than he expected and interest rates had soared; thus, new mortgage payments were double what he had been used to. Mrs. Rister found prices higher than she had been accustomed to, perhaps in part because she was no longer familiar with the markets and shops. The schools were on split session because children were pouring in faster than classrooms could be financed or built. The school board had the same difficulty finding teachers as Juster and Price had had in finding a legal secretary; some teachers weren't quite up to the board's standards, but they had to take what they could get.

Rister, looking at his budget battered and beaten, working longer hours to train a secretary and meet new bankers and new clients, and coming home to a daily tale of woe about food prices and school problems, went to the senior partners for compensation adjustment. They understood and sympathized with the financial realities and met his requests in that respect. They did not see where more money would solve the other problems and declined to grant what Rister looked upon as deserved "combat pay." With job pressures still bearing upon him and now carrying the hurt of a turn-down, Rister's morale rose very little.

Some of the new clients whom Rister attracted had come to the new town to make their fortunes, with minimum capital or experience. Their ideas for complicated business arrangements, plus their need for counsel on almost everything, produced loads of billable time for Rister and his staff. Unfortunately, they were unable to pay the bills. Rister also found that, between his inexperience and the administrative and promotional demands on his time, he was not completing engagements as promptly as he should, and could not find time for billing when he finally did finish the job. The natural result was that the branch office was a financial drain. This was a disappointment to the senior partners, who bore the brunt of the losses. They could not, however, agree to close the office, partly because to do so they have had to abandon hope of recouping their losses, and, more important, to close the office would be an admission of an error of judgment; an admission they did not care to make. Their decision was to grin and bear it, although no one recalls seeing them grin when the branch office is being discussed.

8.3   DEFECTIONS BY BRANCH OFFICE PERSONNEL

Defections by branch office personnel can be a real problem. For reasons discussed under "branch office syndrome," partners may conclude that reasons for leaving the firm outweigh reasons for remaining with the firm. Except in cases of overwhelming loyalty, at this point the partner leaves unless he is constrained by a punitive clause in the partnership agreement. Retention under such circumstances leaves much to be desired, as the person so constrained thereafter goes about his work with the enthusiasm expected of a slave or an indentured servant, which is, in his eyes, his role.

8.3.1   Prevention of Defection

The only preventive for defection is a structure in which each person is at least as well off as a member of the team as he would be under some other arrangement. Formulating such a structure can be one of the most difficult assignments facing management. Working against a solution to the problem is the fact that any good worker, if he looks hard enough, can obtain an offer which is, or appears to be, an improvement upon his present situation. However, except when the firm simply cannot provide a situation in which the potential defector can reach his full potential, it should be obvious that the firm that knows him, that does not have to break him in, that does not have to bear the expense of relocation and reorientation, can place a higher value on his services than can an organization in which he will be, for at least a while, a newcomer.

It behooves management to be constantly vigilant regarding the question of partner job satisfaction. Even those partnerships that conduct regular evaluations of employee job performance, including inquiry into whether the job meets the employee's career goals, frequently neglect to evaluate or even to inquire into partner performance and attainment of career goals. Whereas it is true that partners have more opportunity to express dissatisfaction, it is also true that they are frequently reluctant to complain about unsatisfactory conditions and permit mild dissatisfaction to grow into rancor. The situation is reminiscent of the armed services, wherein any individual needing solace can go to the chaplain and unload his tale of woe; the thinking person wonders to whom does the chaplain turn when *his* problems seem unbearable? There must be someone with partnership managerial responsibility to whom each partner can turn and is invited to turn for resolution of his problems, or at least sympathetic consideration of those problems that cannot be resolved. Rest assured, the discontented partner will seek an outlet somewhere. If it is another partner outside the management ranks, they may commiserate to the extent that you have two potential defectors. If his despair leads him to seek out other career opportunities, he may find them; whether he does or not, it does your image no good to have it noised about the community that there is dissension in the firm. The same danger arises if his confidant is a family member or a friend outside the professional circle.

The only answer to partner dissatisfaction and eventual defection is maintenance of communication to the end that feelings of alienation may be kept within reasonable bounds.

A Case Study on Branch Partner Defection

The senior partners of Juster and Price have decided to hold on to the branch office. Rister, branch office partner, ruing the day he accepted the transfer, gamely struggles with his problems at the office and at home. The new secretary finally learns the job. He has become acquainted with enough of his clients and his business and professional colleagues so that less time is spent in getting to know people, and office productivity rises. Relations at home have improved so that he no longer comes home expecting to find a note "Gone home to mother" taped to the refrigerator. Mrs. Rister, however, keeps him sufficiently reminded of the sacrifices she and the children are making to keep him wondering whether his frequent heartburn comes from an incipient ulcer or is the natural result of a steady diet of cold shoulder and hot tongue.

At the monthly partners' meetings, always held in the home office conference room, progress in the affairs of the branch office is noted. Rister believes that more credit should be given for his efforts. The senior partners, instead, exhibit an "it's about time" attitude. Rister got his biggest jolt when one of his peers asked how much longer Rister would get higher pay when his productivity is only now coming up to the levels of those who continued to labor in the home office, and presumably made the profits which permitted the firm to absorb the branch's losses.

Rister's attitude toward the firm is not improved as he contemplates regularly leaving the partners' meeting for a boring drive back to New City; his partners face no such inconvenience. The ride gives him time to think about the injustice of the situation, his righteous indignation rising with each turn of the odometer.

By this time, the client base is big enough to support the office. To most of the clients, to the business and professional community, Rister *is* Juster and Price. True, he needs the expertise of the firm in some areas, but his calls for help are becoming less frequent as his experience increases. The partnership agreement does contain a pecuniary penalty clause for withdrawal by a partner, but it was written many years ago and is not onerous in today's inflated economy.

This case study could end in several ways. Rister could find similarly disenchanted lawyers in other New City branch offices of metropolitan area firms; if their areas of expertise complement each other, all of them might jump ship at the same time and form a new partnership in New City. Juster and Price could abandon the practice to Rister, or they could send someone else in to salvage what they can.

Rister could be persuaded that his best prospects lie in remaining with Juster and Price. However, whether from an abundance of honorable intent or a fear of litigation or loss of peer respect, Rister might depart from the firm, but on conditions less traumatic to Juster and Price.

Whatever the outcome is, it will be the result of the planning that went into creating the office and assigning Rister to it and the result of constant nurture of the office and particularly of Rister to the end that at every moment all are convinced that actions being taken are in the best interests of all the partners.

8.4 COMMUNICATION BETWEEN MAIN OFFICE AND BRANCH OFFICES

Most of the world's problems can probably be traced to poor communication. This axiom applies to offices of a professional partnership.

Why Communication Problems Arise

Communication problems among offices of a professional partnership arise from these circumstances:

1. The sheer fact of distance;
2. Difference in sizes of operations;
3. Partner's preoccupation with the problems of his bailiwick;
4. Absence of a system of communication, or neglect of the system when one exists.

8.4.1 The Vices of Written Communication

When distance is a substantial obstacle to communication, there must be greater reliance on written material, including manuals and reports. To a degree, these are valuable communication media in any except the smallest partnerships. Formal communication contains within itself at least three seeds of confusion or discontent:

1. The tendency to prepare a policy directive and then fail to keep it up to date or to follow it in a consistent manner so that the persons supposed to be guided by the documents are left more confused than they would be without them;

2. The tendency to proliferate. Those of us who pursue our professions in the private sector castigate the federal bureaucracy for the torrent of rules and regulations with which they inundate the economy. Unfortunately, persons in much smaller organizations who take pen in hand to write with authority are frequently afflicted with a diarrhea of words, too often complicated by a constipation of clear thought;

3. Requiring reports that serve very little purpose. The benefit to be obtained from the report should be compared with the cost of preparing, reading and filing it, and this should be done regularly. If there is not a clear showing of benefit substantially greater than cost, some other form of communication should be devised.

8.4.2 Verbal Communication Must Supplement Written Communication

Written communication alone, no matter how well-designed or conscientiously carried out, is not sufficient for a partnership with two or more offices. Regular meetings, at which all partners get together, should be held, and these should be supplemented by visits to the branches by key people from the home office and to the home office by key people from the branches. In between, phone conversations of the "just to keep you informed" variety can be effective in squelching rumors and avoiding dependence on a grapevine. Meeting sites should be rotated among the main office and the branches to equalize the travel burden, to avoid signaling to the branches that they are lackeys being called to headquarters to report, and to give all partners an opportunity to be reasonably familiar with as many locations as is practical.

8.4.3 The Engagement as a Communication Medium

Communication can be fostered informally by having staff (or partners) assigned temporarily to various locations. Such assignments will be obvious for persons with special expertise. However, peak seasons at different times of the year in different locations, or needs for additional people for engagements that are unique only because of their size, or engagements at a neutral site, provide opportunity for creating task forces of people who do not normally work together.

8.4.4 Illustration of the Engagement as a Mixer

Ulrich and Cumming, Certified Public Accountants, wanted the employees at the branch offices to know and feel familiar with the employees in the main office. The partners observed that at the sit-down dinner Christmas party, usually held in the home office city, the branch people came together, talked with each other, and left together; there had been no breach in the isolation which the party was intended, at least partly, to break down. An informal summer swim party produced results almost as dismal.

Management decided that henceforth it would staff engagements on the basis of geographic location so that serving them would entail travel from either office with a mix of people from two offices. The mix would depend on specific requirements of the engagement and the personnel available. In a typical case, the senior in charge of the engagement and one staff accountant came from the branch; the partner in charge and one staff accountant came from the home office.

The engagement provided the contacts to help break up the office cliques at succeeding social functions. The partner had an opportunity to observe the work of two people whom he otherwise would not have known well. The two people from the branch had their experience broadened by working under the supervision of a partner who otherwise would have been unknown to them. The home office staffer, the newest person on the team, had his experience broadened by working with a senior branch office employee. Since he returned to the home office during delays in the engagement, he served as an unofficial go-between for the senior employee and the partner, transmitting files and messages and generally feeling more important than he might have felt without this experience. Of no small importance, this client, located out of the immediate area of either office, gained a feeling that he was dealing with real team players who know how to use the advantages of the multioffice firm.

8.4.5 Seminars to Build Business and Cement Relations

A law or accounting firm, wanting to improve communication between offices, further its program of continuing professional education, and get in some public relations licks all at one time, can pull off this triple play by sponsoring a seminar. Using a subject such as year-end tax planning or a law change affecting a sizable segment of the community in which the branch is located, the branch office hosts a part-day seminar at which knowledgeable people from the firm present a program. Attendance of branch office staff and of partners and other key people from the main office tends to impress the guests with the resources of the firm. When branch office people have special expertise, the location and roles could be reversed.

Suffice it to say, the program, the site and the hospitality must be of a quality which will create the desired impression.

8.4.6 Introductions Are a Two-Way Street

Typically, the branch office is small and depends on the resources of the home office in situations beyond the scope of the branch. Frequently, the management level in the branch is inexperienced compared to the moguls in the main office. Because of this, it is common practice for the heavy artillery to visit the branch for luncheon or other meetings with clients, prospective clients, bankers or other community leaders to acquaint these VIPs with the firm's higher-ups.

The home office should run this in reverse, bringing in branch staff to meet the influential people in the home territory. It is an educational experience for branchers and a morale builder, too. The good impression which the branch staff can leave, tied in with the show of firm camaraderie, may cause the guests to refer business to the branch, or at least drop the right word to someone else who is a prospective client.

8.5   CONTROL OVER IMAGE AND QUALITY

It is assumed that the branch office will be staffed with adequately trained people and will be properly equipped. In many cases, some or all of the initial staffing will come from people who have served in the home office or another branch office. There is every reason to believe that procedures in effect in established offices will automatically carry over to the new branch. However, such an assumption is unwarranted.

8.5.1 Constant Vigilance Is Required

A 19th century Irish orator proclaimed that "Eternal vigilance is the price of liberty." He could as well have said "Eternal vigilance is the price of quality control and preservation of image." Work of consistently high quality, the kind that projects the image of a first-class professional firm, will not be produced unless high standards are set and all levels in all locations meet those standards. Reference to maintenance of standards in the context of discussion of branch offices might infer that standards are more likely to slip in branch offices. Such an inference is not warranted in every case, but caution is justified for these reasons:

1. Since it was the successful operation of existing offices that made the new office necessary or practical, acceptable standards may be presumed to have existed in the older offices;

2. The established offices should be settled into a routine that permits maintenance of standards, whereas the newer office is more prone to unanticipated crises during which there is a temptation to cut corners, hoping to do things better when the alligators have been driven back into the swamp.

8.5.2 Specific Controls Are Needed

At the minimum, there should be these image and quality control procedures in effect for all offices:

1. Monitoring of compliance with continuing professional education requirements;

2. Review by another partner or his competent designee of all reports or opinions for prima facie compliance with standards;

3. Review of files on a sampling basis for compliance with standards;

4. Monitoring of delivery schedules to be sure that work is being performed within reasonable time specifications;

5. Review of billing and collection, to determine if reluctance to bill indicates concern for client resistance to the amount of the bill in relation to the quality and amount of work which the client perceives to have been done, or if slow (or no) collection definitely signals client dissatisfaction;

6. Observation of the condition of offices, furniture, equipment and files to assure that an efficient workplace not only exists but gives a favorable impression.

7. Assurance that memberships in professional and civic organizations and participation in their activities are not being neglected.

8.6   THE BRANCH OFFICE SYNDROME

Professional firms encounter a branch office syndrome. Like a disease, the branch office syndrome must have a culture, or climate, in which it can develop, a germ to start the infection, and a termination.

The Branch Partner Becomes Estranged

In a typical situation, a professional partnership opens a branch office in a likely spot, sending a junior partner out to colonize. The home office has acquired office space, probably has furnished and stocked the office, and has either hired the initial staff or has assisted the new resident partner in doing so. There are enough clients in the vicinity to maintain a respectable workload and the new partner is encouraged to develop his clients. The firm's reputation is good and the new partner is a practice builder. The firm grows. New staff must be hired, both to service new business and to offset turnover. More capital is required. Billing and collection problems mount. No one from the home office is on a first-name basis with the new clients. The resident partner was promised appropriate staff help from the home office when he has a special problem, or even a personnel overload of routine matters; to his chagrin, he finds that the home office, and perhaps other branches, are having scheduling pains too and that the help he wants is not available.

The resident partner had envisioned a situation in which he would happily serve clients in a new location and when he needed people, or capital, or expertise, he would need only to press a button or pick up a telephone and out they would flow from a cornucopia labeled "Home Office." The vision of the home office as a cornucopia full of goodies dims; he begins to see it as a Pandora's box, from which emerge nit-picking quality control inspectors, and nickel-nursing controllers harping on why his expenditures are so high while his collections are so slow.

The resident partner, comparing himself with local practitioners, sees himself as both required to solve all his problems himself and also to spend much of his time reporting to the home office. His frustration, fueled by self-pity over his predicament, can cause paranoia. He has forgotten that he receives a great deal of personal satisfaction from the success of the office, that his income has risen significantly, and that, as far as money can do it, he is well-compensated for his additional responsibilities. He has forgotten that his partners either took or at least shared in the losses incurred as the branch office was moving up to operating level.

8.6.1 Estrangement Strains Loyalty

At least, the result is strained loyalty. The branch office partner wonders whether his best course of action is to withdraw from the partnership and go it alone. The partnership agreement may (and should) provide for such an eventuality. A logical provision is to permit withdrawal with little or no penalty if the withdrawing partner intends to leave public practice and signs a covenant not to compete. Since it is a practical impossibility to prevent a partner who feels sufficiently independent from withdrawing and becoming a competitor of the firm, the agreement should call for liquidated damages sufficiently stiff to discourage withdrawal, though described as reimbursement to the firm for the losses and expenses incurred if actual withdrawal occurs, with attendant loss of clients and staff and problems of replacement of staff to serve those clients who remain with the firm.

8.6.2 Prevention of Estrangement and Disloyalty

Other than writing into the partnership agreement withdrawal penalties so severe as to handcuff partners to the firm, there are steps that may be taken to prevent or alleviate the "branch office syndrome." The first is to plan very carefully for a branch office before it is opened. The first thing to determine is whether there is a *partnership* reason for creating the branch office. If the office is opened to satisfy the personal ambitions of the person who will run it, and if you expect him to build the practice from scratch or from a nominal base, you can count on the syndrome developing and can predict his eventual withdrawal or his continuance on terms so favorable to him that the branch office serves no firm purpose.

If, however, the branch office will serve branches of clients or if the potential scope of branch office practice is such that it will permanently remain dependent on the home office for some services, then the branch office will not develop the autonomy necessary to nourish thoughts of defection.

Whatever the reason for opening the branch office, there must be a realistic conception of the responsibilities to be borne by the branch manager and of the resources to be provided by the home office. Each should then carry its part of the load. Communication should be maintained so that personnel in home and branch offices feel that they are part of the same organization, sharing each other's triumphs and tribulations. To put it simply, management at home and in the branches must prevent the development of an "us" and "them" dichotomy.

8.7   DUPLICATION OF EXPENSES IN BRANCH OFFICES

Branch Office May Be an Economical Way to Solve a Space Problem

The opening of a branch office entails a set of expenses which parallel and almost duplicate already occurring expenses. A firm outgrowing its space may consider the need for more space as justifying a branch office as a means of avoiding greater occupancy costs in its old location. If you need an additional 1,000 square feet of space to accommodate growth, and if you can serve your clients as well by obtaining space at some distance, then it is probably true that you will incur no more per capita rent expense by obtaining space for a branch office. Unfortunately, that is the only expense which will not increase, both per capita and in total.

Equipment Costs Escalate in the Branch Office

Assuming that the projected personnel growth is five persons, the telephone expense to integrate them into the main office is five extensions, and perhaps one more incoming line; in a branch, five people require more than one incoming line and will require someone to answer the phone and route calls. There will probably be no measurable saving of the main office switchboard operator's time because she has to serve five staff persons, more or less.

Five persons may not require additional tax or other professional library services if added to an existing office. A separate and reasonably complete library will be needed at the new location. Budgets for a branch office not only are frequently low for library requirements, but may overlook the fact that the cost of clerical time for posting updates may exceed the cost of the subscription; this is a complete duplication of cost.

Copying and word processing equipment will probably not be overloaded by adding five staff persons, and lightening their load by five persons will probably not decrease their costs at all. A total duplication of copy equipment costs will result. Branch offices, to be served by word processing or data processing equipment, must have terminals and leased lines, which are costly, or must depend on transmittal of documents by U.S. mail or courier. These are expensive, sometimes slow, and carry the risk of loss of irreplaceable papers.

Evaluating the Cost-Benefit Ratio in the Branch Office

In considering a branch office, management must consider whether the benefits outweigh the additional costs. The most logical reason for opening a branch office is to serve a significant client base already in existence in the distant location. In such a case, the new office will reduce travel expenses and travel time and should remove the morale problems associated with frequent or sustained engagements away from home. Competition may force a presence in the branch location. If, however, the main purpose is to obtain new business, management must recognize that this new business will be obtained at greater cost than would be incurred by adding this volume at an established location. If the new office cannot command a higher fee structure, then it will necessarily be less profitable than the same business obtained by expansion at an existing location.

8.8   CHAPTER EIGHT IN REVIEW

Branch offices are like the little girl with the curl on her forehead: when she was good she was very, very good, but when she was bad, she was horrid! Branch offices provide superior service to distant operations of clients; minimize travel; afford growth opportunity. Branch offices also may consume great amounts of management time; encourage faster alienation of partners and staff; weaken quality controls; cost a great deal of money.

Intelligent management may choose between bane or blessing by selecting branch offices for the right reasons, providing appropriate amounts of support, maintaining a flow of vital information back and forth, and monitoring performance and relations. The mother of a prominent American is alleged to have said "Sometimes when I look at my children, I think I should have stayed a virgin." The management of many a partnership has looked at what it created and joined her in her perplexity. Yet, without the successful solution of the myriad problems of branch offices, the complex economy of the world could not exist. The national and regional CPA firms, as well as the prestigious multioffice law firms, stand as examples to all of us who would venture into distant places to serve our clients better or to improve our own professional standings.

CHAPTER NINE

Management of the Partnership

CONTENTS

INTRODUCTION — 187

9.1 DICTATORSHIP, OLIGARCHY, OR DEMOCRACY? — 187

    9.1.1 Dictatorship, Genesis of Many Partnerships – 187
    9.1.2 Dominant Partner Resists Change – 187
    9.1.3 Partnerships Spawn Oligarchies – 188
    9.1.4 Partnership Democracy Is an Idle Fancy – 188

9.2 DISTINCTION BETWEEN THEORY AND REALITY IN MANAGEMENT OF A PARTNERSHIP — 188

    9.2.1 How Partners Say They Want to Be Managed – 188
    9.2.2 What Partners Really Want from Management – 189
    9.2.3 Management Technique Recognizes Individual Capabilities – 189

9.3 MANAGING PARTNER OR ADMINISTRATIVE PARTNER — 189

    9.3.1 Assigning Responsibility for Chores – 189
    9.3.2 Upgrading Routine Tasks Improves Performance – 190
    9.3.3 Upgrading the Payroll Function – 190

9.3.4   Upgrading the Bookkeeping Function – 190

9.3.5   Make a Clean Sweep for Profit – 191

9.4   THE MANAGING PARTNER   191

9.4.1   How the Managing Partner Functions – 191

9.4.2   Qualities of the Managing Partner – 192

9.4.3   The Managing Partner Leads Toward Well-Defined Goals – 192

9.4.4   Meetings as Goal-Setters – 192

9.4.5   Individual Characteristics and Partnership Goals – 193

9.4.6   Individual Goals Subordinated to Firm Goals – 194

9.4.7   There Are No "Born Subordinators" – 195

9.4.8   Partners Have Different Attitudes Towards Work – 195

9.4.9   Management Must Recognize Productivity – 195

9.5   WHO SHOULD BE A MANAGING PARTNER?   196

9.5.1   A Managing Partner Must Be a Good Administrator – 196

9.5.2   Requisites of a Managing Partner – 196

9.6   ORGANIZATION BY FUNCTION   197

9.7   COMMUNICATIONS   197

9.7.1   The Hazards of Lack of Communication – 197

9.7.2   Communication Should Be Systematic – 198

9.7.3   The Absorption of Communication – 198

9.8   RECONCILING CONFLICTING MOTIVES   198

9.8.1   Partnership Motivators – 199

9.8.2   Conflicts in Motivations – 199

9.8.3   Resolution of Conflicts in Motivation – 200

9.9   PROVISION FOR SHIFTS IN RELATIVE POSITIONS OF PARTNERS   200

9.10   RECORD-KEEPING   202

9.10.1   Records Which a Partnership Should Keep – 202

9.10.2   Records and Partner Compensation – 203

9.10.3   Records to Maximize Profitability – 204

9.11   SUMMARY OF CHAPTER NINE   216

INTRODUCTION

In the organization of a partnership, little thought is given to how it will be managed. The naive will accept Section 18(e) of the Uniform Partnership Act at face value: "all partners have equal rights in the management and conduct of the partnership business." A cynical antithesis would be: "all partners are equal, but some are more equal than others." Partners do not have equal ability or inclination to manage. Seldom will there be time enough for full and equal participation in management, and if there were, the process would be so unwieldy as to be practically unworkable. It is necessary that management of the partnership be delegated and the decisions regarding to whom it will be delegated and the limitations on his authority are crucial to the success of the business.

Some of the questions to be addressed are:

- Will leadership be elected or will it evolve?
- What are the qualifications of the leader, and how shall he be found?
- What organizational form is needed for effective management?
- How can good communication be achieved?
- How will partnership conflicts be discovered and reconciled?
- How will the partnership adjust to shifts in relative positions of partners?
- What record-keeping is needed for effective management?

9.1 DICTATORSHIP, OLIGARCHY, OR DEMOCRACY?

9.1.1 Dictatorship, Genesis of Many Partnerships

Professional firms are frequently formed when an established professional takes in others to assist him and rewards them with a share in the business; usually a share junior to his. In the beginning, he makes all major decisions, perhaps with, but more often without, consultation with his partners. The subordinates accept this, either because they respect his experience and judgment or, more likely, because they have no choice.

9.1.2 Dominant Partner Resists Change

Firms may remain in this mode for many years. Those that do so risk becoming like herds of walruses or elephants, in which the dominant male, by sheer size or strength, relegates all the younger, smaller males to the sidelines. The weaker members of the herd have three choices; they may live in the shadows indefinitely, or they may leave and seek to form a new herd elsewhere, or they await the time when they can successfully challenge the old bull and force him into ignominious retirement. The warning is clear for the partner who will attempt to dominate the firm for an indefinite period with inadequate concession to the potential challengers.

9.1.3 Partnerships Spawn Oligarchies

The firm which is formed around two or more strong partners, or in which a limited number rise to greater prominence than some of their erstwhile peers, is an oligarchy. Oligarchy is a form of government in which the power is vested in a ruling few (frequently a clique). Although I have no statistics to support it, I believe that most larger partnerships operate this way, and that they do so even though there is not even a hint of provision of such a structure in their partnership agreements.

9.1.4 Partnership Democracy Is an Idle Fancy

There may be a partnership somewhere with more than four or five partners that can operate in a democratic manner, meaning that all decisions represent a majority decision, or at least a consensus, of all partners and that all partners share roughly equally in management. There may be such an organization, but I doubt it; and if there is, it is probably heading for trouble. An oligarchy, almost by definition, is an amorphous style, ruled only by the vagaries of the power structure of the moment. With democracy and oligarchy ruled out as techniques of systematic management, we shall concentrate on partnership management by a partner designated by and responsible to the partnership as a whole.

9.2   DISTINCTION BETWEEN THEORY AND REALITY IN MANAGEMENT OF A PARTNERSHIP

9.2.1 How Partners Say They Want to Be Managed

On those rare occasions when they participate in planning the structure and management of their firms, partners invariably say that this is what they want:

1. A strong manager who can carry out positive programs and policies;

2. A centralized management structure in which job descriptions and operating procedures are carefully prepared and strictly followed;

3. Uniformly high quality of product so that the firm displays a positive and united image in the community.

9.2.2 What Partners Really Want from Management

After giving lip service to the concept of centralization, the partners demonstrate by their actions that this is what they want:

1. A managing partner who will exert strong influence over the rest of the organization, but will leave my sphere of operations alone, because it is obvious that I know better than anyone else how to manage my share of the practice.

2. Since my clients (patients) are special and my practice is unique, the people who work with me and the procedures needed to get my job done won't fit a standard mold, so exceptions must be made.

3. Clients (or patients) are more attracted to individual professionals, so my emphasis will be on the personalized approach to professional practice.

9.2.3 Management Techniques Recognize Individual Capabilities

The person who would design and execute the management of a successful professional firm should realize from the outset that the same individual strengths that made the firm strong will negate any attempt to set up a textbook operation in the management area. Geese fly in perfect formation, veering left or right, up or down, as they are led; eagles are never regimented; they soar as they will, seizing the opportunity of each updraft, and they control the high places.

The first thing to learn in management of professional firms is that the system must satisfy the needs and ambitions of its members, rather than that the members will be forced or cajoled into a structure repugnant to their personalities.

9.3 MANAGING PARTNER OR ADMINISTRATIVE PARTNER?

9.3.1 Assigning Responsibility for Chores

Every partnership needs to designate someone to perform those chores that are essential to the successful operation of the firm and that may be left undone if no one is assigned specific responsibility for their accomplishment. These functions may include:

1. Payrolls
2. Accounting (bookkeeping)
3. Bill paying
4. Client (patient, customer) billing and collection
5. Housekeeping, including keeping the office (store, plant) clean and the supply shelves stocked.

These are menial tasks; the kind willingly left to anyone who will assume responsibility for their accomplishment. Important though they are, they do not justify the title of managing partner. If this is the extent of the activity to be performed by one partner, he should be designated as administrative partner and should carry out his function to the greatest extent possible through the efforts of employees.

9.3.2 Upgrading Routine Tasks Improves Performance

The partnership that has more than three or four partners and is content to let the common functions be handled by a partner who is little more than a custodian is missing a great opportunity to better itself. A progressive firm will look at each of these "necessary evil" areas and determine that the areas can be elevated to positive factors in firm betterment.

9.3.3 Upgrading the Payroll Function

Administration of the payroll function can be upgraded into management of the personnel function. Logical outgrowths of a positive attitude toward the partnership's human resources will add these functions to the dull routine of seeing that paychecks are written and payroll tax returns prepared.

1. Recruitment of outstanding employees who will learn faster, produce more and develop into leaders of an expanding business.

2. Development of systems of formal education and on-the-job training, along with effective valuation, so that the firm directs and participates in personnel development rather than leaving it to the individual to lift himself by his own bootstraps.

3. Synchronization of financial rewards, job titles and levels of responsibility with the increase in value of employee services that results from positive personnel practices.

4. Identification of those employees who will be future partners and broadening their training so that they will be prepared for the additional responsibilities that will be thrust upon them when they achieve partnership status.

9.3.4 Upgrading the Bookkeeping Function

Accounting (bookkeeping) can be a chore performed because the Internal Revenue Service requires records, or because you need some way to know how you are doing financially so you can make distributions to the partners. Such a basic system can be a powerful tool for measuring productivity, for profit planning, for spotlighting areas needing improvement.

Through budgeting, the partnership can determine where it wants to go and good accounting can tell the partners whether its goals are being met.

Bills must be paid and someone must pay them. It is not likely that anyone can imbue this function with much glamour or make it a major accomplishment. However, close attention to paying bills can avoid waste. Beyond avoiding paying twice or paying too much, observing to whom you are making payments can tell you if you are giving your patronage to those who are or may be of help to your business. Promptness in payment can mark your firm as a well-managed enterprise; the kind that the rest of the business community wants to buy from as well as to sell to.

Careful attention to client, patient or customer billing can be time well spent. Prompt billing and effective follow-up keep the cash rolling in, and this is no minor consideration when interest rates are at historic highs. Observation of billing and collection practices can tell you which areas of your own practice (business) are following techniques conducive to profitability. Additionally, such observation will pinpoint customers, clients or patients who need to be upgraded or dropped. Finally, careful attention to billing (when there is latitude in setting the amount of the bill) can maximize profitability and can promote good will by the sensitive use of rates or wording.

9.3.5 Make a Clean Sweep for Profit

Whether an office, shop or store is a pleasant and effective place to work often depends on such routine tasks as keeping the place clean, keeping mechanical facilities in good repair and keeping the workplace adequately stocked. Appearances count, not only in the visual impression they make on customer or colleague, but also in setting employee and partner attitudes as to how they go about their duties.

Every administrative chore, then, should be examined and evaluated to see if it can be managed so that a cost center can become a profit center. Gilbert and Sullivan wrote of the cabin boy who polished the brass so brightly that he "became the ruler of the Queen's Na-vee." Management that looks for every opportunity to brighten a corner may be surprised at how often it converts a chore into a challenge.

A progressive partnership will not miss the opportunity to upgrade its administrative function to a management function.

9.4   THE MANAGING PARTNER

9.4.1 How the Managing Partner Functions

The function of a managing partner is analogous to that of the chief executive of a city. Usually that position is held by a mayor. The functions of the job range all the way from the undisputed boss of a far-flung operation to a figurehead who passes out keys to the city and crowns beauty queens. In between is the mayor who functions mainly as presiding officer at meetings of the city council and has some authority in designating department heads and supervising the performance of their duties. As the personal involvement of the mayor moves down the scale, the evolvement and involvement of the professional city manager increases.

9.4.2 Qualities of the Managing Partner

Ideally, the managing partner should be that person who commands the greatest respect from his partners and who is held in high regard in the community. Such esteem augurs well for his chances of leadership without the need for spending an inordinate amount of time in politicking, persuasion, or confrontation. More likely, the partner whose qualities make him best qualified for the role of managing partner is in such demand for client service or is so besieged by calls for community service that he cannot afford the time to manage the firm.

The managing partner should display in balanced amounts the qualities of a pragmatist with those of a theoretician. As a pragmatist, he should have a feel for what his firm's needs and potentials are, yet avoid the tendency to stay with only the familiar, the comfortable, the unimaginative. As a theoretician, he should keep abreast of new ideas in management, drawing inspiration from written texts, from the approaches pioneered in the business schools and from association with his peers in other firms. This association should include brainstorming in structured environments such as seminars as well as one-on-one bouts in his office or that of the other firm's managing partner where specific techniques and procedures can be compared to results. When it comes to using his firm and his partners as guinea pigs for experimentation, he would do well to heed the words of Alexander Pope: "Be not the first by whom the new are tried, nor yet the last to lay the old aside."

9.4.3 The Managing Partner Leads Toward Well-Defined Goals

The managing partner should see his role as leader as requiring him to find out where his partners want and need to be led. He needs to obtain their input as to the firm's goals and philosophies. There are several reasons why this may not be as easy as it sounds, and for these reasons there may not be any one way to obtain valuable help from them.

9.4.4 Meetings as Goal-Setters

The obvious way to find out what the partnership goals are is to hold an extended meeting to hammer out a charter or constitution for the group.

This is a document that differs from the partnership agreement. If the partners have an aptitude for verbalizing, if they will express their real desires, such a session may be very constructive in planning for firm growth, improvement of quality in professional output, or any of those desirable goals which must have firm-wide support to succeed.

It is more likely that holding a long meeting to adopt a unified approach to the firm's problems and opportunities will produce more friction over peripheral issues than harmony over the essentials. The result of such a meeting may be the adoption of a meaningless set of resolutions that endorse Americanism, motherhood and apple pie, but do little for setting goals or defining avenues for accomplishment.

9.4.5 Individual Characteristics and Partnership Goals

If the "town meeting" seems inadvisable or doesn't produce practical results, the managing partner must turn to other techniques to determine his firm's goals. A valuable start can be made by analyzing the wants of his partners, considering these criteria:

1. Age
2. Present and probable economic status
3. Willingness to subjugate personal desires to firm goals and vice versa
4. Appetite for hard work

Typically, the firm will be composed of heterogeneous persons, varying widely when measured by the above criteria. The problem, then, becomes one of setting goals which are, in descending order of desirability, a consensus, a compromise, or a lowest common denominator.

Each of these partner characteristics must be dealt with by the managing partner. To fail to recognize the differences of viewpoints among the partners is to condemn the organization to constant unrest, or worse.

Age, meaning the number of candles on the birthday cake, is not nearly as meaningful as is sometimes supposed. In a professional or executive role, the duties are seldom so physically taxing that age has a serious effect on a person's ability to perform them. Senility is seldom a problem in any organization that has a mandatory retirement age. At the other end of the age scale, a potential partner should not be rejected because he (or she) lacks years if he (or she) has the requisite maturity.

Age is a determinant of attitude because it affects the outlook, encouraging those who are getting up in years to have a short-term outlook on such matters as firm growth. For the younger partner, the various milestones in the shape of birthday candles mark checkpoints for the measuring of attainment of goals. Sometimes these goals are self-imposed; in other cases they result from peer influence, sometimes clearly visible within the firm or the local business community and sometimes, more subtly, from the career comparisons made at the quinquennial college reunions. A rational person will accept the conditions imposed by, or the opportunities presented by age, and work toward a reconciliation of these different points of view. It is a function of the managing partner to understand the significance of age and lead his partners to a constructive acceptance of age as a fact of life.

Economic status desired, already attained or reasonably attainable affects partner attitudes and goals. The desire for economic success and the attendant feelings of security and status are strong motivators, particularly for those who came from humble backgrounds. Insecurity drives some to attain measurable goals as recurring proof of their adequacy. This desire can be a worthy or an unworthy goal; the managing partner need not pass judgment on the moral issue but he must recognize this upward drive if he is to harness it for the benefit of the organization.

Except for those few who never achieve satisfaction as long as there is more money to be made or more status symbols casting their allure, attained economic status can have a profound influence on partner attitude and behavior, exhibited by a desire to maintain the status quo. An obvious reason is that there is a point at which the economic rewards of additional achievement are so diluted by income taxation that they do not justify the exertion. An even better reason is that, once reasonable needs are adequately met, it makes no sense to risk such a halcyon state to grab for the brass ring of unneeded opulence. The economically solid partner is well aware that the high risks inherent in the unlimited liability of partners combined with the dilution of the fruits of success by progressive income, gift and estate taxes make risk-taking almost a heads-or-tails-I-lose proposition. The competent managing partner will realize that the financially sound partner who resists the more aggressive ideas of impecunious junior partners is not necessarily a hopeless reactionary.

9.4.6 Individual Goals Subordinated to Firm Goals

The partnership that will succeed must be composed of partners who will subjugate their personal desires to the firm's goals. The quid pro quo of this is that firm goals must be set to ultimately satisfy the personal desires of the partners. Some of the personal preferences that must be foregone for the common good are: forfeiting the "star" role to emphasize the firm's overall capability; cooperating in a program that has majority support but for which the partner individually has no enthusiasm; postponing personal financial plans to provide the working capital essential to firm operations.

9.4.7 There Are No "Born Subordinators"

Selfishness is an ingrained human trait. It is significant that a main course in nursery school and kindergarten is "sharing." Despite the early emphasis on sharing, it is a virtue seldom fully learned. As a result, a managing partner must frequently continue the curriculum that the toddler's mentor started. He will find a tendency toward selfishness in the younger practitioner, a product of the "now generation," who wants the emphasis of the firm bent in the direction of his interests. He will find an equal desire for privilege and preference in the senior member, a person who reasons that he has earned a priority, that he has "paid his dues." The managing partner who successfully reconciles conflicts in goal-setting must accomplish at least two things; he must make the trade-offs as equitable as possible and he must present them in such a way that persons of diverse leanings will perceive at least an acceptable amount of self-interest in pursuing the common goal.

9.4.8 Partners Have Different Attitudes Towards Work

Different partners have different appetites for hard work. The same person does not approach all phases of his job with equal enthusiasm. The "work" of a business concern sometimes consists principally of the product of one's time and hands, whether it be surgery or plumbing. "Work" certainly includes continuing education; keeping up with what's new. "Work" sometimes consists principally of just being where one is supposed to be. There are those hard workers who will address themselves assiduously to the immediate task, but have no interest in planning or in extending their horizons. There are those who measure effort solely in terms of hours put in. There are those who will, for short periods, work with tremendous enthusiasm and great effectiveness but who insist on generally short hours and frequent time off.

9.4.9 Management Must Recognize Productivity

The women's rights movement has forcefully latched on to the slogan "Equal pay for equal work," but the principle applies to situations where sex is not an issue and should be a cardinal principle in controlling the effort-reward ratio in partnership compensation. It easily follows that there should be greater pay for greater work, and vice versa. "More work" may mean more hours, or more skill, or more productive use of hours and skills. The successful managing partner must find a way to match compensation to value to the firm. This could be the most difficult task he faces because people naturally tend to place a high value on their own contribution and because neither pride nor economic self-interest will permit a person to have the value of his services downgraded in relation to those of others.

9.5   WHO SHOULD BE A MANAGING PARTNER?

A partnership without a good managing partner is like an orchestra without a conductor; the performers may be competent and they may be giving it their best effort, but the result is dissonance rather than a symphony.

9.5.1 A Managing Partner Must Be a Good Administrator

It is a given fact that the managing partner must be a good administrator. He must be much more. We can look to many vocations for his counterpart. We have already turned to music, where he emulates the maestro in causing diverse artists to combine their talents to produce harmony. From the political system, we find him performing the job of presiding officer as well as floor leader, patiently shepherding the elements of a program until it has the support needed for its successful accomplishment. From architecture we take his role as planner of the structure and writer of the specifications. From horticulture we take the role model of the even-handed nourisher of the good growth and pruner of the deadwood or undesirable growth. He needs the talents of the coach to bring out the best in his charges. Finally, he emulates the clergyman by listening to the woes of his flock and by providing a quick burial for the wild ideas and petty peevishnesses that threaten the partnership.

9.5.2 Requisites of a Managing Partner

Perhaps your partnership needs a leader who is a dozen people rolled into one, but you must choose from prospects who are only one person. You have a better chance of choosing the right person if you insist on at least these attributes:

1. He must be willing to give the job his best efforts for an extended term.
2. He must have the respect of his partners.
3. He must be as free as possible from bias and from preconceived positions.
4. He must be able to afford the time for the job.

Your partnership may quickly turn to one of two choices, and either will probably be a mistake. The first is selection of the dominant partner. He is frequently a bad choice because his other duties already consume all his time and because his position may stifle participation in management by others. The second equally bad choice is the youngest, who has fewer other things to do and can therefore find the time. He will not have the influence or the security needed for the position.

It follows that the ideal choice is a person who comes from the center in experience as well as in freedom from bias from any direction. If you have such a person and he also has intelligence, stamina and stability, look no further.

9.6   ORGANIZATION BY FUNCTION

Large businesses are always organized by function; production, sales, finance, transportation, record-keeping, etc. By their very nature, the largest businesses are not set up as partnerships. In the typical partnership, the same person may provide the product, sell it, arrange its financing, deliver it, handle the paper work and eventually collect for it. This may be true even when the partnership business is big enough to benefit from organization by function.

No one can be master of all trades or functions. Almost any business or profession involves a sufficient variety of activities to justify organization by function. Some examples:

- In a construction company: estimating and bidding, administration, on-site supervision.
- In retailing: buying, sales, administration.
- In law practice: litigation, tax, corporate law.
- In an accounting practice: auditing, tax, management advisory services.

The aggressive partner is seldom satisfied unless he participates directly in every firm activity. Careful analysis of the jobs to be done and of his work preferences will convince him that he and his colleagues will get more out of life by concentrating on areas of special expertise.

9.7   COMMUNICATIONS

Since partnerships operate best in an environment of ongoing consensus, it is imperative that partners be fully informed of what is going on. Busy practitioners become absorbed in their particular concerns and tend to neglect things with which they are not immediately involved. Lack of information about such areas makes it even easier to shut them out of the care of the uninformed partner.

9.7.1 The Hazards of Lack of Communication

The hazards of lack of communication are twofold: One is that a neglected area of the partnership operation suffers from a dearth of the talent that broad partner interest could bring to it, thereby being less effective in providing for the best interests of the partnership. The second hazard is more negative; the neglected area is prone to become a risk of malpractice as well as to become or remain financially unrewarding.

9.7.2 Communication Should Be Systematic

Communication can be ordered or disordered. Unless there is provision for proper communication, some sort of grapevine will develop; a source of misinformation and disservice to the firm. Partner's meetings are the logical channel of communication. In any but the smallest partnerships, partners' meetings that are held often enough to communicate a regular flow of information will probably consume too much time. Regular meetings are an absolute must, but as the partnership grows, it will be increasingly hard to obtain participation. Participation in this sense means not only attendance but also having worthwhile input into the proceedings.

Partners can be kept informed in a variety of ways other than by the formal scheduled meeting. Although there may be circumstances justifying having someone circulate among the partners spreading the word on a one-on-one basis, circuit-riding is too time-consuming for general use. It is likely that the message delivered at each stop will be slightly different and create more confusion than coherence.

A newsletter or some other form of regular news release to the partners can be effective. Minutes or digests of department or committee meetings are informative. A "reading file" of significant correspondence or reports may be circulated. All of these have the danger that they will so flood the partners with paper that most of it will be ignored and all of it runs a risk of being put aside for a more convenient time, thereby destroying whatever time value it has.

9.7.3 The Absorption of Communication

Two facts will emerge from any serious study of partnership communication; one is that those who want to keep up with needed information will somehow manage to keep informed. The second fact is that those who are not personally interested in keeping current will manage to remain uninformed. You can lead a horse to water but you can't make him drink; you can provide a partner with information but you can't make him think. The effective manager will do his best to design a cost-effective information system and hope that it will be used; there is little more that he can do.

9.8   RECONCILING CONFLICTING MOTIVES

A program of reconciling conflicting motives requires an answer to these three questions:

- What motivates the partners?
- Are there conflicts in motives?
- Can the conflicts be resolved?

9.8.1 Partnership Motivators

Since a partnership must have a profit motive (there is no such thing as a nonprofit partnership), the existence of an economic motive for participating in the partnership may be assumed. Whereas making a living is alone seldom a satisfying reason for working and risk-taking, it is an essential motive. While dissatisfaction is frequently attributed to other factors, unhappiness with the way the profit pie is sliced is probably the most frequent cause of disagreement.

There are ego-centered motivators. These range from having one's name in the firm name to the amount of exposure to the public inherent in the job. The issue of the name of the firm is very difficult to deal with. Ethical restrictions prohibit legal and accounting firms from adopting names like "Superior Accountants" or "Standard Legal Service." Unless the firm has an historic name not containing names of present partners, there will be a problem. There is an obvious limitation on how long a name may be, so you can't satisfy everyone. Adding names contemporaneously with dropping names is seldom a viable option as a partner is not likely to agree to his name being dropped. Many a potential partnership has foundered on the shoals of selecting the name. There is no easy answer. A partnership that can select any name would do well, from the beginning, to adopt a name like "Quality Construction Co.," or "Emerald City Internal Medicine Associates."

Many partnerships have front-office exposure, as contrasted with back-office or plant responsibilities. Often, one partner has the "dress-up" position, working in the public view to the extent that many customers do not realize that the fellow toiling behind the warehouse or shop door is one of the bosses. Since many businesses operate with a front office or sales area, well-appointed, well-lighted and much in the public view, and also have a proletarian work area, room for conflict exists if status is a motivator. This problem is best solved by having a partnership comprised of people who welcome the diverse roles, or who can at least become resigned to them.

9.8.2 Conflicts in Motivations

Determining whether there are conflicts in motivation can be done by freely discussing the question when the partnership is formed, and updating the conclusions from time to time. This technique requires total honesty of expression by all parties, a condition infrequently encountered.

It is more likely that motivational conflicts will be revealed by astute observations by persons with empathy for their peers.

9.8.3 Resolution of Conflicts in Motivation

Whereas it is obvious that not all conflicts in motivation can be resolved, it is also surprising that so many apparent conflicts turn out to be misunderstandings. In the process of determining the source of conflict, one may also discover the solution. Persons who enter into active partnerships soon realize that their partners' needs must be met insofar as the business can meet them. The discerning managing partner realizes that partners, either from altruism or egoism, will react positively to their calls for identification and resolution of conflict.

9.9   PROVISION FOR SHIFTS IN RELATIVE POSITIONS OF PARTNERS

Other sections of this book have shown how a partnership tends to grow around partners who are centers of influence. The organization is designed, or simply grows, to capitalize on their strengths or cover their weaknesses. It is not unusual for a small partnership to develop a structure that will serve it for many years. It is obvious that such a static organization does not grow. The organization that would grow must accommodate shifts in function, in emphasis and in control.

Shifts in position can affect control (shifts in the power structure) or affect function. Shifts in power come from gaining expertise, or clients or a following. Shifts in function occur because a need must be met or because of a partner's desire to change his work pattern to suit a personal preference.

The partnership must constantly adjust and readjust to changing priorities. Failure to permit shifts in partner functions and relations will, at best, lead to tension as partners feel that their security is under attack or that they are being denied opportunities. Time should be provided to analyze the organization at regular intervals to determine what structural changes are indicated. Each partner should ask himself (and be prepared to defend his answer to) these questions:

- Am I the most effective person in the firm in this position?
- Am I doing what I want to do?
- As the firm's position in the marketplace has changed, have I adapted to the changes?

If the answer to any of these is a strong "no" then appropriate changes should be initiated.

Case Study on Rearranging Work Schedules of Partners

Fall and Spring, C.P.A.s, are the classic case in the "generation-gap" problem as it applies to professional partnerships. Fall epitomizes the generation that started its working career when the lessons of the Great Depression were fresh upon the business community—work hard, invest conservatively, take few chances. Although Spring has modulated his views considerably since his college days, when he supported the protest movements of the Vietnam war era, he still questions many of his older partner's views.

Gradually, they find that age and economics are causing them to reverse their positions as to how the work of the firm should be done. Fall, suspecting that he is losing some of his enthusiasm for hard work and recognizing that he no longer needs the economic rewards of his old work schedule, is looking for a way to do no more than keep the status quo. Spring wants to make his own record, wants to overcome the feeling that so far he has lived in the shadow of his older partner, who brought in more of the clients and has set the style of the business.

Fall's house is paid for; his children are self-supporting. Spring's growing family is reaching the expensive stage for food, schooling, clothes and recreation. In short, Fall will swap higher income for more security; Spring must have more income.

They found a solution by carefully calculating what the firm could earn with Fall working on a reduced schedule and Spring working more; enough to handle the reduction in Fall's load. They amended the partnership agreement to provide for partner salaries equal to this level of income. Income above this level would be shared 25 percent to Fall and 75 percent to Spring, justifying the split by the logic that Spring would carry all of the increased responsibility, but Fall nonetheless must be compensated for the extra risk. With the reduced schedule, Fall would produce 1,500 chargeable hours per year.

This left them with the problem of providing for Fall's retirement. His contacts and his experience justified a charge-out rate considerably higher than that which the firm could charge for a much less experienced person. The partners went to their accountant's dictionary and found that good will is the earning power of an entity with good will over that of an entity without it. They concluded that Fall's contacts and experience were akin to good will because they made his services more valuable than those of the person who would replace him, and that the value of this good will was the capitalized value of his excess earning power. To measure this excess earning power, they reasoned that when Fall left, suddenly or otherwise, he would be replaced by a new partner who presumably would have been the best employee; logically the highest paid employee. Carrying the logic further, they reasoned that a new partner should be willing to forego a substantial increase in earnings for as much as five years to earn a full partnership. They set the initial value of Fall's good will at $300,000, calculated as a spread of $40 per hour for 1,500 hours per year for 5 years.

As a practical matter, a new partner would not be able to survive frozen earnings for 5 years, so the agreement called for payment to Fall over a period of 120 months without interest, and that the payments should be guaranteed payments as described in IRC Section 736(a).

The assumptions above are more the basis for a formula than they are a predictor of earnings of a new partner. Actually, a new partner's salary will be set at a fair figure with an appropriate charge-out rate; if things go well, the bills to clients formerly served by Fall will not drop, but the partner salary cost of earning them will come down. From this spread will come the wherewithal to make the guaranteed payments. If, indeed, the persons who replace Fall can reach his level of competence within 5 years but pay him out over 10 years, with income tax deductions for the payments, they may find little or no discomfort to themselves while making a comfortable retirement for Fall possible.

The reader should note that the formula automatically adjusts for inflation or increase or decrease in Fall's activity. If Fall drops back to 1,200 hours per year, the formula drops to a total of $240,000. If Fall slows down or lets his skills slip so that they can justify only a $30 spread, even with 1,500 hours, his good will will drop to $225,000. On the other hand, the old codger may find that he can work less and work smarter and make himself worth $50 more per hour than the best employee, in which case his 1,200 hour schedule produces $300,000 over 10 years.

The partnership agreement should make it clear that the payments to Fall are deductible under Section 736(a).

The provisions for Fall's retirement may include separate payment for his capital account and/or his share of accounts receivable and work in process.

9.10   RECORD-KEEPING

9.10.1 Records Which a Partnership Should Keep

Record-keeping for a partnership can be categorized three ways:

1. Financial records adequate for tax and credit purposes;
2. Supplemental records to provide more detail for efficient management, such as information to measure productivity or to spotlight profit opportunities or loss potentials;

3. Nonfinancial records, such as minutes or proceedings of partners' meetings or of committees of the partners. These records may include policy manuals or other guides for the internal operation of the firm.

The bare minimum of records necessary for income tax return preparation and for division of profits requires no discussion here. The accounting system should be designed by competent accountants and should produce the required information with a minimum of cost.

The elementary system capable of producing a balance sheet, an income statement and a reconciliation of partners' accounts suffices for preparing income tax returns. It tells you whether you made a profit and tells you if your assets are at least equal to your liabilities, and there it stops. It does not tell you why you didn't do better, or how you can improve either your operating results or your financial condition.

9.10.2 Records and Partner Compensation

Perhaps the most sensitive area in partner relations is the relative compensation to which each is entitled. Even though your agreement may provide for equal shares of profit or loss, it is a fact that partners were seldom created equal and it is even less likely that they will remain equal in their contribution to the firm. Records are needed to measure the relative contributions.

Some services, such as those of managing partner, do not produce units of measurable output such as patient fees, billable hours, or volume of sales. Such services must be compensated in some fashion; perhaps the fairest way is to pay the partner the amount that the same effort would have produced if exerted in producing measurable results.

The value of a partner depends not only on the value of his services but also on his contacts, his standing in the community, his contribution to the image of the firm. Founding or senior partners tend to emphasize reputation as a basis for compensation, down-playing services that are measurable. They have a valid point, but should recognize that much dependence on what they did in the past and too little direct participation in the current scene cause their contacts and their images to fade quickly.

It follows, then, that measurable activity is essential to a long-range compensation policy. Records should be kept of hours worked and the results produced by those hours, if hours of chargeable time are the principal measure of productivity, as they are in most legal and accounting firms. It is, of course, necessary to be very careful in setting different hourly rates to reflect different levels of skill and experience as well as to reflect different working speeds. If patient visits or medical or surgical procedures are the basis for billings, records of partner provision of such services should be kept. Even in an establishment where selling by a partner is an incidental, records of partner sales should be as accurate as those for employees paid by commission.

Partners' salaries, by whatever name designated, are usually based on the assumption that the partner will invest a specified amount of time and effort. Such a salary arrangement is a sham unless there are records to measure compliance and there is a penalty for failure to meet expectations under any but the most unusual situations.

9.10.3 Records to Maximize Profitability

Like other businesses, partnerships should have appropriate cost-accounting systems for the control of manufacturing costs (including costs of building houses or raising tomatoes, if building or farming is your game). Accounting for costs of delivery, advertising, utilities, employee benefits is necessary if those profit devourers are to be controlled and the dollars spent on them directed to where they produce the best results. Since such systems must be designed to serve the needs of the industry in which you transact your business, their design is beyond the scope of this book.

Unlike many other businesses that have excellent records, partnerships are usually small and their records are minimal. While the amount that a partnership spends on any particular expense is tiny compared to that spent by the industrial and financial giants, it is probably true that it spends an equally large percentage of its resources in the various expense categories. It follows that a partnership should be just as careful as General Motors or IBM in seeing that it receives a dollar of benefit for each dollar spent. A partnership's record-keeping and interpretation system should match that of the Fortune 500 Company, not in cost or complexity, but in accuracy and effectiveness in doing these things:

1. Measuring and comparing costs in areas where there is latitude in specifying amount and direction of expenditures;

2. Determining the source of income and the cost of producing it, to the end that you discontinue lines that are unprofitable to you, maximize the profit in continuing operations, and understand and exploit your sources of good new business.

Sample Time and Efficiency Records for a Professional Partnership

Since a professional firm has only its time and its skill to sell, it is imperative that it maintain a record of the units of time provided to the client. The steps involved are:

1. Reporting the time put in by each person who serves clients;
2. Accumulating all of the time devoted to a client;
3. Setting a fee for the service, based on time spent and other appropriate factors;
4. Analyzing why the engagement was or was not completed in such a manner that the firm receives the expected return.

The records illustrated on the following pages serve these purposes:

- Exhibit A – Time Card – used for each staff person to report time worked.

- Exhibit B – Work in process detail ledger – computer prepared, accumulates time from all time cards and other sources such as copying machine or postage charges, automatically extending the hours at a standard rate for each person.

- Exhibit C – Listing of substantial mark-up/down from work in process to billing – shows all deviations over a pre-set minimum resulting from billing the client at a figure larger or smaller than the standard rates for the units of time. Evaluation of this report reveals situations requiring analysis.

- Exhibit D – Explanation of substantial write-up or write-down from work in process (at standard rates) to billing. Analyzes deviation from standard rates; may be used to trigger corrective action or in personnel evaluation.

A professional partnership, having developed figures to show its own results such as number of hours worked by each staff person, number of those hours chargeable to clients, percentages of standard rates realized, salary costs or fringe benefit costs, does not know whether the results are favorable or unfavorable unless it has something with which to compare its results.

Surveys of practice management results are conducted by state societies and by groups of accounting firms. The results are distributed to participants, may appear in the professional literature, or may be available for a fee. The following four exhibits are furnished by and published with the permission of the Texas Society of Certified Public Accountants and are based on a 1981 survey.

These Exhibits show results for the average reporting entity and for the entities in the top 25 percent when ranked by profitability. In interpreting these statistics, for our purposes, individuals are ignored because they are obviously not partnerships.

EXPENSE CODES: 911 - SUPPLIES;   912 - MEALS & MILEAGE;   913 - TEL.;   914 - MISC.;   915 - POSTAGE.

CLIENT NAME	CLIENT #	TOTAL HOURS	EXPENSE AMT.	CODE	1/16	2/17	3/18	4/19	5/20	6/21	7/22	8/23	9/24	10/25	11/26	12/27	13/28	14/29	15/30	31
ST. PETERS ACADEMY INC	01865	24.75			5.50 / 4.75				.25	3.00	7.50 / 3.50	3.50				.25				
EMILY WALKER	01973	3.00			.25				.50 / .25	.25	.25 / .25	.75	.25			.25	.25	.25 / .25	
THEODOSIA SMITH ET AL	01907	1.00			1.00													.50		
HENRY MITCHELL ET AL	01849	2.00			1.00				.25		.25							.50		
ASHLEY HOUSE	01621	5.50			.75					.25						2.50	2.50	1.20	.50	
MARGARET BLACK	01648	10.75							6.50	3.25	.50 / 5.25	5.25	6.75		7.75	.50	.50	2.40	6.25	
JOHN MILLER	01701	26.50									.50						.25			
INDUSTRIAL DESIGN INC	01469	.50															.25	.25		
ACCENT	01000	.25															.50		.25 / .25	
MOSES REYNOLDS	01819	.25																		
KEN KLOPPER	12621	.50																		
CARLYSLE BAILEY	01022	.50																		
ADM-CLERICAL	99000-80	3.00			.25 / .25						.25					.50 / 1.75	1.75		1.00	
ADM-QUALITY CONTROL	99001-80																			
UNIDENTIFIED	99002-80	2.50							.75								.75			
EDUCATION	99003-80											.50						3.50		
PRODUCTIVE	99004-80	4.00																		
VACATION	99005-80																			
SICK LEAVE	99006-80																			
HOLIDAY	99007-80																			
TOTALS:		84.50			6.00 / 7.75				8.25 / 6.75	6.75	9.00 / 8.25	8.25	7.00		8.75	6.75	6.75	9.00	8.00	
DO NOT USE THIS LINE																				

Exhibit A

206

WORK IN PROGRESS-DETAILED

YR EMPL	SERVICE	BILL DATE	DESCRIPTION	HRS	DOLLARS	BILLINGS
01290 - LONG, DR. JOHN			12/31	--------	--------	--------
	51 XEROX	001 04/15	XEROX	0.00	1.89	
				0.00	1.89*	
	52 M & M	002 04/15	MEALS & MILEAG	0.00	10.00	
				0.00	10.00*	
	63 W.PROCE	003 04/15	WORD PROCESSOR	0.00	20.00	
				0.00	20.00*	
			TOTAL	0.00	31.89**	
101		004 04/15	D. MCGRUE	0.50	45.00	
		005 04/15	D. MCGRUE	0.75	67.50	
		006 04/15	D. MCGRUE	9.00	810.00	
				10.25	922.50*	
		101	TOTAL	10.25	922.50**	
295		007 04/15	D. SMITH	1.00	28.00	
				1.00	28.00*	
		295	TOTAL	1.00	28.00**	
309		008 04/15	P HUNTER	18.00	324.00	
				18.00	324.00*	
		309	TOTAL	18.00	324.00**	
395		009 04/15	C SUMTER	2.00	32.00	
				2.00	32.00*	
		395	TOTAL	2.00	32.00**	
600		010 04/15	COMPUTER	1.25	31.25	
				1.25	31.25*	
		600	TOTAL	1.25	31.25**	
602		011 04/15	COMPUTER	0.75	18.75	
				0.75	18.75*	
		602	TOTAL	0.75	18.75**	
		FISCAL YEAR	TOTAL	33.25	1,388.39	
		CLIENT TOTAL WIP		33.25	1,388.39	
		LESS BILLINGS			0.00	
		UNBILLED WORK IN PROGRESS			1,388.39	

Exhibit B

JONES AND SMITH, CPAs
SUBSTANTIAL MARK UP/DOWN
FROM WORK IN PROCESS TO BILLING
OCTOBER, 198X

Client #	Partner In Charge	Client Name	Work In Process	Billing	Mark-Up (Down)
12396	NIM	Easterling, Albert	1,053.25	1,150.00	96.75
15715	KIL	Robinson, Joseph	556.25	390.00	(166.25)
01996	DSR	Yeamans Fuel Co.	4,004.95	4,250.00	245.05
14336	JLG	Francis, Dr. Wm.	944.14	1,145.00	200.86
14690	JMO	Ming, John	230.25	330.00	99.75
14917	JMO	Sanchez, Julius	72.00	120.00	48.00
09477	WBJ	Howell, Bowles, etc.	2,024.10	1,470.60	(553.50)
09073	WBJ	Bft. Co. Water Dept.	549.74	275.00	(274.74)
		Totals	9,434.68	9,130.60	(304.08)

Exhibit C

(Please return to Personnel)

**EXPLANATION OF SUBSTANTIAL <u>WRITE-UP</u>
FROM WIP TO BILL DATED NOV. 12, 198X**

Partner: ___DSR___

Client: ___YEAMANS FUEL CO. #01996___

Work in Process: ___OCT. 198X___ Bill $ ___4,250.00___ WIP $ ___4,004.95___

Explanation of Write-Up:

Possible Future Services _____	Required overtime _____
Consistent Write-Up _____	Dynatax _____
Difficult or Risky _____	Other – Explain below
In lieu of interest _____	
Extra good performance by ___SUE SMITH___	

(Please return to Personnel)

**EXPLANATION OF SUBSTANTIAL <u>WRITE-DOWN</u>
FROM WIP TO BILL DATED NOV. 7, 198X**

Partner: ___KIL___

Client: ___ROBINSON, JOSEPH #15715___

Work in Process: ___OCT. 198X___ Bill $ ___390.00___ WIP $ ___556.25___

Explanation of Write-Down:

New Client _____	Concession to keep client _____
New Employee ___X___	Inefficiency, principally
Fixed Price-Rate too low _____	by persons named below _____
Other Reason _____	

Exhibit D

209

Exhibit E is a statistical profile from which several interesting conclusions may be drawn. The most obvious one is that partner income increases as firm size increases, and that this increase is accomplished with a minor increase in hours worked.

Exhibit F, read in conjunction with Exhibit E, permits conclusions as to the fee volume needed to justify a partnership slot.

Exhibit G shows that the salaries of professional staff as a percentage of fees increase, and partner income as a percentage of fees decreases as firm size increases. If this Exhibit stood alone, one might conclude that paying good salaries is injurious to partner income. Exhibit E, however, shows that partner compensation increases with firm size. One might draw the conclusion that profitability is enhanced by paying superior salaries and relying on staff to do more of the work, freeing partners for partner-level activity.

Exhibit H shows that, while total hours worked by partners in medium and large firms are almost identical, chargeable hours for the larger firms drop noticeably. This is probably caused by devoting more time to management as firm size increases; again, reference to Exhibit E shows that management time is profitably employed. The consistency in average net fees realized per charged hour could lead to a conclusion that firm size permits more profit with no higher unit price (hourly fees) because the tasks can be assigned to the lowest staff level capable of performing them. The smaller the entity, the more likely that persons will work at jobs below their optimum level simply because there is no less qualified person available to perform them.

A Case Study in Use of Accounting and Management Techniques To Increase Efficiency and Accelerate Cash Flow

A CPA firm has just added up the books for the year and finds these results, reporting on the cash method:

Net fees	$1,000,000
Employee salaries	(400,000)
Payroll taxes and fringe benefits	(50,000)
All other expenses	(100,000)
Income available to partners	450,000
Partners' salaries	400,000
Net income for distribution to partners based on units of profit sharing	$ 50,000

The partner who serves as controller attends a practice management seminar and gains the impression that his firm is below average in partner compensation. Being a good accountant, he concludes that unsatisfactory profits (and all partner compensation comes from profits) are the result of inadequate fees or unsatisfactory expenses ratios, or a combination of them.

SIZE OF OFFICE	INDIVIDUAL	NON-NATIONAL			NATIONAL
		SMALL	MEDIUM	LARGE	
1. PARTNERS	1.0	2.2	2.5	3.7	8.5
	1.0	2.1	2.7	4.6	8.8
2. CPA MEMBERS	.7	.8	3.0	7.1	50.0
	.3	.4	1.6	5.8	37.8
3. OTHER PROFESSIONAL	1.8	1.8	3.1	7.9	31.8
	1.1	1.4	3.9	9.6	28.4
4. OFFICE AND NON-PROFESSIONAL	.9	1.2	2.2	4.4	20.5
	.8	1.3	2.3	5.6	17.8
5. TOTAL	4.4	6.0	10.9	23.1	110.8
	3.2	5.2	10.4	25.6	92.8
6. AVERAGE NET INCOME PER PARTNER **	86,944	71,803	97,463	120,788	228,096
	45,445	46,581	58,094	78,256	146,299
7. AVERAGE NET FEES PER FIRM	182,938	298,681	522,568	1,040,109	5,066,531
	99,275	193,584	366,644	973,946	4,351,840
8. AVERAGE PERCENTAGE INCREASE IN NET FEES ***	23.4	22.1	24.5	25.9	27.6
	24.2	24.7	23.0	20.0	27.4
9. AVERAGE SQUARE FEET OF OFFICE SPACE PER PERSON **	319	300	278	238	259
	308	316	272	242	230
10. AVERAGE CHARGED HOURS PER PERSON **	1334	1359	1510	1358	1295
	1137	1265	1305	1313	1249
11. AVERAGE PERCENTAGE OF STANDARD FEES REALIZED	89.2	90.5	95.3	95.0	85.3
	86.8	87.6	89.6	89.5	81.9
12. PERCENTAGE OF RESPONDENTS USING STANDARD BILLING RATES	81.8	78.3	95.2	90.9	100.0
	75.9	83.3	81.7	96.6	100.0

** REPLIES WERE DIVIDED BY NUMBER OF PARTNERS OR PERSONNEL, TOTALED FOR EACH SIZE GROUP AND DIVIDED BY THE NUMBER OF FIRMS IN EACH GROUP TO ARRIVE AT THE AVERAGE

*** PERCENTAGE INCREASE IN NET FEES WAS COMPUTED FOR EACH REPLY, TOTALED FOR EACH SIZE GROUP AND DIVIDED BY THE NUMBER OF FIRMS IN EACH GROUP TO ARRIVE AT THE AVERAGE.

* AVERAGE CALCULATED BY DIVIDING TOTAL OFFICE NET INCOME BY TOTAL NUMBER OF PARTNERS. HOME AND REGIONAL OVERHEAD MAY OR MAY NOT BE INCLUDED IN RESPONSES.

Exhibit E

NET FEES PER PARTNER
UPPER ROW TOP 25 %

FROM	TO	INDIVIDUAL	NON-NATIONAL			NATIONAL
			SMALL	MEDIUM	LARGE	
1	25,000	.0 5.5	.0 2.2	.0 .0	.0 .0	.0 .0
25,001	40,000	1.3 13.0	.0 1.1	.0 .0	.0 .0	.0 .0
40,001	60,000	.0 18.9	.0 13.3	.0 1.2	.0 .0	.0 .C
60,001	70,000	3.9 8.5	.0 16.7	.0 3.7	.0 .0	.0 .0
70,001	80,000	3.9 6.2	4.3 15.6	.0 2.4	.0 .0	.0 .0
80,001	90,000	1.3 5.2	4.3 8.9	.0 3.7	.0 1.1	.0 .0
90,001	125,000	22.1 17.9	39.1 26.7	.0 40.2	.0 8.0	.0 .0
125,001	150,000	13.0 6.5	26.1 8.9	.0 11.0	.0 8.0	.0 .0
150,001	200,000	23.4 9.1	17.4 4.4	47.6 20.7	4.5 31.0	.0 .0
OVER	200,000	31.2 9.1	8.7 2.2	52.4 17.1	95.5 51.7	100.0 100.0
	TOTALS	100.1 99.9	99.9 100.0	100.0 100.0	100.0 99.8	100.0 100.0

Exhibit F

	INDIVIDUAL	---- NON-NATIONAL ----			NATIONAL
		SMALL	MEDIUM	LARGE	
NET FEES	100.0	100.0	100.0	100.0	100.0
	100.0	100.0	100.0	100.0	100.0
PROFESSIONAL STAFF SALARIES - EXCLUDING PARTNERS	19.1	15.8	22.0	25.3	34.0
	15.7	13.2	21.4	26.7	32.4
OTHER SALARIES - EXCLUDING PARTNERS	7.6	5.5	7.2	6.2	5.9
	9.1	8.1	8.2	8.2	7.2
OUTSIDE SERVICES - CONSULTATION, SERVICE BUREAUS, TAX RETURN PROCESSING	2.4	2.7	1.8	1.8	.4
	2.4	2.2	1.9	1.9	.8
PERSONNEL EXPENSES - PAYROLL TAXES, FRINGE BENEFITS, PROFESSIONAL DUES	3.6	4.0	4.7	6.0	6.5
	3.4	4.1	4.8	5.9	5.8
EDP EXPENSES - IN HOUSE OR TIME SHARING	2.2	1.5	1.4	1.4	.6
	2.7	2.2	2.1	2.5	.8
FACILITIES EXPENSE - OCCUPANCY, MAINTENANCE, DEPRECIATION	6.7	6.9	6.1	5.6	6.6
	8.0	8.3	6.9	6.4	6.3
OTHER OPERATING EXPENSES - ALL EXPENSES NOT INCLUDED ABOVE	13.2	10.4	10.7	10.4	7.8
	15.1	12.5	12.5	12.0	17.3
PARTNER SALARIES AND AMOUNT REMAINING FOR DISTRIBUTION TO PARTNERS	47.5	53.3	46.2	43.3	38.3
	44.9	50.4	42.3	36.3	29.5
DO YOUR PARTNERS INCUR PRACTICE RELATED BUSINESS EXPENSES WHICH ARE NOT REFLECTED IN THE FIRM'S INCOME STATEMENT	20.8	26.1	38.1	31.8	.0
	21.8	25.6	22.0	34.5	29.4
UNDER 5 % OF PARTNERSHIP NET INCOME .... % OF YES ANSWERS	75.0	50.0	75.0	85.7	.0
	31.3	56.5	66.7	86.7	80.0
5 - 10 % OF PARTNERSHIP NET INCOME .... % OF YES ANSWERS	.0.	16.7	25.0	.0	.0
	10.4	21.7	22.2	6.7	20.0
OVER 10 % OF PARTNERSHIP NET INCOME .... % OF YES ANSWERS	25.0	33.3	.0	14.3	.0
	58.2	21.7	11.1	6.7	.0

Exhibit G

213

AVERAGE HOURS WORKED FOR LATEST YEAR
UPPER ROW TOP 25 %

	INDIVIDUAL	SMALL	NON-NATIONAL MEDIUM	LARGE	NATIONAL
CHARGEABLE					
PARTNERS-PRACTITIONERS	1534	1576	1543	1454	1047
	1432	1382	1378	1340	957
STAFF	1483	1586	1754	1643	1683
	1299	1483	1618	1605	1515
CLERICAL	900	945	796	903	536
	875	870	812	776	512
TOTAL HOURS					
PARTNERS-PRACTITIONERS	2184	2158	2362	2362	2324
	2104	2151	2307	2310	2192
STAFF	1996	1999	2242	2124	2270
	1793	1969	2113	2159	2121
CLERICAL	1840	1859	2111	2007	2181
	1609	1784	2000	2021	2063
AVERAGE NET FEES REALIZED PER CHARGED HOUR	35.32	36.42	32.94	34.22	37.99
	30.92	31.22	28.34	30.46	37.57

Exhibit H

214

He obtains the results of a regional association of CPA firms' survey of financial results and manages to scrape together figures for his own firm for comparison. He finds this out in comparison of income figures:

- Their fee schedule is in line;
- The ratio of chargeable hours to total hours worked is in line;
- Fee and time write-offs are not more than average;
- Total hours worked are on a par with more profitable firms;
- Employee salaries and other expenses are in line.

Even though income statement analysis showed no reasons for unsatisfactory profits, our controller was not satisfied. He compared balance sheet figures, and noticed that the more profitable firms had about 25 percent of their annual net fees tied up in work and process and accounts receivable, whereas his firm had 40 percent of annual net fees tied up. (Even though these figures were not on the cash basis books, they were available.)

Making inquiries and "guesstimation" revealed that the practice produced its net fees from these sources:

Opinion audits, including tax returns	40%
Compilations and reviews, including tax returns	35%
Write-up work	15%
Tax returns only	10%

Work in process records are kept on an in-house computer on a monthly input basis. Bills are prepared reasonably promptly after work in process figures are obtained, and with few exceptions, clients are billed once a year.

Inquiry revealed that most engagements involving financial statements (75 percent of the firm's work) were completed by the 15th day of the 3rd month after the client's year-end. Field work was usually completed within 6 weeks after the client's year-end, and the remaining month was consumed with preparation of reports, preparation of tax returns or financial statements. The average engagement consumed 35 hours of staff and clerical time after completion of field work.

The controller quickly made two observations which, without any changes in the work schedule, substantially accelerated the cash flow. The first was to put all write-up work on an interim billing so that clients paid in regular installments, usually monthly, as the work was done. This change alone, affecting 15 percent of the work load, accelerated payment of about $100,000 per year. The second change was even easier to effect, since it consisted of changing the time record period to end on the 15th day of the month (or 16th or 17th when those were tax return due dates). Eliminating the half-month lag between delivery of product and having time records available for billing speeded up the collection process enough to reduce work in process/accounts receivable by 1/24th of a year's fees.

A final realization was that it didn't make sense to spread 35 hours of statement and return preparation and review time over a period of a month. Some of that 35 hours went into preparing drafts of financial statements for insertion of figures from adjusted trial balances. It took a year to phase it in, but after the phase-in a word processor spit out statement and report drafts ready for current year figures, plus such modification of wording and arrangement as was needed. Work was logged from statement and return preparers to typists and processors, to proofreaders and reviewers, so that the month formerly required was cut by half. This placed the finished product in the hands of the client weeks earlier than he had been accustomed to receiving it. He welcomed the extra time to review the work before the tax due date, and the firm was able to bill that much earlier.

Even though none of this required particularly sophisticated techniques, it reduced average tied-up capital from $400,000 to $200,000; this was a one-shot increase in profit of $200,000, plus an annual benefit to the partners of a perpetual return on the extra capital left from the $200,000 after their income taxes were paid.

9.11 SUMMARY OF CHAPTER NINE

Unless there is to be a duplication of functions, even chaos, the partnership must be organized and managed. Management is usually thought of as operation through managers. A manager is usually thought of as someone appointed from above and given authority over underlings. In a partnership, the partners are both the source of that authority and the persons to be managed. The person who manages a partnership must be a leader, in the sense that leaders derive their authority from the desire of others to be led and the selection of that person to lead them.

The leader must keep the group purpose visible and must maintain cohesion in working toward that purpose. Cohesion, simply "sticking together," implies a common bond, a willingness to work together. When individual goals conflict with the common goal, there must be ways to resolve the conflicts and keep the structure from coming unglued. Cohesion requires logical organization and acceptance by each partner that in furthering the common goal he is obtaining a personal benefit. Finally, good management requires a score-keeping system, both to plot strategy and to tell which partners are players and which are only spectators.

CHAPTER TEN

Estate Planning and Administration Aspects Of a Partnership Interest

CONTENTS

INTRODUCTION   219

10.1 VALUATION OF A PARTNERSHIP INTEREST   219

    10.1.1   Valuing a Partnership Interest When There Is No Established Market – 219

    10.1.2   IRS Rules for Valuing an Interest in a Partnership – 220

    10.1.3   The Practical Aspects of Valuing a Partnership Interest – 220

    10.1.4   Value of Underlying Assets Alone Is Seldom Determinative of Value of a Partnership Interest – 221

    10.1.5   Income and Cash Flow Are Determinants of Value of a Partnership Interest – 221

    10.1.6   Economic Circumstances of the Partner Influence the Value of This Interest – 221

    10.1.7   Valuing an Interest in a Tax Shelter Partnership Presents Special Problems – 222

    10.1.8   Timing and Security Factors in Valuing a Partnership Interest – 222

10.2   PARTNERSHIP INCOME AS INCOME IN RESPECT
        OF A DECEDENT   223

        10.2.1   Income in Respect of a Decedent Is Taxed
                  Twice – 223
        10.2.2   Double Taxation of Partnership Income –
                  224
        10.2.3   Reducing the Double Tax on Income in
                  Respect of a Decedent – 225
        10.2.4   Tax-Saving Options Concerning Guaran-
                  teed Payments Are Available to a Partner –
                  225
        10.2.5   Payments for an Interest in the Partnership
                  as Income in Respect of a Decedent – 226

10.3   GIFTS OF PARTNERSHIP INTERESTS   227

10.4   A WRAP-UP OF CHAPTER TEN   228

INTRODUCTION

We have stated before that there is a no such thing as a nonprofit partnership because the Uniform Partnership Act says that a partnership must be organized for profit. It is logical that a profitable venture will increase in value or it will fail to increase in value only if it distributes its profits to its partners. In that case, the proceeds of distribution are presumed to increase the net worth of the partners. A partnership, then, can be expected to increase the gross estate of the partner, creating estate tax problems or estate planning opportunities.

There are exceptions to this general assumption. One is exemplified by the situation in which a partner makes the wry comment "we didn't intend for this to be a nonprofit organization; it just turned out that way." The other is in the tax-shelter partnership, the main attraction of which is its ability to produce large tax losses. A tax-shelter partnership interest frequently has very limited salability, and is difficult to value in the absence of a market. Its biggest drawback to an estate may be that it was designed to shelter the income of the high-bracket decedent but is now owned by an estate or heir with minimal income tax problems and maximal cash flow needs.

10.1 VALUATION OF A PARTNERSHIP INTEREST

For either gift tax or estate tax purposes, a partnership interest must be valued at its fair market value at the appropriate date—the date of the gift, the date of the decedent's death or the alternate valuation date.

If interests in a partnership are regularly bought and sold, the price of a similar interest on the appropriate date sets the value of the subject interest. Only rarely is there an active market for interests in partnerships.

10.1.1 Valuing a Partnership Interest When There Is No Established Market

There is an old saw to the effect that there are always two prices: one when you are buying and another when you are selling. There are, therefore, *three* prices to consider in valuing a partnership interest, the third price being the sometimes arbitrary price which the estate or gift tax examiners will accept. If there is a price at which buyer and seller want to trade and they do indeed trade at that price, the value is fixed for tax purposes, assuming that the parties are unrelated and/or the price was arrived at in arm's length negotiations.

10.1.2 IRS Rules for Valuing an Interest in a Partnership

Reading the gift tax and estate tax instructions tells you what the examiners will need to be convinced that the partnership is valued fairly. These instructions say that "the value of a gift is the fair market value of the property on the date the gift is made. The fair market value is the price at which the property would change hands between a willing buyer and a willing seller, when neither is forced to buy or to sell, and when both have reasonable knowledge of all relevant facts."

The gift tax instructions do not specifically cover valuing a partnership interest. However, the estate tax instructions are more helpful in insuring compliance when they say "When an interest in a partnership or unincorporated business is reportable, attach a statement of assets and liabilities for the valuation date and for the 5 years preceding and statement of the net earnings for the same 5 years. Good will must be accounted for. In general, the same information should be furnished and the same methods followed as in valuing close corporations." The instructions refer to these instructions for valuing stock in close corporations: "Apply the rules in the Section 2031 regulation to determine the value of inactive stock and stock in close corporations. Complete financial and other data the estate uses to determine value should be submitted with the return, including balance sheets (particularly the one nearest to the valuation date), and statements of the net earnings or operating results and dividends paid for each of the 5 years immediately preceding the valuation date."

10.1.3 The Practical Aspects of Valuing a Partnership Interest

The appraiser of a partnership interest for estate or gift tax purposes is faced with an imposing task. In placing a value on the interest, he must ask himself "what gives this interest its value?" He will give himself this answer:

1. Its equity in the underlying assets
2. Its potential for future profits
3. Its cash flow
4. Any special situation that may have a bearing on its value
5. The manner in which one or more of the above interact to give value to the interest

The observations made in these paragraphs may be applied in the context of the partner who is attempting to arrive at a value for inclusion in an agreement for the redemption or sale of his partnership interest. If he is successful and a firm buy-sell agreement is in force at the time of his death, there should be no tax problem with valuation. If the interest must be valued in the absence of an inter vivos agreement for the purchase and sale of the interest, his executor should consider these practical aspects in arriving at a value which is reasonable for tax purposes as well as for assigning a value for the interest which is as fair to the heirs as is the value placed on stocks, bonds or real estate.

10.1.4 Value of Underlying Assets Alone Is Seldom Determinative of Value of a Partnership Interest

Very seldom will value of underlying assets be the sole determinant of value of a partnership interest. This is true for the same reason that value of underlying assets is not the sole determinant of value of stock in a corporation: unless the partner has absolute control of the partnership, he can't get at the assets so they have no inherent value to him.

10.1.5 Income and Cash Flow Are Determinants of Value of a Partnership Interest

Assets of a partnership are usually valuable only for what they promise in the way of future benefits. For illustration, we look at a real estate partnership owning one building rented under a long-term lease with the rental roughly equal to the debt service and all insurance, repairs and taxes being borne by the tenant. A single minority partner cannot demand his share of the assets, and he gets no cash until the mortgage is retired many years hence. Such an interest is worth the present value of the proportionate interest in the underlying assets upon the retirement of the mortgage. To obtain the present value, you must assume a value at the expiration of the mortgage and a rate of interest for the intervening years. Even under "normal" conditions such a calculation is at best a shrewd guess. Under conditions of high inflation and high interest, the estimate has all the precision of a crapshooter's roll. Nonetheless, appraisers are called upon every day to attest to such values and vast sums of taxes are paid (or avoided) on the strength of such estimates. If that were not complication enough, you may consider that the size and type of income or loss generated can make identical interests of greater or lesser value to two individuals in materially different tax brackets. The tax-shelter partnership with no cash flow but large depreciation pass-through was attractive to the high-bracket decedent; it is the last thing needed by his family that suddenly finds itself in reduced circumstances.

10.1.6 Economic Circumstances of the Partner Influence the Value of This Interest

The estate planner must value a partnership interest from the angles of its value to the person whose estate is being planned during his peak income years, during his declining years, and as a resource of his estate. There is no easy answer to placing a value on a partnership interest because its value depends on who has it and under what circumstances, and how the partnership interest will serve its owners as circumstances change.

10.1.7 Valuing an Interest in a Tax-Shelter Partnership Presents Special Problems

The executor and his professional advisors are faced with an immediate and practical problem in valuing tax-shelter partnerships. The problem is the valuation to be placed on them for estate tax purposes and the suitability of the interest as an asset of the estate or of the heirs. If the interest clearly should not be held, prompt efforts to dispose of it may produce a sale that will fix the estate tax value and effect prompt disposition of a no longer good investment. Since tax-shelter partnerships are usually limited partnerships, there should be no legal barrier to sale of the interest.

If a prompt decision to sell cannot be reached or if a buyer is not forthcoming and the estate is subject to estate tax, the executor is well advised to place the lowest possible valuation on the interest to avoid a capital loss upon its eventual sale. It might be argued that a maximum estate tax valuation furnishes higher basis to permit larger pass-through of losses or to minimize future capital gains when the interest is sold. Such an argument will not hold water for two reasons. First, basis to permit deduction of losses traditionally comes from the partner's share of partnership liabilities, not from basis acquired by purchase or inheritance. Second, the maximum capital gains tax is 20 percent and the minimum rate at which U.S. estate tax can be paid is 32 percent. Add in the fact that estate taxes are paid almost immediately and that capital gains taxes are deferred until the time of sale and you must reject the idea that there can be any merit in paying more estate tax than the legal minimum.

10.1.8 Timing and Security Factors in Valuing a Partnership Interest

In negotiating the sale of a partnership interest, the participants must keep in mind the dollar amount to be paid and the schedule of payments. The usual result is an extended payout with little or no interest. Payments to be received far into the future are worth less than payments receivable immediately. The fact that the payments are unsecured calls for further discount in their present value.

In a partnership in which there is a substantial equity in real estate or in other assets with long-term values, a retiring partner or partners entering into a buy-sell agreement should consider backing up the agreement with a security interest in partnership assets. There are practical limitations on what can be done here. The first is that placing a lien on partnership property may so restrain the ongoing business as to adversely affect its ability to survive and make payments. The second is that the only security available may be a second mortgage. A second mortgage on an office building in the early years of a 30-year first mortgage has so little value to a partner retiring for age that he could obtain very little security from it.

Perhaps a buy-out agreement can be backed with life insurance. Insurance on the life of an active partner provides a cushion against the double blow of losing his services and commencing payments to his estate. Insurance on the lives of remaining partners performs a function similar to that of credit life insurance. Life insurance, however, does very little for the retiring partner or his former partners if all are hale and hearty during the payout period.

Disability insurance intended to relieve the pressures of meeting payments to a former partner can add security to a retirement plan. The insurance can be on the partner about to retire, to replace payments otherwise due from the partnership, or on the remaining partners to assure their abilities to pay.

Life and disability insurance premiums are not tax-deductible expenses of a partnership. This makes them expensive ways of providing security, though the tax-free receipt of their proceeds may be an offsetting advantage.

Funding and securing buy-outs is more properly a subject to be addressed under planning for retirement of a partner. The subject is touched upon here because the existence or absence of security factors has a measurable effect on the valuation of partnership interests.

10.2 PARTNERSHIP INCOME AS INCOME IN RESPECT OF A DECEDENT

IRC Section 61(a)(14) provides that gross income, (from which the deductions allowed by Sections 62 and 63 are subtracted to arrive at taxable income) includes "income in respect of a decedent." Section 691 states the general rule that gross income that was not included in the final return of the decedent because the income was not taxable to the decedent, because of his method of accounting, shall be included in the return of the estate or other heir who receives the income. This seems only fair; the income was earned, the decedent didn't pay tax on it, so his heirs will pay the tax.

10.2.1 Income in Respect of Decedent Is Taxed Twice

The problem with income in respect of a decedent is that the income receivable is included in the decedent's gross estate. The receivable, when collected, is subject to income tax. Section 691 provides partial relief by permitting a deduction for estate tax paid on income in respect of a decedent. Since a deduction is not the same as a credit, there is an incidence of double taxation inherent in the taxation of income in respect of a decedent.

We can show how the tax works with this illustration. A lawyer, practicing as a sole proprietor, who files his return on the cash basis, is owed $1,000 for legal services. The client pays the $1,000 shortly after the lawyer dies. If the lawyer's taxable estate was between $150,000 and $250,000, the estate tax attributable to the $1,000 will be $320. If the income of the lawyer's estate is distributed to and taxable to the widow, she will report the $1,000 as taxable income reduced by the $320 estate tax. Assuming a maximum 50 percent rate, the federal income tax on it will not exceed $340. It is clear that combined estate and income tax takes $660 out of a $1,000 item of income in respect of a decedent. These figures are lower than will be encountered in many situations because 32 percent is the lowest rate at which estate tax can be paid.

If we change the $1,000 to rent due and the deceased landlord left a taxable estate of $1,001,000, the estate tax becomes $410. If the highest income tax rate applies, income tax takes 50 percent of the $590 which ended up in the residue of the estate. When $295 disappears into the coffers of the income tax collectors, $705 has been wrung out of $1,000 inheritance. Include state inheritance or estate taxes and administrative expenses such as executor's commission, and the $1,000 has shrunk to almost nothing.

10.2.2 Double Taxation of Partnership Income

The problem of double taxation of income in respect of a decedent is not peculiar to partnerships. In both illustrations above, the $1,000 is depicted as something other than partnership income. It was shown that way to illustrate the dollar effect without complicating the illustration with the timing of partnership income earned by a decedent. The problem of double taxation does concern partners. It behooves partners and their advisors to understand the problem and to plan for minimization of these taxes and to understand how the fact that income earned by a partner in the partnership year up to the date of his death and not received by him, but received by his heir, invariably is income in respect of a decedent.

It is possible to get a deduction for estate tax on an asset that is not in the estate. Income in respect of a decedent is the share of partnership income for the partnership's tax year earned up to the date of the partner's death. If we assume that the pre-death share of income was $40,000, that is the amount of income in respect of a decedent. The partner may have withdrawn and spent or given away $30,000 so that the asset value of his partnership income account is only $10,000; so estate tax is levied on $10,000 but deduction for estate tax on $40,000 is allowable.

To bring the tax cost of double taxation of income in respect of a decedent into perspective, we shall look again at the illustration of $1,000 of rental income. If the taxpayer had collected the rent, he would have been subject to $500 tax on it. If the remaining $500 were in his taxable estate at his death, the estate tax cost would have been $205. The total tax cost of $705 is the same as if the collection had constituted income in respect of a decedent.

10.2.3 Reducing the Double Tax on Income in Respect of a Decedent

The problem then is not in whether an asset of the estate will produce income in respect of a decedent when collected, but in whether one of these taxes can be avoided. We must start with the assumption that tax on income cannot legally be avoided. We know that there are many ways to avoid estate taxes. Our problem becomes one of how to avoid or minimize either or both of the onerous taxes.

Stockholders of corporations may freely transfer shares to family members to reduce the donor's estate or to spread the dividend income around. Sole proprietors (or investors) have considerable control over timing of income as well as of receipt or disposition of income, thereby having opportunity to control (or at least affect) items that may or may not otherwise become items of income in respect of a decedent. An example of the latter is the person of advanced years or failing health who considers the effect of taxation of inherited installments when deciding for or against election of the installment method of reporting gain from a sale.

10.2.4 Tax-Saving Options Concerning Guaranteed Payments Are Available to a Partner

Since decisions in a partnership must be made by or in the interests of at least a majority of the partners, there is less chance of arranging transactions for the sole benefit of one partner. However, a partner does have some options that affect the probability of income in respect of a decedent.

His first option might be that of when to get out of a partnership. A partner in a cash basis professional firm may have a substantial share of accounts receivable and work in process to be paid to him shortly after retirement or death. He may also have guaranteed payments of significant amount, with payment to commence after retirement or death. If he dies with his boots on, every cent of this is includible in his gross estate (though perhaps at a discounted value) and in the taxable income of his heir. The heir presumably is his estate; an assignment of income during lifetime is uncommon and would serve no current income purpose, as the assignment of income doctrine would cause the income to be taxed to him. Therefore, it is unlikely that he has contracted to have his income paid directly to an heir while he is alive.

IRC Section 706(c)(2)(A)(ii) provides that the taxable year of a partnership with respect to a partner who dies shall not close prior to the end of the partnership's taxable year. Since practically all partnerships and practically all individuals file their returns on the calendar year, even as to a partner who dies in December, all the income earned in his final year may be taxed to his estate. Unless the first year of the estate's fiduciary return ends on December 31 and the income is distributed or distributable to his widow, his final joint return will show no income from the partnership. The income may be taxed to the estate, which pays tax at the high married-filing-separately rates, or the partnership income may pass-through to the widow in the following year when she may be taxed at single rates.

A partner can avoid such a problem by retiring and taking most or all of his income from the partnership while he is alive. Under those circumstances, he may take advantage of joint rates, or tax shelters, or increased charitable contributions. He can then dispose of the after-tax money by inter vivos gifts, removing it from his gross estate.

A partner who expects to receive guaranteed payments may minimize income tax on those items of income in respect of decedent by bequeathing them to a low-bracket taxpayer, such as his minor child. He may avoid estate and income tax on income items by bequeathing them to a charity. A person familiar with U.S. Form 706, Estate Tax Return, will recognize that a testamentary gift to a charity is includible in the adjusted gross estate, thereby maximizing the marital deduction. The charitable deduction, along with the marital deduction, serves to reduce the adjusted gross estate to the taxable estate. A person who expects his estate to be in the high estate brackets and his heirs to be in high income tax brackets should consider bequeathing income in respect of a decedent, including his benefits as a retired partner, to a charity, because the taxes otherwise are so high that he can well afford to be generous.

10.2.5 Payments for an Interest in the Partnership as Income in Respect of a Decedent

Payments for an interest in the partnership, sometimes described as payments for good will or Section 736(b) payments, or installments resulting from the sale of the interest to someone other than the partnership, may continue after death of the partner. If the partner was reporting capital gain from the principal portion of such installments, the gain included in principal payments received after his death is income in respect of a decedent to the heir who receives them. The exclusion from taxable income of part of the capital gain requires exclusion of part of the estate tax attributable to income in respect of decedent. This can be illustrated by the case of a former partner who died before receiving the last 10 payments of $1,000 each on a liquidation of his interest under Section 736(b). We assume that he had no basis in the installments so that he was reporting $1,000 as long-term capital gain from each installment received. We shall assume that the 10 payments are included as assets of his estate at their face value of $10,000, and that estate tax at the marginal rate of 34 percent is paid on them. If the heir collects all 10 payments in one taxable year when the capital gain exclusion is 60 percent, the deduction would be figured as $10,000 minus $3,400 times 60 percent, equalling $3,960. The significant point is that a substantial part of the advantage of partial taxability of capital gains is cancelled out by a proportionate reduction of the deduction for estate tax on income in respect of a decedent.

10.3 GIFTS OF PARTNERSHIP INTERESTS

Partnership interests are personal property. Assuming that the partnership agreement permits it, partnership interests may be sold, given, or bequeathed. It is essential that the right to free transferability of a general partnership interest be carefully provided for in the agreement. Otherwise, the provision of Section 18(g) of the Uniform Partnership Act will prevail: "no person can become a member of a partnership without the consent of all the partners." The Uniform Limited Partnership Act suggests that a limited partnership may provide for assignment of interest by including this clause in the Uniform Limited Partnership Act (Section 2(a)x): "The right, if given, of a limited partner to substitute an assignee as contributor in his place, and the terms and conditions of the substitution."

In theory, given the right to do so, a partner may include partnership interests in his estate planning with as much ease as he might plan for any other undivided interest in property. It is inconceivable that a general partnership would grant unlimited powers of substitution. Since, however, the persons to whom a partnership interest might be given or bequeathed are known, there should be no great problem in having them admitted upon receipt of an interest by gift, bequest or sale. It should be even easier to give at least a capital interest to a person who is already a general partner. Obviously, an interest in a professional partnership can be transferred only to a person licensed to practice that profession.

A gift of a partnership interest falls under the same rules, from the gift tax point of view, as any other gift of property. The gift is valued at the fair market value of the interest. The rules for valuing a gift of a partnership interest are discussed in paragraph 10.1.1.

10.4   A WRAP-UP OF CHAPTER TEN

The partner who has worked hard to create an estate in which a partnership interest is a major asset should aggressively plan a defense against its shrinkage or disintegration upon his death.

There are at least three threats to the value of a partnership interest upon the death of the partner:

1. The unwillingness or inability of the surviving partners to preserve the value of the interest;

2. Subjection of the partnership interest to more than minimal estate taxation;

3. Subjection of the partnership interest to more than minimal income tax in the hands of estate or heirs.

Every partnership should have a binding buy-sell agreement. Such an agreement should insure that the partnership interests retain their value and provide an unassailable valuation for estate tax purposes. A happy balance must be struck between requiring the top dollar for the interest and setting a value which the surviving partners can and will honor.

When the value of the partnership interest has been agreed upon, the character of the purchase price, as payment for the interest or as guaranteed payments, must be determined. This may be stated backwards—the character of the payment may be a strong determinant of a fair price.

Although no one can foresee the future, partners should exert their best efforts to plot a course that will place the maximum after-tax dollars in the pockets of their heirs and extract a minimum of after-tax dollars from the partnership treasury. Skillful resolution of these apparently opposing yet closely related problems requires a working knowledge of terms like guaranteed payments, payments for interest in the partnership, and income in respect of a decedent. This chapter is intended to place these terms and their tax significance in the vocabulary of the partner's estate planner and to point out the hazards of being unfamiliar with them.

CHAPTER ELEVEN

Tax-Shelter Partnerships

CONTENTS

INTRODUCTION   231

11.1 WHY TAX SHELTERS ARE ATTRACTIVE   232

    11.1.1   Tax Savings Alone Are Not Enough – 232
    11.1.2   Who Can Benefit from Tax Shelters? – 233
    11.1.3   The Benefits of a Tax-Sheltered Investment
            – 233

11.2 COMPARISON OF THE LIMITED PARTNERSHIP
      WITH OTHER ARRANGEMENTS FOR
      ORGANIZING TAX SHELTERS   236

    11.2.1   Sole Proprietorships, General Partnerships,
            and Corporations Don't Quite Have It – 236
    11.2.2   Limited Partnerships Fill the Bill – 237
    11.2.3   Limitations on the Limited Partner – 237

11.3 HOW TAX SHELTERS ARE SOLD   237

    11.3.1   Tax Shelters Bring Money and Talent To-
            gether – 237
    11.3.2   Tax Shelters and the Securities Laws – 238
    11.3.3   The Prospectus of a Tax Shelter – 239
    11.3.4   Participation in a Tax Shelter May Draw
            IRS Fire – 239
    11.3.5   Buying Tax Shelters on the Easy Payment
            Plan – 240

11.4 ORGANIZATION AND OPERATION OF THE
LIMITED PARTNERSHIP   240

    11.4.1   Limited Partners Are Excluded from Management – 240

    11.4.2   Characteristics of the General Partner – 241

    11.4.3   Compensation of the General Partner – 241

    11.4.4   How Costs Are Shared and Deductions Are Allocated in the Real Estate Partnership – 242

    11.4.5   How Costs Are Shared and Deductions Are Allocated in an Oil and Gas Drilling Program – 242

    11.4.6   Allocations Should Not Unduly Place General and Limited Partners in Adversary Roles – 243

    11.4.7   How Costs Are Shared and Deductions Are Allocated in an Oil and Gas Income Program – 244

    11.4.8   Sharing of Income and Cash Flow – 246

    11.4.9   The General Partner's Potential Conflict of Interest – 246

    11.4.10   The Limited Partners' Defense Against Conflicts of Interest – 247

    11.4.11   Prospectuses Disclose Conflicts of Interest – 247

11.5 LEVERAGE   248

11.6 ECONOMIC HAZARDS OF A LIMITED
PARTNERSHIP   248

11.7 OTHER KINDS OF TAX-SHELTER LIMITED
PARTNERSHIPS   249

11.8 CHAPTER ELEVEN REVIEWED   249

INTRODUCTION

"Tax shelter" conjures up an image of a bloated plutocrat exploiting devious schemes to hide money from the tax collector, using techniques that, if not illegal, are at least reprehensible. Equally common is the view that tax shelters make sense only for the rich.

A simple definition of a tax shelter is that it is an investment which either produces totally and permanently nontaxable income, or defers taxation of income with no significant reduction in the amount of tax eventually paid, or causes the same amount of income to be taxed at a lower rate.

The simplest and safest tax shelter is investment in sound obligations of states and their subdivisions; interest from such investments is completely and permanently free from U.S. income tax. The tax-exempt feature permits them to be issued with lower interest requirements than taxable investments; a person in a relatively low tax bracket would be better off investing in higher-yield taxable securities. Because of their limited appeal and because they have no connection with partnerships, tax-exempt bonds will not be considered further as tax shelters.

The next simplest tax shelter is an investment in which a disproportionately large part of the tax deductions are claimed in the early years so that the deductions therefrom reduce taxable income of the investor, perhaps to the point that other income of the investor is "sheltered" by the excess deductions. An illustration is the investor who acquires personal property for rent to others, borrowing some or all of the required funds. Accelerated cost recovery (depreciation) is available and interest payments are higher in the early years. Even though the cash inflow is constant over the life of the lease, the taxable income is lower in the early years so that the investor has the use of his tax-deferred income for a long time. Whether the useful life coincides with the depreciable life, or the investor sells the asset, the ordinary income is exactly the same. Even though taxable income is the same over the life of the investment, the investor might benefit from the rate differential of low rental income (or losses) in his peak earning years followed by high rental income when he is retired and his other sources of income have tapered off.

A third kind of investment permits deductions therefrom to be offset against ordinary income with the expectation that these deductions will be recouped in a transaction taxed at less than ordinary income tax rates, usually as long-term capital gains.

The limited partnership is an ideal investment vehicle for tax shelters because it alone can pool the investments of many people, pass all of the tax attributes through to the partners, and still limit the investor's liability for loss to the amount he has invested.

This chapter will show why tax-shelter limited partnerships are attractive and for whom they are suitable investments. It will describe the roles of investor, general partner, and sponsor. It will show how tax shelters are sold and how they are organized and operated to serve the different and sometimes conflicting aims of the parties.

A separate chapter will explain the tax treatment of income, deductions and credits as it affects the limited partners and general partners, and will point to some of the land mines that the tax laws have planted on this particular road to financial success through skillful management and tax avoidance.

11.1   WHY TAX SHELTERS ARE ATTRACTIVE

Few things could be more obvious than why tax shelters are attractive: they are seen as ways to save taxes, and everyone likes to save taxes. However, there are many things that are almost universally considered to be desirable, but not everyone has them or even wants them. Why not? Because they can't afford it; it is not useful to them; it does not fit their style of living; they shy away from it because they do not understand it.

It follows that tax shelters are for those who can afford them; for those for whom the device provides a useful service; for those who are willing to take the risks necessary to obtain the benefits. It also follows that an intelligent answer can be obtained only by those who have at least a basic understanding of the term "tax shelter."

11.1.1 Tax Savings Alone Are Not Enough

If saving income taxes were the only reason for tax shelters—a widely held belief—there would be no justification for them, as the ventures that we describe in this chapter are large, complicated and risky. You can lose all of your investment, but since income tax rates are never 100 percent, you cannot recoup a total loss by tax savings. Therefore, we must conclude that tax shelters are attractive because they save taxes in addition to having other beneficial characteristics.

To illustrate this point, let us assume that an investor has $10,000 to invest and expects to pay income tax at 50 percent. He expects a 12 percent return, and will choose between completely safe but income taxable U.S. Treasury obligations and a real estate tax shelter. He will retain the investment for five years. The Treasuries produce $6,000, of which half goes for taxes. In this particular case, he pays an 8 percent sales commission to purchase his interest. His income (and cash flow) from the investment is nothing in the first two years, $1,000 in the third year, $1,200 in the fourth year, $1,500 in the fifth year and $2,300 long-term capital gain when he sells out to get his $9,200 investment back at the end of the fifth year. In each case he has received $6,000 income, but in the latter case, it cost him $800 to get in, and this he did not recover. From the real estate investment he received $3,700 ordinary income (less taxes of $1,850) and $2,300 of long-term capital gain (less taxes of $460). He has $3,700, less $1,850, plus $2,300, less $460, reduced by the $800 commission for after-tax income of $2,890. He netted only $2,890 from a risky investment compared to $3,000 from a secure investment.

Investments in tax shelters are never this predictable, and the investor hopes for more than a simple return. However, this little story should point out that tax savings alone do not justify a tax-shelter type of investment.

11.1.2 Who Can Benefit from Tax Shelters?

If our definition of tax shelters were broad enough to include home ownership, life insurance and tax-deferred annuities, we could say that tax shelters are attractive to anyone who pays income taxes. Because of the risks involved, we take the position that the typical tax shelter is attractive only to the higher-bracket taxpayer who is a person of considerably more than average means. A prospectus for an oil and gas offering confirms this opinion by saying "Subscriptions will be accepted only from persons representing that (a) they have a net worth of not less than $200,000 (exclusive of home, furnishings, and automobiles) or (b) they have a net worth of not less than $50,000 (exclusive of home, furnishings, and automobiles), and some portion of their taxable income for the previous year was (or some portion of their estimated taxable income for the current year will be) subject to Federal income tax at a rate of not less than 50% without regard to investment in the Drilling Partnership." Obviously, most American taxpayers cannot benefit from such a tax shelter because they can't buy into it. Those who squeak by the requirements, or those who have located an opportunity with less stringent requirements, should weigh the risks and benefits very carefully before committing themselves to a tax-shelter investment.

11.1.3 The Benefits of a Tax-Sheltered Investment

Although some of the benefits listed below accrue to investors who do not use limited partnerships, and though some of the benefits have nothing to do with taxes, the following are associated with the limited partnership type of venture that is usually the vehicle of a tax-sheltered investment:

    1. *Deferral of Taxation* – Large deductions for depreciation and

interest in the early years postpone taxation for an extended period of time, permitting the investor to use his money rather than paying it in the coffers of the Internal Revenue Service. With luck and strategic tax planning, the investor might time the eventual receipt of ordinary income from the shelter so that the tax will be minimal, such as taking the income just before a net operating loss carryover expires.

2. *Converting Ordinary Income into Long-Term Capital Gain* – A well-located property may appreciate in the economic sense while tax depreciation lowers its basis. A well-maintained property may hold its original value or lose value at a rate slower than tax depreciation. For whatever reason, a gain on the sale of nonresidential property, up to the amount of depreciation taken, will be ordinary income; any excess will be capital gain. However, gain on the sale of residential property will be recaptured as ordinary income only to the extent that deductions under the accelerated method exceed those that would have been allowable if the straight-line method over 15 years had been used. We call this converting ordinary income into capital gain, a most lucrative creation of tax alchemy.

3. *Keeping Up with Inflation* – If it is to produce a real return to the investor, a property must throw off income or increase in value at a rate equal to at least a desirable rate of return plus the rate of inflation. Many tax shelters invest in real estate or in oil or gas properties. Inflation causes almost any tangible asset to increase in value; good site selection, maintenance, and management tend to cause a property's value to increase faster than the rate of inflation. A good tax-shelter program brings the advantages of sound capitalization and good planning (in both the pre-completion and post-completion phases) to the project; it is unlikely that many individuals could obtain either while going it alone.

4. *Leverage* – In many tax shelters the limited partners put up only enough money for the down payment, with the rest of the acquisition price coming from borrowed funds. Just as a light touch on a long lever will lift a heavy load, a small equity will bring a large project into being. The result is that the opportunity of profit is multiplied manifold. An illustration shows how this works:

Cautious Investor buys an apartment project for $100,000 and sells it a few years later for $200,000. Ignoring depreciation for simplicity, Cautious Investor has doubled his money.

Leveraged Investor buys an apartment project for $100,000 with $20,000 cash and a mortgage for $80,000 and sells it a few years later for $200,000. Ignoring depreciation and principal payments on the mortgage, we say that he receives $200,000 and pays the mortgage, keeping $120,000. His $20,000 investment has increased sixfold.

Tax-shelter investments are normally leveraged to the hilt.

5. *Percentage Depletion* – In the mid-1920s, Congress, to encourage exploration for and extraction of mineral resources, added to the Internal Revenue Code a provision permitting owners of mineral properties, including oil and gas, to deduct a reasonable allowance for depletion. Depletion may be based on cost or expressed as a percentage of gross income from the property; whichever method produces the greater deduction is to be used. Percentage depletion may exceed the basis of the property. The percentage applicable to various minerals is specified by Section 613 of the Internal Revenue Code.

To illustrate that an unglamorous resource like coal can rival the riches of the Comstock lode when taxes are taken into effect, we shall look at the experience of Thatcher, who paid $600,000 for rights to mine an estimated 600,000 tons of coal. He may deduct cost depletion of $1 per ton of coal sold. If coal sells for $10 a ton, cost and percentage depletion is the same, since coal is subject to depletion at 10 percent of selling price. However, the price of coal has risen, so the average selling price is $20. Mr. Thatcher deducts $2 per ton and may deduct $1,200,000 if he mines the estimated 600,000 tons. If he is fortunate and the right yields more than 600,000 tons, he keeps right on deducting 10 percent of the gross sales price.

Percentage depletion is a technical subject; depletion is limited to 50 percent of the taxable income from the property, and percentage depletion in excess of cost depletion is a tax-preference item.

Percentage depletion is a tremendous boon to natural resource tax shelters, which have received a great boost from concern over energy sources, such as oil, gas, coal and shale.

6. *Professional Management* – An investor who recognizes the benefits of tax-sheltered investments realizes that he does not know where to find investment opportunities and if he could locate them he would have neither the time nor the expertise to profit from them. The syndicator (the person who puts the deal together) and the general partner (who may be the same person) represent themselves as having located the opportunity and being able to build, finance, and manage the project. This scarce talent may be utilized for the benefit of a large number of passive investors. It may also lead to the skinning of a large number of innocent lambs. The quality and integrity of management are the *sine qua non* of a large tax-shelter investment.

7. *Investment and Other Tax Credits* – Investment credit and fuel production credit may be passed through to the investor by the limited partnership. The value of the investment credit will be minimal in a real estate investment because real estate is generally not eligible for the credit. The value of the investment credit will also be minimal in

an oil and gas drilling program because most of the investor's money goes for items of overhead and intangible drilling costs which produce little or no investment credit.

Investment credit and fuel production credit could be significant in an oil and gas income program or in ventures involving purchase of large amounts of capital equipment for the partnership's own use. Partnerships organized to be lessors of personal property may be committed to pass investment credit through to lessees.

11.2 COMPARISON OF THE LIMITED PARTNERSHIP WITH OTHER ARRANGEMENTS FOR ORGANIZING TAX SHELTERS

The typical tax shelter brings together an investor who has money and needs relief from high taxes with a person who has property or expertise appropriate to that particular investment. The man with the deep pockets wants a limit to his risk and access to the tax-saving features of the investment. The other party wants capital and an opportunity to be paid for his entrepreneurial talents.

11.2.1 Sole Proprietorships, General Partnerships, and Corporations Don't Quite Have It

The first arrangement that might occur to an investor is to enter the deal as a sole proprietor or individual investor. He might reason that in the event of success he makes all the profits, and, win or lose, the tax breaks are all his. The first drawback is that his role exposes him to unlimited liability. The second drawback is that few single investors have enough to invest to pull off a worthwhile project. The third drawback is that he would have difficulty hiring the experts needed and could not police or evaluate their performance if he did.

A large general partnership could answer the second and third drawbacks mentioned in the preceding paragraph, but any prudent person would blanch at the prospect of assuming the unlimited liability of a general partner in association with strangers in a field in which the investor is a tyro.

At first glance, a corporation seems to be a viable investment medium. Liability is limited; stockholders do not have to know anything about running the business; the potential for raising capital is unlimited. Unfortunately, corporations are taxpayers in their own right. The tax advantages that the venture is intended to create inure to the corporation, which probably could not use them. A corporation whose shareholders had elected to be taxed under Subchapter S of the Internal Revenue Code could be considered, but the limitation on the number of shareholders and the restrictions on who may be shareholders severely limit the use of such corporations.

11.2.2 Limited Partnerships Fill the Bill

There is a creature of statute, a hybrid of the general partnership and the corporation, that meets all the requirements for the structuring of the tax shelter. The number of investors is not limited, all but one may have his liability limited to the amount of his investment, and the organization, itself not subject to income tax, passes all income, deductions and credits through to its owners with considerable latitude in how it does that. This unincorporated association of two or more persons who carry on a business for profit, is, of course, the limited partnership. Partners may be individuals, trusts, foundations, corporations or other partnerships.

11.2.3 Limitations on the Limited Partner

The limitations on limited partners encompass more than the amount which is at risk. The limited partner must take the role of passive investor; he participates in management at the peril of being held liable as a general partner. Although this prohibition against active management insulates the general partner from perhaps well-meaning but unwelcome meddling, it gives him power that may not be used for the best interests of the limited partners. The limited partners who suspect a conflict of interest or even malfeasance are restrained from taking steps to protect themselves by reluctance to assume general partner liability, especially if the questioned activities have already caused the partnership to list, if not to show signs of sinking.

11.3 HOW TAX SHELTERS ARE SOLD

An individual contemplating investment in, say, real estate, might consider selecting and purchasing property on his own and hiring management to supervise it effectively. He might, but he probably won't. To make a "do it yourself" project out of his investment, he must first locate a property and do a feasibility study to determine the property's potential. If the property seems suitable, he must acquire the building, or build it if it isn't already built, do battle with zoning boards, hire lawyers, find financing, find tenants, maintenance men, gardeners and managers.

11.3.1 Tax Shelters Bring Talent and Money Together

Since few investors would tackle such a project, and even fewer could pull it off, the usual arrangement is that a person or persons with expertise put the deal together and then sell it to potential investors. Depending on the size of the project, the developer may seek investors himself, or the organizers may place the project with a brokerage house to use its considerable contacts to put the package together and sell it.

In the typical large limited partnership tax shelter, a brokerage house (or a joint venture of them) solicits the purchase of partnership interests by its clients. It has found a property and a developer, has hired lawyers, has filed the necessary documents with state and federal securities commissions, and has prepared a prospectus as a necessary selling tool. For its services, the sponsor (broker) will receive an underwriting commission, frequently 8 percent of the price of the unit of partnership interest.

11.3.2 Tax Shelters and the Securities Laws

The federal securities laws consider a partnership interest in a tax shelter offering to be a "security." This means that the sponsor (promoter) must comply with the Securities Act of 1933. The Act requires registration with the Securities and Exchange Commission in Washington of every offer to sell or sale or delivery of a security and of a prospectus relating to a security unless an exemption under the Act is available. The two exemptions cover private offerings or intrastate sales. Private offerings may not be generally advertised or solicited. The issuer of the security must have reason to believe that the person to whom an offer is made is a sophisticated investor or is able to bear the risk of the investment. The Securities Act is very technical and penalties for its violation are severe. Its provisions are beyond the scope of this work; it is sufficient to say here that the issuer or purchaser of a public limited partnership should make himself sufficiently aware of the Act's provisions, as well as those of applicable state securities laws.

The sponsor wants to avoid trouble with the feds; he also wants to keep his customers happy. He recognizes, and his customers should recognize, that every venture has some risk. However, a sponsor (promoter, broker) can minimize risk by exercising "due diligence" to reasonably assure quality in the offering. A sponsor may fulfill his responsibility for due diligence by doing these things:

1. Reviewing the general partner's abilities, strengths, and integrity;
2. Having a review of the economics of the program by outside consultants specializing in real estate, petroleum, or whatever the program invests in;
3. Continually monitoring the program to ensure that no problems develop as the program matures.

After satisfying himself that the program is of a quality suitable for offering to its clients, the sponsor will insist, and the prospectus will cite, that the program is offered only to clients having income or net worth appropriate to the risks inherent in the offering.

11.3.3 The Prospectus of a Tax Shelter

Offers to sell limited partnership interests in tax shelters registered with the Securities and Exchange Commission are made only through a prospectus. The prospectus will contain information on subjects such as:

1. The degree of risk assumed by the investor;
2. A description of the number of partnership shares to be sold;
3. Information about the general partner;
4. A description of the property to be acquired;
5. Method of financing the project ("leverage");
6. How the funds raised will be spent, including sponsor's commission;
7. How profits will be distributed;
8. Conflicts of interest;
9. Tax aspects of the offering;
10. Compensation of the general partner;
11. A description or a copy of the partnership agreement, covering matters like transferability of limited partnership interests or removal of the general partner;
12. Financial statements of the partnership, and;
13. The "track record" of the general partners and promoter.

A prospectus is not light reading. An investor is tempted to rely on the broker's sales pitch and not read the prospectus. The point has already been made that tax-shelter investments are not for the person of limited means. The complexity of reporting income from tax shelters is such that the nuisance of it offsets advantages from a small investment. It follows, then, that a person should not consider investing less than several thousand dollars in a tax shelter; if you are going to invest enough to make it worthwhile, you are going to invest enough to justify diligent study of the prospectus.

11.3.4 Participation in a Tax Shelter May Draw IRS Fire

Another reason for not investing paltry sums in a tax shelter is that you expose your own tax return to audit when you make such an investment. Remember that partnerships pay no income taxes; the IRS, when it adjusts the income of a partnership must go to the returns of the partners to collect the additional tax. Tax-shelter partnerships, by their very nature, push the tax laws to their limits (sometimes beyond the limits). The person who has a substantial income but a minor investment in a particular tax shelter exposes his whole tax picture to audit merely because he is a limited partner. The exposure may be a high price to pay for minimum returns.

11.3.5 Buying Tax Shelters on the Easy Payment Plan

Subscriptions to limited partnership interests are usually payable in full at the time of subscription or in periodic equal installments up to a few months after the effective date of the program.

Some programs with high subscription prices allow investors to pay a part of their total subscription as a down payment and to pay the balance over a specified period of time, from months to years. Sometimes the installments coincide with the time when the project expects to need cash. If, however, the purpose is to make the subscriptions more salable and the money is needed up front, then the partnership must borrow the money, using the subscriptions as collateral. It is not uncommon for the subscriber to be called upon to post collateral or to furnish a bank letter of credit to guarantee his subscription. The bank charges a fee for this service.

Each investor who has not fully paid for his subscription is personally liable for program debt to the extent of his unpaid balance. Under the at-risk limitations of the Internal Revenue Code, the investor's assumption of program debt is considered a contribution of money by the investor, so he is allowed a current deduction for costs associated with the debt.

11.4   ORGANIZATION AND OPERATION OF THE LIMITED PARTNERSHIP

To accomplish its purposes, a limited partnership must be properly organized and operated. Even the highest attainment of tax objectives is for naught if the investors lose all their money. Aside from tax objectives, the purpose of a limited partnership is to achieve maximum profit with minimum liability.

11.4.1 Limited Partners Are Excluded from Management

The price of limited liability is exclusion from management. Under state law, any limited partner who oversteps the legal boundaries of his participation in the operation of the partnership may be stripped of the mantle of limited liability. State courts may hold the partnership to be a general partnership if they determine that it has been improperly formed, structured or managed. Beyond the amount of investment by the limited partners, the general partner takes all the risks. The quid pro quo is that he has the exclusive right to run the business or manage the property. Limited partners, of course, have a right to be kept informed including the right to look at the books and records. Considering the fact that the investment function of the partnership (building the apartments, drilling the well) involves spending huge amounts of money in a short period of time, the financial records will tell what went wrong, but only after it is too late to do anything about it. Even when there is warning of impending trouble, limited partners should consider carefully the risk of being classified as general partners if they attempt to influence the actions of the general partner. The clear warning here is to be very careful in picking the general partner—that is your last chance to control your investment.

11.4.2 Characteristics of the General Partner

The general partner may be an individual who has substantial experience and operating skill. The general partner may be a corporation formed for the sole purpose of being the general partner in this particular limited partnership. Obviously, a new corporation has no experience and no skill. In that case, the investor looks at the record of the individuals who will be officers and directors and of the experts whom it has engaged for marketing studies, site acquisition, architectural, engineering, geological, legal and accounting services. A corporate general partner must have substantial assets (other than its interest in the partnership) which are reachable by creditors of the limited partnership. Revenue Procedure 72-13, CB 1972-1, 735 defines substantial assets and also places limits on the percentage of the corporate general partner's stock which may be owned by the limited partners.

The general partner may be a limited partnership itself.

If the Internal Revenue Service determines that the general partner is a "straw man," it will declare that the partnership is a sham and will declare the entity to be an association taxable as a corporation, with disastrous tax consequences. (See Chapter Two, 2.4)

11.4.3 Compensation of the General Partner

A general partner may receive start-up fees, ongoing fees, and a capital gains split. In addition to compensation received in cash, the general partner may be rewarded for his services by being given an interest in the partnership's profits or capital even though he has contributed no capital. If the partner receives an interest in capital, he has ordinary income to the extent of the value of the capital interest. The regulations imply that there is no taxable income if the interest received for services is an interest in profits only as distinguished from an interest in capital.

In a real estate partnership, the general partner might be paid a commission on the purchase of properties for analyzing, structuring and negotiating investments. He will be entitled to an annual management fee for rendering day-to-day management services for the partnership, to include bookkeeping and preparation of reports. Additionally, he may receive a property management fee similar to that paid to real estate agents for collecting rents and maintaining the property. He may receive a fee similar to that received by real estate agents upon sale of the property.

In any public offering, the sponsor (who might be the general partner) will be paid a commission on the sale of partnership interests. This usually ranges from 7 percent to 8½ percent of the offering price.

In an oil and gas program, the general partner may receive a management fee paid out of initial contributions, or a percentage of gross receipts, or a per-well fee as operator of partnership wells, or some combination of these.

11.4.4 How Costs Are Shared and Deductions Are Allocated in the Real Estate Partnership

The sharing of costs in a typical real estate limited partnership is straightforward; the limited partners pay them all and the general partner doesn't pay any. Here is the way one prospectus says it will spend the money.

Gross offering from proceeds (from sales of limited partner interests)	$12,500,000
Less: underwriting commissions and organizational expenses	375,000
Amount available for investment	$12,125,000
Prepaid expenses, property start-up expenses, reimbursements to general partner for cash advances	$ 6,237,260
Cash payments for equity in property	5,262,740
Real estate commissions	625,000
Proceeds expended	$12,125,000

It is clear from this illustration that the general partner makes only temporary advances which are repaid to him (in this case without interest) from the proceeds of sales to limited partners. The limited partnership illustrated here was formed to acquire unspecified properties so the total purchase price of properties in which an equity would be acquired is not known; the prospectus in the section "Use of Proceeds of Prior Limited Partnerships" indicates that equity usually was 15 percent to 20 percent of property cost.

11.4.5 How Costs Are Shared and Deductions Are Allocated in an Oil and Gas Drilling Program

The situation is different in an oil and gas program. The income tax "quick fix" which the limited partners seek is accomplished by having them pay for and allocating to them the non-capital, currently deductible outlays. The costs allocated to the limited partners are usually referred to as "intangible drilling costs." These are incurred for items that in and of themselves have no salvage value—labor, fuel, hauling and supplies which are used in the drilling, shooting and cleaning of wells, clearing of ground, draining, roads, surveying and geological services, construction of such derricks, tanks, pipelines and other physical structures as are necessary for the drilling of wells and the preparation of wells for the production of oil and gas. Intangible drilling and development costs also include reimbursement of general and administrative overhead of the general partner.

Capital costs include those items that must be capitalized under federal income tax laws, such as depreciable and salvageable equipment on producing wells, including casing, tubing, separating and pumping equipment.

Operating costs include the monthly recurring costs of producing, marketing and transporting as and if and when oil is found.

A study made by a CPA firm and reported in a national magazine shows the typical allocation of costs in a "functional allocation partnership," the type described above as:

Costs	Limited Partners	General Partners
Organization offering costs	100%	none
Management fees	100%	none
Intangible drilling	100%	none
Tangible drilling	none	100%
Post completion costs	60%	40%
Dry hole costs	100%	none

In this example, revenues are allocated 60 percent to limited partners and 40 percent to general partners.

11.4.6 Allocations Should Not Unduly Place General and Limited Partners in Adversary Roles

Some investors, and some sponsors, believe that interests of limited and general partners are likely to be more compatible if the general partner shares in some of the costs which might have been allocated to (and paid by) the limited partners. A prospectus for an oil drilling program provides that the general partner will contribute in cash 10 percent of the capital contributed and that the division of costs and revenues will be:

Costs	Participants	General Partner
Formation fee	90%	10%
Acreage acquisition	90%	10%
Intangible drilling and development costs for drilling and completing wells	90%	10%
Capital costs for drilling and completing wells	90%	10%
Operating costs	75%	25%
General and administrative overhead	75%	25%
All other costs	75%	25%

In this case, income from temporary investment of offering proceeds and from sale of leases would be allocated 90 percent to the participants and 10 percent to the general partner. All other income would be allocated 75 percent to the participants and 25 percent to the general partner. You can see that the bulk of the costs are borne by partners who carry 90 percent of the costs and those same partners get 75 percent of the income. The odds favor the success of the general partner. He, of course, earns this point spread for his services.

11.4.7 How Costs Are Shared and Deductions Are Allocated in an Oil and Gas Income Program

A different cost-showing arrangement is provided for an oil and gas income fund. Such programs buy producing programs and therefore do not incur the intangible drilling costs which are the "big bang" of the tax-shelter program. Promotional literature for one income fund puts it this way:

Question: "If this investment has income, should it be considered a tax shelter?"
Answer: "No, the XXXXX Income Program is not intended to provide significant tax benefits to investors such as those generated by investments commonly known as tax shelters. However, the general partner anticipates that over the life of the partnership there will be some tax benefits generated from operating expenses, depletion, depreciation and availability of investment tax credit, as well as a minimal amount of intangible drilling deductions throughout the property's development phase."

The limited partnership is an appropriate vehicle for an income program, even though it declares that the program is not a tax shelter. This is set forth in one program's promotional literature:

> Question: "Why is XXXXX purchasing income producing properties through limited partnerships?"
> Answer: "Partnerships serve as a means of increasing XXXXX's buying ability in terms of properties offered. In addition, through the partnership sharing arrangements, partnerships provide the company with an opportunity for growth."
> Question: "Why is a limited partnership form used?"
> Answer: "A limited partnership offers to the participant many of the benefits of direct ownership of oil and gas properties, such as taxation only at the partner level and flow-through of depletion. In addition, it affords much of the benefit of limited liability usually present in a corporation."

The difference in emphasis of a drilling program vs. an income program is illustrated in the "Investor Qualifications" required by two offerings:

- Income Fund: Income subject to U.S. taxation at 36 percent or net worth of $100,000
- Drilling Fund: Income subject to U.S. taxation at 54 percent or net worth of $225,000

Clearly, the different funds are aimed at different markets.

With the different emphasis from a drilling fund comes a different division of costs and revenues. One prospectus allocates the 7 percent sales commission to the limited partners' investment and allocates all other costs 15 percent to the general partner (who provided 15 percent of the total after-commissions capital) and 85 percent to the limited partners. All revenues are shared 15 percent-85 percent. Another prospectus shows the contribution of partners in an income fund, for each $10,000 subscribed by limited partners:

Limited partners' subscriptions	$10,000
Less: sales commission	(792)
reimbursement of offering costs and selling expenses	(458)
Limited partners' net subscriptions	8,750
Less: 1% management fee	(100)
General partners' 1% contribution	88
Partnership capital available for producing property transactions	$ 8,738

As you can see, the general partner has put up $88 for each $10,000 of limited partner investment. The general partner pays 10 percent of general and administrative and operating costs and the limited partners pay 90 percent. The partners will split revenues 10 percent-90 percent until such time as the limited partners have received as their share of partnership net revenues an amount equal to 100 percent of their subscriptions to the partnership. Thereafter, 15 percent of costs and revenues shall be allocated to the general partner.

11.4.8 Sharing of Income and Cash Flow

The section on sharing costs included sharing of income in the examples used. In all cases, income is shared according to formula from the first dollar of income to the last.

A variation is the "reversionary interest" method under which the general partner typically pays 1 percent of all costs. Only 1 percent of the revenue would go to the general partner until the limited partners get all their investment money back, after which income is split some other way, such as 80 percent to the limited partners and 20 percent to the general partners. Under the "carried interest" method, the general partner puts up perhaps 1 percent of all costs and gets 10 percent to 15 percent of net revenues from the first. In the "promoted interest" variation, the general partner puts up 5 to 15 percent of total costs and receives 20 to 40 percent of total net revenue from the beginning.

The variety of income-sharing arrangements places the investor in a quandary. There are obvious advantages in having the limited partners who take most of the risks get first priority on the profits, either in timing or in percentage. However, cutting the general partner out of the early returns undeniably dampens his enthusiasm for spending his time or his money on a project that seems to be a poor prospect for a long run.

11.4.9 The General Partner's Potential Conflicts of Interest

The general partner may have allegiances that may make it difficult for him to put the interests of the limited partner investors first. A person may be general partner of several oil and gas programs. When leases are made available to him, he must choose which partnership gets which. He may have a long-time connection with interests that own or hold under lease properties adjacent to that of the limited partnership. Will he use the partnership's funds for the exploratory wells, expecting to drill from the adjacent land when the area is proved? In an oil program where the limited partners have incurred the non-capital drilling costs, the general partner might elect not to incur the capital costs (which he would bear) of a marginal well; to incur the costs would bring some return to the limited partners but would cause him to expend more than he would get back.

In a real estate development, the general partner could have a connection with contractors or others whose interests are adverse to those of the limited partners. He could have a limited partnership incur costs of feasibility studies to determine the suitability of an area, then use the results as a basis for developing, for other interests, a project in the area studied. He could become overextended in the commitment of his time so that he might have to slight one of his projects, or he could favor one project over another at rent-up time. He might base the decision on whether to dispose of a property on the effect of his decision on his future compensation rather than on what is best for his investors.

11.4.10 The Limited Partners' Defense Against Conflict of Interest

Ultimately, the investor must depend on the integrity of the general partner. Besides carefully reviewing his record, the limited partner is advised to look for whatever contractual protection he can get, such as a prohibition of certain activities or relationships, or requiring the general partner also to have limited partnership interests so that his economic interests will be penalized to some extent by having conflicting interests in his two roles. Partnership agreements should have provisions to mitigate conflicts of interest. Additionally, the general partner has a fiduciary duty to act fairly with respect to the limited partners.

11.4.11 Prospectuses Disclose Conflicts of Interest

Concern about conflicts of interest is not a manifestation of paranoia on the part of a timid investor. The fact that it is very real is borne out by the attention devoted to conflicts of interest in a separate section of limited partnership prospectuses. Prospectuses reveal these potential conflicts:

> The feasibility of completion of any well will be determined by the general partner and completion will require further payments to the general partner whether or not the well is profitable.
> The general partner will be a party to several contracts for sale of oil or gas. He may fulfill a contract using the partnership's production when a better price could possibly have been obtained elsewhere.
> The general partner may be the general partner of other limited partnerships and conflicts of interest may arise as to the timing and development of drill site acreage.
> The general partner may transfer to the partnership less than a full working interest in leases; he may transfer the remainder of the interests to outside parties so as to accrue a greater profit.
> The general partner will not devote his (its) exclusive efforts to oil and gas properties in which the partnership participates; it may be

advantageous to him to favor one entity over another since the income participation of the general partner may vary among entities.

11.5 LEVERAGE

"Leverage" refers to the use of borrowed funds to acquire a property much larger than could be obtained if the investors provided the entire capital. Under the income tax laws, general partners are permitted to deduct a share of partnership losses up to the amount of their basis, consisting of their investments plus their shares of partnership debt. Limited partners may add shares of partnership debt only when the debt is "nonrecourse"; that is, no partner is personally liable for the debt. Since deduction of early stage losses is a raison d'être of a tax shelter, maximum borrowing of the nonrecourse kind is very desirable. The term "nonrecourse" generally is not found in prospectuses. The nonrecourse feature is indicated by words like "The remedies of the holder of the Note are limited to the real property subject to an all-inclusive deed of trust."

11.6 ECONOMIC HAZARDS OF A LIMITED PARTNERSHIP INTEREST

A limited partnership is subject to all of the economic hazards to which the business is subject, regardless of its legal form. Competition may be worse than expected; financing may not be available at affordable rates, or may not be available at all; neighborhoods may deteriorate; tenants may be hard to find; environmental problems may be insurmountable; wells may be dry holes; management may be incompetent; construction may incur delays or cost overruns.

Limited partnership interests are not always freely transferable. They may be subject to delays or to a requirement that the general partner consent. Since a sale or exchange of 50 percent or more of the interests in a partnership within a 12-month period will terminate the partnership (Internal Revenue Code Section 708), the general partner may find it prudent to withhold consent under certain conditions. Limited partnership interests may not be assignable to a minor.

Bankruptcy of the general partner will terminate the partnership.

There is almost never a market for limited partnership interests; they are perhaps the most illiquid of assets. Bankers may not welcome them as collateral. Some limited partnerships attempt to mitigate this problem by including a Right of Presentment under which the general partner is required to buy back the limited partner's interest. There are restrictions on such repurchase, including limitation on the volume of repurchase.

It is generally understood that one of the great advantages of a limited partnership is that the liability of the partner other than the general partner cannot exceed his investment; that is, he can't lose more than he put it. This is not necessarily so; some limited partnerships permit additional assessments when things go wrong, and the penalty for not meeting an assessment call is stiff. Even when no right of assessment is provided, if things get bad enough, the limited partners may be faced with the necessity to ante up more capital to keep from losing what they already paid in, with no assurance that the ante won't also go down the drain.

One additional hazard is that the investor's economic or tax needs may change drastically so that the reason for being an investor in the limited partnership has lost its validity. The lack of liquidity prevents him from taking any of the steps he could take with almost any other investment, such as to sell it or to borrow against it.

11.7 OTHER KINDS OF TAX-SHELTER LIMITED PARTNERSHIPS

This chapter has concentrated on the two most common forms of tax shelter, real estate and oil and gas programs. The number and variety of tax shelters is limited, apparently, only by the imagination and selling skills of those who will, for a consideration, bring together those who have money and need tax relief and those who need money and can devise ways to produce tax losses that will either escape the scrutiny of the Internal Revenue Service or, it is to be hoped, survive it.

Other tax-shelter limited partnerships are involved in:

1. Equipment leasing
2. Farming, including cattle feeding and breeding
3. Research and development
4. Movies, books, records, art, tapes
5. Mining, including metals and coal

11.8 CHAPTER ELEVEN REVIEWED

Tax shelters are not for everyone, but any person who pays oppressive income taxes or who expects to be badly hurt by estate taxes and inflation owes it to himself and to those for whom he must provide to find out what a tax shelter offers and the hazards he will face when he seeks its refuge.

He will find that there is a wealth of information available for his guidance in selecting an investment. He should read and ponder and invest with the Latin words "caveat emptor"—let the buyer beware—always in his mind. He must realize that for every opportunity there is a risk. He will be naive if he does not realize that the people with whom he will deal invited him into the shelter for their purposes, which may or may not be compatible with his.

Another Latin phrase, "Semper Fidelis"—always faithful—is the motto of the U.S. Marines who proudly sing of how they landed in Tripoli to put an end to the depredations of Mediterranean pirates. Even at their heyday of preying on American business, the pirates of the Barbary Coast probably never approached the assaults on American wealth now being mounted daily by the twin dangers of taxes and inflation. It is also true that the ethics of some of those who organize and operate tax shelters would be highly admired by the Tripolitanian plunderers.

The investor who prepares himself, who is aware of the opportunities and the hazards, can make tax shelters a productive part of his portfolio.

CHAPTER TWELVE

Income Tax Aspects
Of a Tax-Shelter Partnership

CONTENTS

INTRODUCTION   253

12.1 SAVING TAXES OR DEFERRING TAXES   254

 12.1.1 Deferring Taxes Has the Effect of an Interest-Free Government Loan – 254

 12.1.2 Use of a Partnership Increases the Size of the Government Loan and Has Other Advantages for a Lessor of Equipment – 256

 12.1.3 Equipment Leasing Invites IRS Attack – 258

 12.1.4 Saving Taxes by Changing the Form of Taxation – 258

 12.1.5 Economic Advantages of Real Estate Investment Complement the Tax Advantages – 260

12.2 PASS-THROUGH OF TAX ATTRIBUTES   261

 12.2.1 Partners' Distributive Share Items – 261

 12.2.2 Schedule K-1 Contains Other Information – 262

12.2.3   Disclosure Reveals Adverse Features of a
Tax Shelter – 262

12.3 WHAT TO DO WHEN THE PASS-THROUGH OF
TAX ATTRIBUTES TURNS THE VENTURE INTO A
NEGATIVE TAX SHELTER   264

12.4 AT-RISK RULES   265

12.4.1   At-Risk Rules Prior to 1976 – 265
12.4.2   1978 Changes in the At-Risk Rules – 265
12.4.3   At-Risk Rules Can Have Delayed Effect –
266
12.4.4   Other Effects of the At-Risk Rules – 266
12.4.5   Real Estate and the At-Risk Rules – 267

12.5 PRE-OPENING EXPENSES   268

12.5.1   Organization Expenses, but Not Syndication Expenses Are Amortizable – 268
12.5.2   Construction Period Interest Is Capitalized
and May Be Amortized – 269
12.5.3   Start-up Costs Are Capitalized and May Be
Amortized – 270
12.5.4   Costs of Obtaining Financing Generally
Are Capitalized and May Be Amortized –
270

12.6 A LIMITED PARTNERSHIP RISKS BEING TAXED AS
AN ASSOCIATION   271

12.7 CHAPTER TWELVE SUMMARIZED   272

INTRODUCTION

A person should decide on whether a tax-shelter limited partnership is an investment compatible with his economic circumstances and his financial goals. Simply put, this means: can he afford it and does he have the temperament to make an investment over which he will have no control and which risks being so illiquid that he cannot get out at a time of his choosing?

Only after he answers that question in the affirmative is he ready to consider the tax aspects of the tax-shelter limited partnership. For the right person, the limited partnership is an unmatched vehicle for minimizing or timing the tax impact of a successful venture or using the tax saving to reduce the sting of the dream that turned into a nightmare.

The magic words "tax shelter" account for much, if not most, of the appeal of limited partnerships as investment vehicles. This principal asset of this medium has become its greatest problem, for three reasons:

1. The competition to produce ever greater tax breaks has caused promoters (and participants) to tread ever further onto the thin ice of compliance with the tax laws;

2. The Internal Revenue Service and the Congress, both to curb shady practices and to protect the revenue, have adopted complicated and dangerous restrictions on tax-avoidance practices, and;

3. "Investors" have become so attracted by the tax-savings features that they have embraced schemes which, except for the favorable tax aspects, would be rejected as uneconomic, if not downright fraudulent.

By reducing the maximum tax rate on unearned income from 70 percent to 50 percent, the Economic Recovery Tax Act of 1981 has reduced the tax savings possible through use of a tax shelter and, in theory, should make tax shelters less attractive. A major brokerage firm's newsletter made these observations: "The 70% bite discouraged income-oriented investors while encouraging risk-oriented tax shelters. The 50% maximum will be an incentive to consider investments with good current yields and may well eradicate some of the more exotic tax shelter schemes."

The same newsletter also said: "One of the avowed intentions of the tax law was to avoid or minimize tax "loopholes" and abuses. In general, transactions should have economic merit—that the taxpayer will make money—rather than to be structured strictly to avoid or dodge taxes."

Maybe so. However, little if any lessening of interest in tax shelters is expected. There are several reasons for this, one being that with many

253

people, avoidance of taxes is a fixation; they neither know nor care how much they are saving; the fact that they think they are saving taxes is excuse enough. Another reason is that while a 50 percent rate is less onerous than a 70 percent rate, having the federal and state governments take over half of one's income is not a situation to be taken lying down. A final reason to believe that tax shelters will not go the way of the Edsel is that promoters will be quick to point out that when the tax shelter pays off, the tax bite will be so much lower under the new law.

12.1   SAVING TAXES OR DEFERRING TAXES

12.1.1 Deferring Taxes Has the Effect of an Interest-Free Government Loan

A buy now, pay later philosophy has been characteristic of the American ethic for at least the last forty years. Whatever the fiscal soundness of this philosophy for an individual or a nation, it is a fact that the interest-free use of money is almost as good as owning money.

Sophisticated tax advisors frequently recommend investments as tax shelters with the full knowledge that the investor will pay no less income tax, but that the payment of tax will be deferred for several years so that the investor is in effect making an interest-free loan from Uncle Sam. A very simple illustration can show how this will work. Financier is interested in putting his money out at 10 percent interest. Entrepreneur needs a machine with a 5-year life and is willing to pay 10 percent interest and, since he is not looking for tax deductions, is willing to forego tax advantages that might arise from his ownership of the property. Financier could lend the money and obtain security by taking a chattel mortgage on the machine. If he does, he lends $10,000 and gets back $12,750. His profit, in the form of interest income, is taxed to him (loan made October 1):

First year	$ 247
Second year	886
Third year	712
Fourth year	519
Fifth year	307
Sixth year (9 months)	79
Total	$2,750

Financier looks for an arrangement that gives him the same overall income and the same cash flow, and is told that he can buy the machine and rent it to Entrepreneur for 5 years at $2,550 per year under a net lease, meaning that Entrepreneur maintains and insures the machine and pays property taxes on it. By using accelerated cost recovery system depreciation, Financier creates this taxable income pattern for himself.

	Rent	Deprecia-tion	Taxable Income (Loss)
First year	$ 638	$ 1,500	$ (862)
Second year	2,550	2,200	350
Third year	2,550	2,100	450
Fourth year	2,550	2,100	450
Fifth year	2,550	2,100	450
Sixth year (9 months)	1,912	0	1,912
	$12,750	$10,000	$2,750

The difference in taxable income in the first year is $1,109; Entrepreneur, in the 50 percent tax bracket, defers payment of taxes of $555, money that he can invest to make more money.

Unfortunately for Financier, this scheme won't work. The IRS would hold that, rather than a lease, this transaction is a sale and purchase. The effect of denial of lease status is denial of depreciation deduction and taxation of the interest element as interest. Authority is found in Revenue Ruling 55-540 1955-2 CB 39, which says that the existence of *any* of the six following conditions would cause the transaction to be treated as a sale and purchase:

(a) Portions of the periodic payments are made specifically applicable to an equity to be acquired by the lessee.

(b) The lessee will acquire title upon the payment of a stated amount of "rentals" which under the contract he is required to make.

(c) The total amount which the lessee is required to pay for a relatively short period of use constitutes an inordinately large proportion of the total sum required to be paid to secure the transfer of the title.

(d) The agreed "rental" payments materially exceed the current fair rental value. This may be indicative that the payments include an element other than compensation for the use of property.

(e) The property may be acquired under a purchase option at a price which is nominal in relation to the value of the property at the time when the option may be exercised, as determined at the time of entering into the original agreement, or which is a relatively small amount when compared with the total payments which are required to be made.

(f) Some portion of the periodic payments is specifically designated as interest or is otherwise readily recognizable as the equivalent of interest.

Our example would pass the first five tests, but fail the sixth. Classification of a lease as an operating lease (permitting deduction of rental payments) or as a capital lease (requiring capitalization by the lessee) frequently depends on the lessee's right to acquire the property at a bargain price upon expiration of the lease. Revenue Ruling 55-540 specifically refutes such an argument by saying:

> The fact that the agreement makes no provision for the transfer of title or specifically precludes the transfer of title does not, of itself, prevent the contract from being held to be a sale of an equitable interest in the property.

If the Financier's lease deal had not run afoul of Revenue Ruling 55-540, it would have been even better if he could have claimed investment credit. Since 1971, Internal Revenue Code Section 46(e)(3) has denied investment credit to individuals, partnerships, Subchapter S Corporations and personal holding companies unless the property subject to the lease was manufactured or produced by the lessor; or the term of the lease, including options to renew, is less than 50 percent of the useful life of the property; and during the first year of the lease, the deductions which are allowable to the lessor solely by reason of Section 162 (other than rents), exceed 15 percent of the rental income produced by the property. Since interest, taxes and depreciation are allowable under Sections 163, 164 and 167 respectively, it is hard to find enough Section 162 expenses in a "net lease" to exceed 15 percent of the gross rentals.

Financier did not intend to use borrowed money to leverage the proposed lease. If he had, he would have found that property subject to a net lease (property on which Section 162 expenses do not exceed 15 percent of gross rentals) is, under Internal Revenue Code Section 163(d)(4)(A), held to be investment property and not property held for use in a trade or business. This brings the deduction for interest under the limitation on interest on investment indebtedness and may make the deduction for interest much less desirable.

12.1.2 Use of Large Limited Partnership Permits Tax Advantages That Are Not Feasible for a Smaller Entity

Financier becomes convinced that he can't get the advantages of fast cost recovery and investment credit on an individual lease and that forming a partnership with a few friends to acquire equipment for lease won't improve the prospects. Yet, he recalls seeing advertisements for large tax-shelter limited partnership engaged in equipment leasing. He recognizes that most limited partners would be noncorporate taxpayers, and wonders what magic the large limited partnerships have to get around the rules.

His inquiry leads him to the brochure published by a limited partnership, to this paragraph:

Tax Benefits; Depreciation, Interest Deductions, Investment Tax Credit. Initially, the Partnerships will use accelerated depreciation on equipment and change to the straight line method when it would mean more favorable deductions to investors. In the early years, it is possible that depreciation may generate losses in excess of the "tax-sheltered" distributions which could be used to offset other taxable income.

The Partnerships will borrow approximately one dollar to add to each dollar of investor equity. Interest deductions on these loans will be passed on to the Limited Partners.

Seemingly, the limited partnership offers all three benefits that are denied to Financier as an individual or as a partner in a small entity.

The prospectus provides the answers. It defines leases as; "operating leases," short-term leases under which the lessor will receive aggregate rental payments in an amount that is less than the lessor's purchase price of the equipment, and; "full payout leases," long-term leases under which the noncancellable rental payments due during the initial term of the lease are at least sufficient to recover the purchase price of the subject equipment. It continues to say that, because operating leases are for terms insufficient to recover the purchase price of the equipment, in order to recover a partnership's investment in such equipment the partnership will, on termination of an operating lease, either have to obtain a renewal from the original lessee, find a new lessee, or sell the equipment.

The prospectus further warns that, in order for the limited partners to be eligible to take the investment credit on equipment, the term of the lease must be less than 50 percent of the equipment's useful life, and therefore the partnership cannot give the lessee a renewal option in the original lease. This factor may inhibit customers from entering into leases with a partnership. If the partnership cannot induce the lessee to extend the lease, the partnership may have to find a new customer or sell the property; if obsolescence is severe, this may be very hard to do.

The prospectus warns that Section 162 expenses, including management fees, maintenance costs, insurance, legal fees, supplies and accounting fees, may not exceed 15 percent of gross rental income, throwing the claiming of investment credit into jeopardy and risking treatment of interest expense as investment interest.

It is clear that limited partnerships are subject to the same restrictions as an individual investor or small partnership, restrictions that are sufficient to effectively close the equipment leasing field to the small noncorporate taxpayer. How, then, do they accomplish their purpose?

They do it because their size and structure permit them to do things that the small investor can't do, including:

1. Purchasing in quantity to minimize acquisition costs;

2. Having the sales force to resell lessees upon lease termination, or make some other advantageous disposition of the property;

3. Having enough leases to spread the risk of getting stuck with unwanted equipment;

4. Furnishing enough services to have Section 162 expenses in excess of 15 percent of gross rentals;

5. Better access to financing.

In other words, no magic; just the innate ability of the capitalist free enterprise system to permit marshalling of money and ability for a common good.

12.1.3 Equipment Leasing Partnership Invites IRS Attack

Equipment leasing is one of the tax shelters that gets close surveillance from the Internal Revenue Service. All publicly traded limited partnerships take precautions to assure limited partners that tax results will materialize as predicted. Sometimes, they obtain a ruling from the Internal Revenue Service, at least on the point that the partnership will not be taxed as an association (see Chapter Two of this book). In all cases, legal opinion is obtained as to probable tax consequences. Prospectuses contain the caveat that such opinions are not binding on the Service, that the opinions are based on facts that may change and on law and regulations that may change.

12.1.4 Saving Taxes by Changing the Form of Taxation

Taxes can be saved by paying tax on only part of the income or at a lower rate, even if the gross receipts that appear on the income tax return are the same.

In our preceding simple illustration of Financier and Entrepreneur and their leased machine, there was no opportunity to convert ordinary income into more favorably taxed income or to avoid tax on any part of the income. This is true because Section 1245 of the IRC taxes any part of gain on sale of personal property as ordinary income to the extent that the gain is attributable to depreciation allowed. Only in the unlikely event of selling the machine for more than original cost could Financier obtain capital gain treatment from this transaction.

Real estate leases offer the opportunity to take an ordinary deduction now and to recover the expense later at a capital gains rate. This break comes because, for property acquired before 1981, Section 1250 of the Internal Revenue Code taxes gain on sale as ordinary income only to the extent that accelerated depreciation exceeds straight-line depreciation. We may illustrate the advantage by having Financier obtain a building for $100,000 and net lease it to Entrepreneur for a rental that will give Financier a 10 percent return. Entrepreneur exercises an option to buy the building at the end of 10 years for fair market value as determined by appraisal. For simplicity we ignore nondepreciable land and salvage value. The useful life of the building for tax purposes is 20 years and 150 percent declining balance method is used for tax purposes.

	Rent	Deprecia-tion	Taxable Income
First five years	$ 57,960	$ 32,282	$ 31,840
Second five years	57,960	21,869	36,091
Sub-total		54,151	
(Switch to straight-line depreciation)			
Third five years	57,960	22,925	35,035
Fourth five years	57,960	22,924	35,036
	$231,840	$100,000	$131,840

The advantages to Financier are that he reports taxable income of only $25,678 in the first five years compared to the $47,686 that he would have reported if he had loaned $100,000 to Entrepreneur at 10 percent simple interest, thereby achieving the advantage of keeping the use of his money by deferring payment of income taxes. The second advantage would be in how the proceeds of sale upon exercise of option are taxed:

Sales price	$75,000
Basis ($100,000 − $54,151)	45,849
Gain	29,151
Gain attributable to excess of accelerated over straight-line depreciation	4,151
Gain taxable as long-term capital gain	$25,000

The Economic Recovery Tax Act of 1981 changed the rules to recapture as ordinary income accelerated cost recovery system depreciation in excess of 15-year straight-line taken on residential realty and all accelerated cost recovery system depreciation taken on nonresidential realty. However, with buildings eligible to be written off over 15 years, a taxpayer might decide to forego depreciation at greater than straight-line rates to insure capital gain treatment upon disposition of the property. This is how Financier fares:

	Rent	Deprecia-tion	Taxable Income
First five years	$ 57,960	$ 33,334	$ 24,626
Second five years	57,960	33,333	24,627
Sub-total		66,667	49,253
Third five years	57,960	33,333	24,627
Fourth five years	57,960	0	57,960
	$231,840	$100,000	$131,840

In the first five years, Financier reports taxable income of only $24,626 compared to the $47,686 that he would have reported if he had loaned $100,000 to Entrepreneur at 10 percent simple interest. If Entrepreneur exercises his option to buy the building at the end of ten years for $75,000, Financier's gain is computed:

Sales price	$75,000
Basis ($100,000 – $66,667)	33,333
Long term capital gain	$41,667

This result is an even better deal than Financier would have gotten on a building acquired before 1981.

In this illustration, no money was borrowed. In most cases, real estate deals are financed heavily with borrowed funds. In such cases, a noncorporate partner should be aware that, unless expenses deductible under Internal Revenue Code Section 162 exceed 15 percent of the gross rentals, the property will be considered to be subject to a net lease and the interest expense will be deemed to be investment interest.

12.1.5 Economic Advantages of Real Estate Investment Complement the Tax Advantages

Limited partnerships dealing in rental properties expect to achieve for their investors the benefits which Financier got. Financier, by combining his funds with those of many others, expects to achieve the additional advantages of:

1. Professional management, including enhancement of value by skillful development, maintenance and management
2. Spreading risk over multiple properties or tenants
3. Obtaining leverage benefits of nonrecourse financing

In one of the previous examples, Financier enjoyed a gain of $29,151 on $100,000 invested; in the other, he enjoyed a gain of $41,667 on $100,000, a fine frosting on the cake of his intended 10 percent annual return.

If he had obtained 80 percent financing, he would have invested only $20,000 to achieve these largely capital gains. Promoters of real estate ventures encourage the idea that their expertise and connections will increase the likelihood of sale at a profit through better site selection, construction economies, more favorable financing, better management and adroit terms of sale. Against this, Financier must weigh the sales commission, the general partner's compensation, and the risks of conflict of interest between general partner and limited partners.

12.2 PASS-THROUGH OF TAX ATTRIBUTES

The most obvious tax advantage of a partnership over other forms in which business might be transacted is that a partnership pays no income taxes; all items of income, deduction, or credit are passed through to the partners for inclusion on their returns. These items may be allocated in any manner upon which the partners agree, providing that the allocation has substantial economic effect. (See Chapter Four, 4.8.6.)

12.2.1 Partner's Distributive Share Items

A glance at Schedule K-1, Internal Revenue Form 1065, Partner's Share of Income, Credits, Deductions shows the distributive share items of particular interest to a tax-shelter limited partnership. These include:

- Net short-term gain (loss)
- Net long-term capital gain (loss)
- Oil and gas depletion
- Property qualified for investment credit
- Property used in computing a prior year investment credit (recapture)

In addition to the items listed above, there is, of course, the allocation of ordinary income. The determination of ordinary income can be made only after the partnership has made many elections, presumably selecting the treatment most advantageous to the partners. These include:

- Cash or accrual method of accounting
- Straight-line or accelerated method of depreciation
- Election to amortize organization expenses
- Election to claim fast write-off of restoration of historic structures
- Ownership or leasing of buildings and equipment
- Contracting out or in-house performance of functions

An investor, with the help of appropriate counsel, should select a tax-shelter partnership investment after considering the partnership's management and accounting policies and its tax elections to be sure that they are compatible with the aims of the investor.

12.2.2 Schedule K-1 Contains Other Information

The partnership is required to inform the Internal Revenue Service of several other matters. The purpose of this disclosure is to be sure the partner (and the government) are informed about items that might limit the partner's deduction of his share of partnership deductions. Schedule K-1 contains information concerning:

- Basis and "booked" value of property contributed by a partner, or distributed to a partner
- Changes in the partner's interest in capital or profits
- Partner's share of partnership liabilities, divided between recourse and nonrecourse
- Tax preferences, including accelerated depreciation, depletion, and excess intangible drilling costs
- Interest on investment indebtedness
- Excess expenses from net lease property

12.2.3 Disclosure Reveals Adverse Features of a Tax Shelter

The purpose of such disclosure is to make sure that the partner is aware not only of the tax attributes that made the partnership attractive to him, but also that he knows when the tide has turned against him and reports the adverse effects of a tax shelter, particularly as the tax shelter matures and becomes more like a leaky roof. The adverse features of a tax shelter that has outlived its usefulness include:

- Taxable income exceeding cash flow (the depreciation has all been used up)
- Ordinary income resulting from sales at a profit when profit is attributable to depreciation of personal property or accelerated depreciation of real property
- Taxation of previously deducted losses (because basis is reduced by partnership retirement of its debt)

Use of financing, particularly nonrecourse financing, is the mainstay of the real estate tax shelter. It is also the source of at least two of the adverse features just mentioned. For example, a real estate limited partnership might be put together to construct an apartment project that will cost

$1,000,000 with 80 percent financing. Rents are to cover debt service on a 10 percent mortgage ($92,642 per year), operating expenses and a 20 percent return on a partner's investment. Assuming operating expenses of $100,000 per year, gross rent must be $232,642 per year, and cash flow will be $40,000 per year. We use a 15-year life and assume the entire investment is depreciable at straight-line rates. Net income is figured this way:

	Gross Rents	Operating Expenses	Deprecia- tion	Interest	Taxable Income (Loss)
First five years	$1,163,210	$ 500,000	$333,334	$ 381,018	$(51,142)
Second five years	1,163,210	500,000	333,333	328,010	1,867
Third five years	1,163,210	500,000	333,333	240,778	89,099
Fourth five years	1,163,210	500,000		103,034	560,176
	$4,652,840	$2,000,000	$1,000,000	$1,052,840	$600,000

In this illustration, cash flow at $40,000 per year, or $200,000 for the last five years, would not be adequate to pay income taxes of $308,097 which would be imposed on taxpayers in a 10 percent state and 50 percent federal tax bracket.

Much to his surprise, a partner can have taxable income when there is no income or loss to the partnership passed through to him. This occurs when the partner loses basis because partnership liabilities have been reduced. The 10 percent partner has these facts:

Purchase price of	$ 10,000
Partner's share of partnership liabilities	90,000
Basis of partners interest available for deduction of losses	100,000
Partner's share of losses in 1 -3	100,000
Partner's basis at end of year 3	$ -0-

In year 4, the partnership breaks even and makes no distribution to partners, but uses favorable cash flow to reduce the debt. This partner's share of the reduction in debt is $8,000. Under IRC Section 752(b) a decrease in the partner's share of the liabilities of the partnership is considered as a distribution of money to him. Under IRC Section 731(a)(1) a distribution of money to a partner, to the extent that the distribution exceeds the adjusted basis of his interest in the partnership, causes income, usually taxed as capital gain.

In this instance, the receipt of $8,000 taxable income was triggered by the reduction of debt by action of the partnership. The partner could, by his own action, cause a reduction of debt. He could despair of the interest ever panning out and sell to the partnership or to someone else for $10,000, thinking that he has merely recouped his investment and has broken even; not so. He has received $10,000 actual cash and a constructive distribution of $90,000 so that his gain is $100,000. He should note that he has received deductible ordinary losses of $100,000 at a cost of capital gain taxation of $100,000, which is not a bad deal.

12.3   WHAT TO DO WHEN THE PASS-THROUGH OF TAX ATTRIBUTES TURNS THE VENTURE INTO A NEGATIVE TAX SHELTER

The ideal tax shelter throws off cash plus tax deductions. A less successful shelter throws off deductions, with the cash going to reduce debt. A venture that throws off little or no cash and produces taxable income is a leaky shelter indeed. Before that stage is reached, the clever investor will have located the exits.

It is basic to the use of tax shelters that the investor doesn't stay aboard until the property is fully depreciated or the mortgage is paid off. He bails out when the large tax deductions taper off, hopefully at capital gain rates. However, IRC Section 1250 provides that gain, to the extent that it is due to depreciation in excess of straight-line, is taxable as ordinary income for real estate acquired before 1981. For real estate acquired after 1980, if the accelerated method is used, all or part of any gain on disposition may be ordinary income. If the straight-line method is used, all gain on disposition will be capital gain. The investor should seriously consider limiting himself to partnerships that will elect straight-line depreciation if capital gains are a principal objective.

The smart investor can improve his position by being alert to a future need to dump a tax shelter and do it at a time most advantageous (or least disadvantageous) to him. A taxpayer may find himself in a loss or low-income year, or may have an expiring contribution carryover. He has the opportunity to "create" income by disposing of his tax shelter.

The peculiarities of the alternative minimum tax provide an interesting opportunity to "create" income to be taxed at 25 percent when it would otherwise be taxed at 50 percent. Von Trapt is in a shelter that has richly blessed him with ordinary deductions but is about to start giving his losses back to him as ordinary income. For the current year he anticipates low ordinary income but also a capital gain large enough to invoke alternative minimum tax. It is a fact that when alternative minimum tax applies, additional income costs only a 25 percent tax. Since Von Trapt's accountant has already determined that this situation exists, he suggests that Von Trapt dispose of his tax shelter in this year.

A taxpayer pursuing such a strategy should realize that paying a tax now, even at 25 percent, may be a poor bargain if the time at which tax at 50 percent might have been payable is so deferred that the interest value of the money spent before it had to be paid has eaten up the tax saving. He also should determine that he will not incur investment credit recapture which could have been avoided by delaying the disposition. A compromise move would be disposition of less than one-third of the partnership interest, achieving almost one-third of the desired tax benefit but no recapture.

12.4   AT-RISK RULES

12.4.1 At-Risk Rules Prior to 1976

Prior to the Tax Reform Act of 1976, investors in tax shelters could, through the medium of nonrecourse financing, increase the basis of their partnership interests and use that basis to permit deduction of losses far in excess of the actual investment made or risk taken. The Revenue Act of 1976 ended that opportunity for some taxpayers by limiting the deduction for losses on four kinds of investment to the amount that the investor had paid in or for which he was personally liable—called the amount "at-risk"—in four areas of investment.

1. Holding, producing or distributing motion picture films or tapes;
2. Certain kinds of farming;
3. Leasing any personal property subject to depreciation recapture;
4. Exploring for, or exploiting, oil and gas resources as a trade or business or for the production of income.

IRC Section 465, which added these "at-risk" provisions to the Code, did not cover the holding of real property for use in a trade or business or for the production of income. Also, the restriction applied only to taxpayers other than corporations that were not exempt from tax under Subchapter S or were personal holding companies. Therefore, Section 465 applied to all partners except "regular" corporations.

12.4.2 1978 Changes in the At-Risk Rules

In 1978, the Code was changed to apply the at-risk rules to any activity engaged in by a taxpayer in carrying on a trade or business or for the production of income, except that the holding of real property continued to be exempt from the at-risk rules. This permits the continued use of nonrecourse financing for real estate ventures. The 1978 amendments added corporations in which five or fewer individuals own more than 50 percent of the stock to the "tainted" investor class.

Investors in tax-shelter partnerships dealing in other than real estate need to be familiar with the limitations imposed by the at-risk rules. Investors are at-risk for an activity to the extent of their cash, the adjusted basis of other property contributed to the operation, and for loans on which they are either personally liable or for which they have pledged property other than property used in the activity. A taxpayer is not considered to be at-risk on loans from related parties or from a person who has an interest in the activity.

12.4.3 At-Risk Rules Can Have Delayed Effect

As usual, there are traps for the unwary in the form of recapture of deductions previously taken. This occurs when the amount at-risk has been lowered. This could come about by distributions to the investor, a switch from recourse to nonrecourse debt, or commencement of a guarantee of the investor's debt. Two simple stories illustrate how recapture can occur.

Mervin puts $50,000 cash into a business subject to the at-risk rules. His share of losses is $40,000. The business distributes $15,000 to Mervin. His at-risk amount has dropped to $10,000 before the distribution so he is required to pay income tax on $5,000.

Erven puts $10,000 cash into a business subject to the at-risk rules and raises another $10,000 worth of capital with recourse debt. Erven deducts $12,000 of losses in the business' first two years. In the third year, Erven manages to convert the debt, which is still $10,000, into nonrecourse debt. His amount at-risk has dropped to $10,000, so the $2,000 by which losses deducted ($12,000) exceed the $10,000 still at-risk becomes taxable income.

12.4.4 Other Effects of the At-Risk Rules

A loss deduction that has been recaptured is a suspended deduction that may be taken in a succeeding taxable year to the extent that the at-risk amount is restored.

In any taxable year, deductions are not disallowed to the extent that there is income from the activity.

The determination of the amount the partner-taxpayer is at-risk in cases where the activity is engaged in by a partnership is made as of the close of the taxable year of the partnership.

The provisions of Section 465 and the Regulations thereunder are intended only to limit the extent to which certain losses in connection with covered activities may be deducted in a given year by a taxpayer. Section 465 does not apply for determining the adjusted basis of a partner's interest in a partnership.

An amount is not at-risk to the extent the taxpayer is protected against economic loss by an agreement or arrangement for compensation or reimbursement to him of any loss which he may suffer. Therefore, a partner is not at-risk with respect to any partnership liability to the extent the partner would be entitled to contributions from other partners if the partner were called upon to pay the partnership's debt.

The amount at-risk in an activity of a partner who lends the partnership money for use in the activity shall be increased by the amount by which that partner's basis in the partnership is increased under Regulation 1.752-1(e) due to the incurrence by the partnership of that liability. The amount at-risk of any other partners shall not be increased as a result of the loan.

The incurrence by a partnership of debt for which none of the partners is personally liable and for which assets used outside the activity have not been pledged as security does not increase the partners' amount at risk. Fairly enough, repayment of such debt by the partnership does not decrease the partner's amount at-risk.

Section 465 had no bearing upon the allowability of investment credit or upon the determination of basis of depreciable property. The Economic Recovery Tax Act of 1981 provides that no investment credit will be allowed to partners or partnerships for amounts invested in qualifying property to the extent the amounts invested are not at-risk.

The disallowance of deductions under Section 465 cannot be circumvented by shams such as putting in money to increase the amount at-risk just before the end of the year and pulling it out just after the new year begins.

12.4.5 Real Estate and the At-Risk Rules

The holding of real estate is excluded from the at-risk rules. However, when a trade or business involves both the holding of real property and the provision of personal property and services that aren't incidental to making the real property available as living accommodations, (example; a restaurant or casino in a hotel), the holding of the realty will be treated as a separate activity to which the at-risk rules do not apply while the other activities will be treated as an activity to which they do apply. The taxpayer will have to allocate income and deductions among the activities.

Proposed Regulation 1.465-42 makes an interesting distinction between an individual investment in an activity falling under Section 465 and a similar investment by a partnership. An individual taxpayer's interest in several motion picture films or video tapes is considered a separate activity in each so that the individual has a separate Section 465(d) loss and a separate amount at-risk with respect to each film. In the case of a partnership, all films and video tapes in which the partnership has an interest are considered as one activity of the partnership.

12.5 PRE-OPENING EXPENSES

Since the object of a tax shelter is obtaining the fastest possible write-off of deductions attributable to the property, an investor must know the rules for expensing, amortizing or capitalizing costs incurred before the property becomes operational. Such costs include:

- Organization expenses
- Selling and syndication expenses
- Construction period interest
- Start-up costs
- Cost of negotiating and obtaining loans

12.5.1 Organization Expenses, but Not Syndication Expenses Are Amortizable

Organization and syndication expenses are covered in Subchapter K, the partnership section of the Internal Revenue Code. Section 709 provides that organization expenses may be deducted ratably over a period of sixty months or more beginning with the month in which the partnership begins business. If the partnership is liquidated before the end of the sixty-month period, the undeducted balance of organization expenses may be deducted at the time of liquidation.

Syndication fees are not deductible when incurred, and they may not be amortized.

The Committee Report ('76 Tax Reform Act – P.L. 94-455 10-4-76) distinguishes between organization and syndication expenses in these comments:

> The organizational expenses subject to the 60 month amortization provision are defined as those . . . incident to the creation of the partnership, chargeable to the capital account, and of a character which, if expended in connection with the creation of a partnership having an ascertainable life, would be amortized over that period of time.
>
> The capitalized syndication fees, i.e., the expenditures connected with the issuing and marketing of interests in the partnership, such as commissions, professional fees, and printing costs, are not to be subject to the special 60 month amortization provision.

The proposed regulations expand on the Committee Report's definitions:

> The following are examples of organizational expenses within the meaning of section 709 and this section: Legal fees for services incident to the organization of the partnership, such as negotiation and preparation of a partnership agreement; accounting fees for establishing a partnership accounting system; and necessary filing fees. The following are examples of expenses that are not organizational expenses within the meaning of section 709 and this section: Expenses connected with acquiring assets for the partnership or transferring assets to the partnership; expenses connected with a contract relating to the operation of the partnership trade or business (even where the contract is between the partnership and one of its members); and syndication expenses.
>
> Syndication Expenses. Syndication expenses are expenses connected with the issuing and marketing of interests in the partnership. Examples of syndication expenses are brokerage fees; registration fees; legal fees of the underwriter or placement agent and the issuer (the general partner or the partnership) for securities advice and for tax advice pertaining to the adequacy of tax disclosures in the prospectus or placement memorandum; accounting fees for preparation of representations to be included in the offering materials; and printing costs of the prospectus, placement memorandum, and other selling and promotional material. These expenses are not subject to the election under Section 709(b) and must be capitalized.

12.5.2 Construction Period Interest Is Capitalized and May Be Amortized

Construction period interest and taxes must be capitalized as required by IRC Section 189. Section 189 permits such costs to be amortized over a period of from four to ten years, depending on when the costs are incurred and the type of property involved.

The fact that Section 189 requires "individuals" to capitalize construction period interest and taxes and goes on to say that electing small business corporations and personal holding companies are treated as "individuals" has caused some to question whether partnerships come under Section 189. After all, you may ask, Congress used the word "individuals" instead of the usual "taxpayers" and specifically included Subchapter S corporations, corporations that are taxed much like partnerships. Why then did it not specifically mention partnerships if it intended to bring them within the reach of Section 189? Wording in the report of the Staff of Joint Committee on Taxation 94th Congress, plus the fact that partnerships pass taxation on to their partners, leads to the conclusion that to the extent that individuals are partners, Section 189 is effective and to the extent that regular corporations are partners, Section 189 is not effective.

Example: Executive Office Park, a limited partnership, incurs $100,000 construction period interest and taxes prior to completion of its office park late in 1983. Interest expense is allocated to limited partners. Corporate partners hold 50 percent of the partnership interests and individuals own the rest. The corporate partners may deduct $50,000 interest expense for their return year which includes December 31, 1983. Individual partners may deduct their pro rata shares of $5,000 in each year 1983 through 1992.

12.5.3 Start-Up Costs Are Capitalized and May Be Amortized

Start-up costs have triggered controversy between taxpayers who wanted deductions for expenses incurred during the construction or rent-up period and the Internal Revenue Service which held that Section 162's allowance of deduction for expenses incurred in carrying on a trade or business required that there be a going concern, not one which was preparing to get going. The courts supported the IRS in several cases. Congress ended the controversy in 1980 by adding Section 195 to the Code to permit an election to amortize start-up expenditures over a period of not less than sixty months, beginning with the month in which the business began. Start-up expenditures are defined in Section 195 as any amount paid or incurred in connection with investigating the creation or acquisition of an active trade or business or creating an active trade or business and which, if paid or incurred in connection with the expansion of an existing trade or business in the same field would be allowable as a deduction for the taxable year in which paid or incurred.

12.5.4 Costs of Obtaining Financing Generally Are Capitalized and May Be Amortized

Since maximum leverage is an integral part of so many tax shelters organized as partnerships, the deductibility of costs of obtaining that financing is an important consideration. These costs will be discussed in three categories:

- Costs of negotiating and obtaining the loan
- Commitment fees
- Points

Costs of negotiating and obtaining loans include legal fees and title insurance, appraisal and survey fees, brokerage fees and government agency fees such as FHA, GNMA (Ginny Mae) fees and FNMA (Fannie Mae) fees. Such costs are payments for services and are not deductible as interest. They must be capitalized and amortized over the life of the loan.

Example: The developers of Hazy View Apartments, a limited partnership, arranged financing for $4,155,000. Of this, $3,700,000 was expended for land, site improvements or building, and $155,000 was retained for working capital for the rent-up period. The sum of $400,000 was deducted by the lender and the broker who arranged the thirty-year mortgage loan for commission and legal and other costs. The developers' accountant turns to his *Prentice-Hall Federal Tax Handbook* and finds "commissions, fees and printing costs paid in one year by a taxpayer in securing a loan for 10 or 15 years covered by a mortgage on property to be leased are deductible ratably over the period of the loan, even though the taxpayer's accounts are kept and the return made on the cash basis." What, he asks, does "ratably" mean? The dictionary says "proportionately.' Does that mean in proportion to the principal balance outstanding, a sort of "rule of 78"? This would bunch the write-off in the early years, a desirable conclusion; or proportionately to principal payments, delaying the deduction to the later years. Further research shows that "ratably" means straight-line over the life of the loan. In this example, the amortization deduction is $13,333.33 per year. If the debt is retired after 10 years, the unamortized balance of $266,666.70 is charged off in the year of retirement.

Commitment fees are paid to the lender for making money available for financing. Although commitment fees are not deductible as interest, they are deductible when paid or accrued as business expenses under Internal Revenue Code Section 162 or as investment expenses under Section 212.

"Points" are a discount exacted by the lender; the lender takes a note and mortgage for $100,000, but advances only $97,000. If the lender renders services for the points, it is clear that the points must be amortized over the life of the loan. If, however, services are charged for separately, and it can be established that the points are solely for use of money or forbearance, then the loan charge may be deductible as interest in full in the year paid or accrued.

12.6   A LIMITED PARTNERSHIP RISKS BEING TAXED AS AN ASSOCIATION

Chapter Two, section 2.4 of this book warns that a partnership may so nearly resemble a corporation that it is taxed as an association; that is, it is taxed on its income at corporate rates. Promoters of tax-shelter partnerships are acutely aware of this danger, realizing that such classification or reclassification would destroy all of the advantages for which the medium of the limited partnership was chosen.

The investor should look in the "Tax Aspects" of the prospectus for a statement that a ruling as to partnership status has been obtained from the Internal Revenue Service, or that an opinion of legal counsel has been obtained. The Service, of course, may not concur in the opinion of counsel. An additional risk is that the economic situation may shift so that a partnership that was not classed as an association may develop too many corporate characteristics. Among the inadvertent changes that may threaten taxation as an association is that of financial reverses of a corporate general partner so severe that it no longer has sufficiently substantial net worth to meet the requirement of "substantial assets which could be reached by a creditor of the limited partnership."

12.7   CHAPTER TWELVE SUMMARIZED

The dictionary defines "shelter" as "something beneath, behind or within which a person, animal or thing is protected from storms, missiles, etc; refuge." Primitive man built huts to protect himself from the elements and built simple fences to prevent marauding animals from carrying off his meager possessions. Medieval man constructed moats and battlements to protect himself and his property from other men bent on taking away what he had accumulated. Modern man, armed with the most sophisticated technological and financial skills, has learned how to accumulate wealth of which his ancestors did not even dream. Alas, changes in technology or financial conditions can strip him of his possessions or destroy their value faster than the marauders of old could render his ancestors destitute. Worse yet, the modern tax system is as confiscatory as any assessment made by the publican or seigneur of old.

The investor now has to protect himself from inflation and from his own ineptitude in carrying out investment plans. If he saves the fruit of his labors from those perils, he must still face the insatiable demands of a tax system designed not only to meet the fiscal demands of government but also to distribute the wealth for supposed social gains.

Primitive man built his kraals and Middle Ages man erected his fortifications after giving consideration to the amount and value of his possessions and to the size, cunning, and ferocity of the attacker. This strategy decrees that the investor of the 1980s must carefully consider what he is trying to protect—usually his income or his estate—and the violence of the assault upon him, usually expressed as a rate of tax.

The attack on the tax shelter involves more than the frontal assault of high tax rates. The designer of the shelter must be alert to attacks on his flank, from the directions of denying him a deduction because he has an insufficient amount at-risk. He must be ready for the siege tactic of allowing him his deduction for early-period expenses, but allowing them only over a period of years so long that the tax deduction is starved of its value.

Just as defense tactics evolve to meet new military weapons, tax strategists must be prepared for changes in the tax and economic climate. Lower tax rates and lower inflation will remove some of the urgency and the appeal from tax-shelter planning of the past few years. However, the most likely scenario is that taxes and inflation will still consume more of the higher-bracket taxpayer's income and estate than will any other expense. The need for good tax planning will abate hardly at all.

APPENDIX A

Sample Partnership Agreement: Professional Partnership

This sample partnership agreement illustrates terms under which a group of professionals may pool their resources and talents to form and operate a professional practice. A more detailed sample agreement for a professional partnership will be found in the *Management of an Accounting Practice Handbook* published by the American Institute of Certified Public Accountants.

Agreement made and entered into this _____ day of _____, 19XX among _____ of _____, _____; _____ of _____, _____ and _____ of _____, _____.

Article 1

Name of the Partnership

The name of the partnership is _____, _____, and _____, Certified Public Accountants. Upon the death or permanent retirement from public practice of any of the partners whose names appear in the firm name, the remaining partners may continue to use the name of the deceased or retired partner as part of the name of this partnership. If a partner withdraws from the partnership for any reason other than permanent retirement or death his name shall be removed from the firm name. The name of the firm may be changed by agreement of a two-thirds majority of the partners.

Article 2

Address of the Partnership

The principal address of the partnership is _____, _____, _____.

275

Article 3

Business of the Partnership

The business of the partnership is the practice of public accounting, including the ownership of real or personal property to be used in the partnership business.

Article 4

Term

The partnership shall commence on _____ , 19XX, and shall continue until dissolved.

Article 5

Termination of the Partnership

The partnership may be dissolved at any time by agreement of the partners, in which event the partners shall proceed to promptly liquidate the business of the partnership. The assets of the partnership shall be used and distributed in the following order:

a. to pay or to provide for the payment of all partnership liabilities and for the expenses of liquidating the partnership;

b. to pay to partners any undrawn shares of partnership income;

c. to equalize the capital accounts of the partners.

Article 6

Management

Except when the express terms of this agreement require that decisions shall be made by votes of the partners, the management of the firm is vested in the managing partner. Unless specified otherwise in this agreement, all decisions to be made by the partnership shall be made upon a majority vote of the partners, with votes based on units of participation as specified in Article 10, or by a two-thirds majority vote of the partners. A successor may be elected for a definite or indefinite term.

The managing partner shall make every reasonable effort to keep each partner advised of all pending problems, prospective decisions, and actions taken.

The partners shall meet at regular intervals, and may meet at other times upon the call of the managing partner. The managing partner shall call special meetings upon the demand of any two partners. The managing partner shall give reasonable notice of regular or special meetings and the call shall give notice of the substance of any matter expected to require a vote of the partners.

At each meeting of the partners every partner shall have one vote for each unit of participation held by him. A quorum shall exist if partners holding a majority of such units are present in person or voting by proxy or by written instructions. Any partner shall have the right to object to the holding of any meeting when he must be absent because of serious illness or because of a scheduling conflict which he cannot resolve with reasonable effort. No business shall be transacted at any meeting which is held over the objection of any partner unless the partners determine by a two-thirds majority vote that the stated business shall be transacted.

At any meeting only the votes of those present and voting or voting by proxy or written instructions shall be counted to determine whether a required majority vote has been cast.

Article 7

Accounting and Records

The partnership shall maintain proper and complete books of account on the cash receipts and disbursements method of accounting, open to inspection at any time by any of the partners or the legal representatives of any of the partners. The accounting year shall begin on January 1 and shall end on December 31.

A partner who withdraws from the firm under any conditions under which he will not receive guaranteed payments shall be entitled to have custody of client files appropriate to clients who will continue to be served by him.

Partnership books and records shall remain in the custody of the partnership but shall be available to former partners at reasonable times for reasonable purposes.

Client files must be maintained for the benefit of all persons who have been partners during any year affected by the files. Client files must be maintained in their original form for a reasonable length of time, not to exceed four years from the time the documents therein were created. Files in their original form or on microfilm or microfiche must be maintained for an additional three years.

Article 8

Bank Accounts

The partnership shall maintain a bank account or bank accounts in such bank or banks as may be agreed upon by the partners. Checks shall be drawn on the partnership bank account for partnership purposes only and shall be signed by any partner.

Article 9

Capital

The capital of the partnership shall be contributed in cash by the partners as follows: _____ $25,000

——————— $25,000
——————— $25,000

The total capital of the partnership shall be maintained at a level adequate for the reasonable needs of the partnership as determined by a majority vote of the partners. A separate capital account shall be maintained for each partner. The capital required from each partner shall be in proportion to his voting units as specified in Article 10. A partner shall be entitled to be paid interest monthly on his capital account at the rate of ——% per annum, and such interest shall be considered to be a distribution of the profits of the partnership.

Upon the withdrawal of a partner for any reason, he or his heirs or assigns shall be paid the balance in his capital account in 36 equal monthly installments without interest, the first such payment being due on the first day of the second month after the month in which the withdrawal occurs.

A newly admitted partner shall be permitted to pay in the amount of capital required over a period not to exceed —— years and his minimum contribution to capital for each of the three years shall be ——% of his income from the partnership.

Article 10

Profit and Loss

The net profits of the partnership shall be divided among the partners on the basis of the units of participation specified in this Article. The profits and losses of the partnership shall be determined in the manner in which the partnership reports its income and expenses for federal income tax return purposes except that partners' salaries, interest on capital accounts, contributions and any other expenses not deemed to be expenses for federal income tax returns shall be expenses for the purpose of determining profits and losses of the partnership.

An individual drawing account shall be maintained for each partner and profits or losses shall be credited or debited to the individual drawing accounts as soon as practicable after the close of each year. Credit balances shall be distributed to partners within ten days after determination that a credit balance exists. The partners may, by majority vote, decide to make distributions at any time from reasonably anticipated profits. Debit balances shall be removed by payment within ten days after it is determined that a debit balance exists. Debit balances remaining after the expiration of the ten days shall bear interest at the prime rate in effect at the ——————— National Bank of ——————— on the date on which restitution became due.

Partners shall receive salaries, including bonuses, in amounts which are determined from time to time by a majority vote of the partners. Regular salaries shall be paid on the last business day of each month. Bonuses to partners shall be paid within ten days of their award.

Units of participation in profits and losses shall be awarded by a two-thirds majority vote of the partners based on one unit per $100 of required capital. Increases in individual capital accounts required by changes in units of participation shall be paid within ten days of the award of additional units. Decreases in capital accounts caused by changes in units of participation shall be paid to partners within ten days of the reduction in number of units

Article 11

Expenses Incurred by Partners

Each partner agrees to provide himself with an automobile and to use it as necessary in the performance of his duties. He agrees to obtain and pay premiums on liability insurance in the amount of coverage set by the partners. A partner shall be reimbursed for automobile expenses directly incurred in carrying on his practice at the rate set by the Internal Revenue Service in effect at the time the travel is incurred.

A partner may be reimbursed for expenses incurred in carrying on his practice. A partner must retain documentation required by the Internal Revenue Service for travel and entertainment expenses. Any expense that is not allowed as a tax deduction shall be allocated to the partner responsible for incurring the expense and shall be charged against his share of distributive income.

It is agreed that a partner may incur expenses that he deems to be appropriate in carrying on his practice but for which he will not be reimbursed by the partnership. Such expenses include part of automobile expenses, home telephone, dues in other than professional and trade societies and house charges of social clubs.

Article 12

Admission of Partners

A person may become a partner in this firm upon election by 75 percent of votes of all partners. For this purpose each partner has an equal vote. Admission of a partner shall be effected by an amendment to this agreement and a vote for admission of the proposed partner is signified by affixing one's signature to the amendment. The amendment shall specify the initial capital requirement of the new partner and shall specify the profit sharing units initially allocated to him.

An applicant for admission as a partner must hold a valid certificate and/or license to practice as a Certified Public Accountant in some state in which this firm has an office.

An amendment to this agreement to admit a new partner may be presented to the partners for signature thirty days after all partners have been notified in writing that the person will be proposed for partnership.

Article 13

Withdrawal and Retirement

A partner may withdraw from the partnership upon reasonable notice to the firm, which will not be required to exceed ninety days. If the withdrawing partner continues in the practice of public accountancy and maintains an office within fifty miles of any office of this firm, or opens such an office within two years of withdrawal, he shall be assessed the costs associated with his withdrawal, including a reasonable allowance for personnel costs for all persons except himself. If the withdrawing partner and the remaining partners are unable to agree on the amount of costs, the withdrawing partner shall forfeit or repay one half of his capital account in lieu of any other determination of costs There shall be no assessment of costs in any case wherein partners holding more than twenty five percent of the units of profit sharing withdraw simultaneously or within such a period of time that the withdrawals may reasonably be assumed to have been in concert.

A partner may retire on any December 31 after his 60th birthday and must retire not later than the last day of the calendar year in which he reaches age 65. A partner retiring under this provision at any time before the date on which he must retire shall give at least sixty days notice of his intention to retire.

A retired partner may request or be requested to remain with the firm as a consultant. Terms of the employment must be approved by a 75 percent majority vote of the continuing partners.

A partner must retire when he is unable because of physical or mental illness to perform the duties of a partner and it is probable that such illness will be permanent. If any partner, including the partner whose disability is being considered objects to a partner retiring or being required to retire for disability then a determination of disability may be made upon a 75 percent majority vote of all partners except the partner whose disability is being considered. A medical certification of permanent disability must be furnished to the partnership before a vote on disability may be taken.

In the event of partial or extended nonpermanent disability, the requirements for active participation in the affairs of the partnership set forth in this Article may be waived by a majority vote of all partners except the partner whose disability is being considered.

Withdrawal or retirement of a partner will not cause dissolution of the partnership.

Article 14

Payments to Retiring or Deceased Partners

The salary of a partner who becomes sick or disabled shall not be reduced for ninety days after onset of the disability. If he is unable to resume at least two-thirds of his normal schedule after ninety days salary continuation, his salary shall be reduced by one half until such time as he returns to a normal work schedule or the passage of six months. After the expiration of six months at half salary, salary payments shall cease and payment of his capital account shall commence.

In addition to payment of his capital account, a retired or deceased partner shall be paid guaranteed payments (as defined in Section 736(a) of the Internal

Revenue Code). Each monthly guaranteed payment shall be one one hundred twentieth (1/120) of the lesser of:

1. The sum of all of his salary and bonus payments for the three (3) years preceding the year of retirement or death, or;

2. One hundred fifty percent (150%) of a figure equal to the net fees received by the partnership in the calendar year preceding the year in which death or retirement solely by reason of age occurred or reduced salary payments commenced divided by the total number of profit sharing units outstanding as of the first day of that year and multiplied by the retiring or deceased partner's profit sharing units outstanding as of the first day of that year.

No interest shall be included in guaranteed payments. Payments shall commence on the first day of the month following the month of retirement or death.

In addition to payment of his capital account and guaranteed payments as provided in this article, a retired partner or the estate of a deceased partner shall be paid a share of accounts receivable and work in process as of the date of retirement or death equal to collections on same divided by the total number of profit sharing units outstanding as of the date on which death or retirement occurs multiplied by the retiring or deceased partner's profit sharing units oustanding as of date of retirement or death.

No interest shall be included in such payments. Payments will commence on the twentieth day of the month following retirement or death and shall continue for as long as there are collections on said accounts receivable and work in process.

A retired partner or the representative of a deceased partner is required to accept payment of his capital account and payments as provided in this Article as full payment for his interest in the partnership. In consideration for making the required payments the partnership shall own all files, furniture and equipment and good will of the partnership.

For purposes of determining the share of partnership profits or losses for the portion of the year up to the date of death only, a determination of partnership income for the year to date shall be made and this determination shall be the basis for distribution of profit (or assessment of loss) as provided in Article 10. The estate of a deceased partner will not share in profits or losses incurred after his death.

Article 15

Expulsion of a Partner

A partner may be expelled from the partnership upon suspension or revocation of his license to practice as a certified public accountant by any state board of accountancy, upon his conviction of a felony, or of his pleading of nolo contendere to any charge which would constitute a felony, or his adjudication as a bankrupt.

A partner may be expelled upon unanimous vote of all partners except himself for gross inefficiency or for conduct discreditable to the firm.

Upon expulsion, a partner is entitled to be paid his capital account balance as provided in Article 9 and his share of work in process and accounts receivable as provided in Article 14. He shall receive no other payments and shall have no rights in partnership property except as provided in Article 9.

Article 16

Military Service, Sabbatical Leave and Elected Office

A partner who is involuntarily called into military service shall be placed on leave without pay for the duration of his military service.

A partner who requests leave for voluntary military service or for other temporary employment may request a definite or indefinite leave of absence without pay. Leave may be granted by a majority vote of the partners other than the partner requesting leave and such vote may be taken after consideration of the facts and circumstances. If the leave is not granted, the partner will be considered to have withdrawn voluntarily.

Article 17

Duties of Partners

Each partner shall devote his best efforts to serving professionally the firm and its clients. Each partner shall devote substantially all his normal business time to such services. A partner shall not perform for compensation any services that are in competition with the firm, and shall not become engaged in any activity that may reasonably be expected to bring discredit upon the firm. Any partner may object to any outside activity of any other partner and the activity may be prohibited by the majority vote of all partners voting. For this purpose, the partner whose activities are being considered shall not vote.

Each partner will at all times comply with all provisions of the Code of Professional Ethics of the American Institute of Certified Public Accountants and the corresponding rules of any state society of which he is a member and of the boards of accountancy of every state from which he holds a license to practice as a public accountant.

Article 18

Limitations on Partners' Powers

No partner may without the consent of the other partners
(a) Borrow money in the firm name or utilize partnership property as security for such loans;
(b) Assign, transfer, pledge, compromise, release or submit to arbitration any claims or debt due the partnership in an amount greater than $XXXX;
(c) Hypothecate or sell substantially all of the property of the partnership;
(d) Lease or mortgage any partnership real estate, or contract to do so;

(e) Borrow against or agree to sell his interest in the partnership;

(f) Commit the partnership as endorser, surety or guarantor;

(g) Commence litigation to collect any fee or to enforce any contract.

Article 19

Review of Reports and Correspondence and Acceptance of Clients

Any partner has the right to review any report or correspondence issued or to be issued by the partnership and to object to the issuance of same. Any partner has the right to object to the acceptance or retention of any client. If the objection cannot be satisfied after discussion with the managing partner, the matter will be settled by majority vote of the partners. The managing partner is obligated to arrange for a vote on such matters with sufficient promptness to avoid unnecessary liability to the partnership.

Article 20

Life Insurance

The partnership may take out and carry life insurance on the life of any partner. Premiums on such policies are an expense of the partnership allocated to all partners except the insured. Cash values or proceeds on each policy shall be allocated to partners to whom the premiums expense was allocated according to the formula under which the numerator is the sum of all premium expense allocated to a partner and the denominator is the sum of all premium expense.

(Note: If payments under Article 14 are to be made from life insurance proceeds, additional provisions of the agreement are needed to specify the disposition of insurance proceeds, restrictions on borrowing against cash value or on cashing policies and on the right of a withdrawing partner to purchase policies on his life).

Article 21

Arbitration

Disagreements arising from this agreement or the breach thereof shall be arbitrated according to the rule of the American Arbitration Association and judgment upon the award rendered may be entered in any Court having jurisdiction hereof.

Article 22

Amendments to This Agreement

This agreement may be amended by an amendment signed by partners holding 75 percent of the profit sharing units specified in Article 10. An amendment to this Agreement may be presented to the partners for signature thirty days after all partners have been notified in writing of the substance of the proposed amendment. Notice may be carried by unanimous consent of the partners.

Amendments to admit a new partner are governed by the provisions of Article 12.

Article 23

Interpretation

The Agreement shall be governed by the laws of the State of

_____.

Reference in this Agreement to the masculine gender shall be read to refer to females where appropriate. Use of the singular shall be read to include the plural where appropriate.

WITNESS WHEREOF, the parties have hereunto set their hands this _____ day of _____, 19 _____.

Witnessed:

_____   _____
_____   _____
_____   _____

APPENDIX B

Sample Partnership Agreement: Nonprofessional General Partnership

The sample agreement illustrates the terms under which a group of investors may bind themselves to carry on a real estate venture. Since an investment in real estate does not involve the close personal relationships encountered in a service partnership, particularly a professional partnership, matters such as expulsion of a partner or specifications for a mandatory buy-sell agreement upon death, retirement or disability are not needed.

State of _____
County of _____   Partnership Agreement

1.   The name of the partnership is 666 Main Street Company
2.   The business of the partnership is to acquire, improve and lease office buildings and to do all things incident or necessary thereto.
3.   The principal office of the partnership is located at 666 Main Street in the City of _____, _____.
4.   The name and place of residence of each partner is:

Ashley and Bull, P.A.
666 Main Street, _____, _____

Aaron Ashley
521 Country Club Road, _____, _____

Sutton Bull
711 Custer Place, _____, _____

5.   The partnership shall continue as long as two partners, including any new partners who may be admitted under the terms hereof, shall survive, unless it is sooner terminated by mutual consent of all partners.
6.   The partnership shall maintain books of account at its principal

office and all the partners shall have the right to inspect such books at reasonable times.

The partnership shall close its books and file its income tax returns for the year ending December 31.

7.   The books of the partnership shall be maintained on the cash method.

8.   Ashley and Bull, P.A., and Aaron Ashley have each contributed $10,000 cash to the capital of the partnership. Sutton Bull has contributed land with an agreed value of $40,000, subject to a mortgage with a principal balance as of the date of this agreement of $30,000. The income tax basis of the land is $30,000; gain or loss upon the sale of the land shall be allocated among the partners so as to avail the partnership of the tax treatment specified in Internal Revenue Code Section 704(c)(2) and Regulations issued thereunder. Capital may be increased or decreased by a vote of the partners with a two-thirds majority vote required. No interest shall be paid on capital accounts.

9.   The partners shall receive no compensation, but shall share in the profits and losses of the partnership equally. Profits shall be distributed at least annually; however profits shall not be distributed when, in the opinion of the managing partner, such distribution will unreasonably deplete the working capital of the partnership.

10.   All monies belonging to the partnership's common funds shall, as soon as practicable after receipt, be deposited to the credit of the partnership in such bank or banks or other depositories or in money market funds as the partners may from time to time select, and shall not in any circumstances be retained by a partner or be deposited to the credit of any individual whatsoever.

11.   All withdrawals from the common funds of the partnership shall be made by means of checks or drafts upon the partnership's account, signed by any partner, provided that no partner shall sign a check or draft in his own favor except by consent of the other partners.

12.   The day-to-day management of the partnership's affairs shall be entrusted to a partner to be chosen each year by a unanimous vote of the partners. A partner may succeed himself in this office. All checks, drafts, contracts, leases, mortgages and other instruments of a like kind shall be signed by the managing partner, except as herein otherwise provided. The managing partner may authorize any other partner to discharge his managerial functions, including the signing of checks, contracts, etc., temporarily or permanently, in whole or in part, and in any event he shall deputize another partner to act for him during any absence from the business of one week or longer. In the event of the withdrawal, retirement or death of the managing partner during his term of office, the remaining

partners shall forthwith choose one of their number to complete the unexpired term.

13. It shall be the duty and responsibility of the managing partner to keep the other partners informed at all times of the progress of the partnership's affairs by means of:

a. regular meetings of all partners held not less frequently than once in each calendar quarter, and

b. periodic financial reports and statements.

In matters involving substantial expenditures or material changes in partnership policy, the managing partner shall obtain the assent of a two-thirds majority of the partners thereto before undertaking the same.

14. Each partner for himself hereby agrees and covenants that:

a. he will not personally make, draw, accept or endorse any promissory note, bill of exchange, lease, contract or other engagement for the payment of money or its equivalent by the partnership, nor pledge the credit of the partnership in any way whatsoever except as authorized herein.

b. any breach of this Clause by him shall entitle the others to recover from him any expense in which they may be involved as a result of such breach, and

c. he hereby consents to a judgment for such recovery in the court having jurisdiction.

15. New partners may be added to this partnership only with the consent of and on terms agreeable to partners holding two-thirds of the capital interests.

16. No partner, other than by bequest, may assign, pledge or mortgage his interest in the partnership either in whole or in part without consent of partners holding two-thirds of the capital interests. Such consent shall not be unreasonably withheld.

17. Disagreements arising from this Agreement on the breach thereof shall be arbitrated according to the rules of the American Arbitration Association and judgment upon the award rendered may be entered in any Court having jurisdiction hereof.

18. This agreement may be altered or amended at any time by means of supplements executed with the same formality as this agreement and made part hereof. Any partner proposing a change to this agreement must submit the substance of the proposed change to all the partners at leas. thirty days before the proposed effective date of the change and no change may be made without the consent of partners holding two-thirds of the capital interests.

19. This agreement is entered into pursuant to and shall be controlled by the laws of the State of _____ .

In Witness whereof the parties have signed this Partnership Agreement this _____ day of _____ , 19_____ .

_____ , President

For Ashley and Bull, P.A.

_____

Aaron Ashley

_____

Sutton Bull

APPENDIX C

Sample Partnership Agreement: Agreement of Limited Partnership

AGREEMENT OF LIMITED PARTNERSHIP OF _____

Article I

Formation of Limited Partnership

The parties hereby enter into a Limited Partnership under the provisions of the Uniform Limited Partnership Act of the State of _____ , and the rights and liabilities of the partners shall be as provided in that Act as herein otherwise expressly provided.

Article II

Name

The firm name under which the Limited Partnership shall be conducted shall be _____ or such other name as the General Partner shall hereafter designate in writing to the Limited Partners.

Article III

Business

The business of the Partnership is to invest in, acquire, hold, maintain, operate, improve, develop, sell, exchange, lease and otherwise use real property and interest therein for profit and to engage in any and all activities related or incidental thereto.

Article IV

Names and Addresses of Partners

The name and address of the General Partner is _____ ,

_____ , _____ . The names and addresses
of the Limited Partners are

_____

_____

_____

_____

_____

_____

_____

_____

_____.

_____

Article V

Term

The Partnership shall continue until April 1, _____ unless sooner
terminated as hereinafter provided.

Article VI

Principal Place of Business

The principal place of business of the Partnership shall be _____
_____ , _____ , _____ .
The General Partner may from time to time change the principal place of business
and in such event the General Partner shall notify the Limited Partners in writing
within thirty days of the effective date of such change. The General Partner may in
its discretion establish additional places of business of the Partnership.

Article VII

Capital and Contributions

Each of the Partners shall contribute to the capital of the Partnership money
as follows:
  a. General Partner. No capital contribution shall be made by _____
     _____ as General Partner.
  b. Within ten (10) days following execution of this agreement each Limited
     Partner shall make a cash contribution of $50,000. There is no agreement as
     to when the contribution of each Limited Partner is to be returned.

Article VIII

Distributions and Compensation

"Net Cash Receipts" shall mean all cash revenues of the Partnership (other than capital contributions or proceeds of any sale or refinancing of Partnership properties) less the sum of the following to the extent made from such cash revenues received by the Partnership: (i) all principal and interest payments on mortgage and other indebtedness of the Partnership and all other sums paid to lenders and (ii) all cash expenditures incurred incident to the normal operation of the Partnership's business.

To the extent Net Cash Receipts are distributed, the General Partner will be entitled to a distributive share and a management fee for managing the business and affairs of the Partnership, each share and fee to be determined as follows: ninety percent (90%) of the Net Cash Receipts being distributed will be paid to the Limited Partners in equal shares; five percent (5%) of such Net Cash Receipts will be paid to the General Partner as its management fee; and five percent (5%) of such Net Cash Receipts will be payable to the General Partner as its distributive share of such Net Cash Receipts.

"Net Cash Proceeds" shall mean the cash proceeds realized by the Partnership upon the sale or refinancing of Partnership properties after (i) payment of all expenses of such refinancing or sale, including real estate commissions, if applicable and (ii) the payment of indebtedness relating to the property sold or refinanced.

When and as the Partnership sells or refinances Partnership properties, the entire Net Cash Proceeds resulting therefrom which are available for distribution shall be distributed to the Limited Partners in equal shares, until they shall have received from Net Cash Proceeds in total an amount equal to their original capital contributions, plus any deficiency in a cumulative distribution of eight percent (8%) as of the end of the calendar quarter next proceding the date of such distribution. Thereafter, any Net Cash Proceeds available for distribution shall be distributed eighty five percent (85%) to the Limited Partners in equal shares and fifteen percent (15%) to the General Partner.

Partnership distributions, if any, will be made at least quarterly to the Partners recognized on the books of the Partnership as of the last day of the immediately preceding calendar quarter.

Article IX

Allocations of Profits and Losses

Each item of the Partnership's income, gain, loss, deduction or credit from operations will be allocated five percent (5%) to the General Partner and ninety five percent (95%) equally among the Limited Partners. When a property is sold or otherwise disposed of, gains, losses, deductions or credits will be allocated one percent (1%) to the General Partner and ninety nine percent (99%) will be allocated to the Limited Partners equally.

Article X

Books

The Partnership shall maintain full and accurate books at its principal office or such other office as shall be designated for such purpose by the General Partner, and all Partners shall have the right to inspect and examine such books at reasonable times. The books shall be closed and balanced at the end of each taxable year. Annual statements, showing the net profits and losses of the Partnership for the fiscal year and indicating the share thereof of each Partner for income tax purposes, shall be prepared by the accountants for the Partnership and distributed to all the Partners within a reasonable time after the close of each fiscal year.

Each Limited Partner shall have the right to demand and receive true and full information of all things affecting the Partnership, and a formal account of Partnership affairs.

Books shall be kept and financial statements shall be prepared on the cash method and shall be in accordance with accounting procedures appropriate for federal income tax returns.

Article XI

Fiscal Year

The fiscal year of the Partnership shall end on the thirty-first day of December in each year.

Article XII

Partnership Funds

The funds of the Partnership shall be deposited in such bank account or accounts, or invested in such interest-bearing or noninterest-bearing investments. as shall be designated by the General Partner. All withdrawals from any such bank accounts shall be made by the duly authorized agent of the General Partner. Partnership funds shall not be commingled with those of any other person.

Article XIII

Status of Limited Partners

The Limited Partners shall not take any part whatsoever in the management of the business or transact any business for the Partnership, shall contribute no services to it and shall have no power to sign for or to bind the Partnership. The Limited Partners shall not be required to contribute any further capital to the Partnership beyond the amounts set forth in Article VII nor shall they be liable for any debts or obligations of the Partnership beyond said amounts.

Article XIV

Powers, Rights and Duties of the General Partner

The General Partner shall manage and control the Partnership business and shall devote such time to the business of the Partnership as shall be reasonably required for its welfare and success. The General Partner may (on behalf of the Partnership) execute any notes, contracts, agreements, shares, bonds, debentures and other instruments and documents of or for the Partnership. No person shall be required to inquire into the foregoing authority of the General Partner to sign, seal and deliver, any document pursuant to the provisions of this paragraph. The General Partner shall not assign, mortgage, sell or otherwise dispose of his interest as a General Partner, except as otherwise provided herein.

Without the prior approval of Limited Partners, who are entitled to at least 66 2/3% of the net profits and losses of the Partnership to which all of the Limited Partners are then entitled under this Agreement, the General Partner shall not (i) sell, assign, transfer, exchange, lease or otherwise dispose of all or any part of any real property owned by the Partnership, (ii) mortgage or otherwise encumber all or any part of the real property owned by the Partnership or (iii) obligate the Partnership, contractually or otherwise in an amount in excess of Ten Thousand Dollars ($10,000).

The Limited Partners hereby consent to the employment, when and if required, of managers and other agents, accountants and attorneys, as the General Partner may, in his discretion, from time to time, employ.

Article XV

Transfer of Interests by Limited Partners

A Limited Partner may assign the whole or any part of his Interest in the Partnership (but only in whole Interests), and such assignment shall confer upon the assignee the right to become a substituted Limited Partner, in the following manner and subject to the following conditions:

(i)   An instrument of assignment executed by both the assignor and the assignee of the Interest satisfactory in form to the General Partner shall be delivered to the General Partner.

(ii) Each assignment shall be effective as of the last day of the month during which the General Partner actually receives the instrument of assignment which complies with the requirements of subparagraph (i).

(iii) No assignment shall be effective if such assignment would, in the opinion of the General Partner, result in the termination of the Partnership for purposes of the then applicable provisions of the Internal Revenue Code of 1954.

(iv) No assignment shall be effective if the assignment would, to the knowledge of the General Partner, violate the provisions of any applicable state securities law.

(v)   No assignment to a minor or incompetent shall be effective in any respect. Except as herein provided, there shall be no right to admit an additional General or Limited Partner.

Article XVI

Notices

All notices and demands required or permitted under this Agreement shall be in writing and may be sent by certified or registered mail, postage prepaid, to the Partners at their addresses as shown from time to time on the records of the Partnership. Any Partner may specify a different address by notifying the General Partner in writing of such different address.

ᴀrticle XVII

ᴀmendments

The Agreement may be amended by the General Partner without the consent or approval of any Limited Partner if (i) the amendment is solely for the purpose of clarification and does not change the substance of the Agreement, or (ii) the amendment is necessary or appropriate to satisfy the requirements of the Internal Revenue Code with respect to partnership or any Federal or applicate state Securities Laws or Regulations and the amendment does not adversely affect the interest of Limited Partners. Any amendment made pursuant to this Article XVII at the option of the General Partner, will be effective as of the date of this Agreement.

Any other amendments may be made only by the General Partner submitting to all of the Limited Partners prior written notice of the proposed amendment and a statement that the proposed amendment will become effective forty-five (45) days after mailing of the notice by the General Partner to the Limited Partners. If any such notice is given, the amendment will become effective at the expiration of the forty-five day period unless prior to the expiration of that period the owners of a majority in interest of the Limited Partners shall object in writing to the proposed amendment.

If the owners of a majority in interest of the Limited Partners shall object in writing in such forty-five (45) day period, such proposed amendment shall not become effective. No amendment will be made without the consent of a majority in interest of the Partners if such amendment would (i) change the Partnership to a general partnership, (ii) change the respective rights or obligations of the General Partner or the Limited Partners, or (iii) change the respective participation of the Partnership as determined in accordance with Article VIII and Article IX of the Agreement.

Article XVIII

Dissolution of the Partnership

The happening of any one of the following events shall work an immediate dissolution of the Partnership:

(i)   The death, insanity, bankruptcy or termination of interest of any Limited Partner shall not cause the dissolution of the Partnership. The bankruptcy of the General Partner or the termination of the General Partner as a partnership under _____ law (unless, if permitted by law, a substitute General Partner is elected by Limited Partners holding a majority of the outstanding Interests owned by Limited Partners);

(ii) The sale by the Partnership of all interest in real estate, including notes received upon sales of properties;

(iii) The agreement by Limited Partners holding a majority of all the then-outstanding Interests owned by Limited Partners to dissolve the Partnership; or

(iv) The expiration of the term of the Partnership as provided in Article V of this Agreement.

Article XIX

Replacement of the General Partner

The General Partner shall have the right to retire from the Partnership at the end of any calendar year, provided written notice of such intention to retire shall be served upon all the other Partners at the office of the Partnership at least three (3) months before the end of the calendar year.

Article XX

Counterparts

This Agreement may be executed in several counterparts, each of said counterparts constituting an original and all together one certificate.

Article XXI

Agreement Binding Upon Successors

This Agreement is binding upon the parties hereto, their respective heirs, executors, administrators, and assigns.

IN WITNESS WHEREOF, the parties have hereunto set their hands and seals as of the _____ day of _____ , 19____ .
Signed in the presence of:

_____   _____
Witness

_____   _____
Witness

_____   _____
Witness

_____   _____
Witness

_____   _____
Witness

_____   _____
Witness

Index

A

Accounting, 189, 190
Accounting year, 40
Accrual basis, 70
Accumulations of earnings, 24, 27
Administrator, 196
Admission of partners:
  "clone" of existing partners, 98
  employees as source, 98
  founding partners, 97–98
  limited partnership, 9
  need, 98
  relatives as source, 98
  screening applicants, 98–99
  terms, 99–100
  when you find right person, 99
Aggregate of partners, 8, 10
Allocation:
  premiums and proceeds, 103
  retroactive, 87–88
  tax effects, 80–83
"All Savers Certificates," 28
Amendment, partnership agreement, 40
Appreciated inventories, 118
Arbitration, 111–112
Art, 249
Assets:
  basis, 29, 126–131, 137–141, 144, 146
  contributed, 82–83
  disposition, 154–159
  intangible, 114
  selling all or part, 158–159
  tangible, 113–114
  transfer in incorporation, 154
  underlying, equity in, 220
Associations, 34–36, 271–272
At-risk rules, 265–268
Attitudes towards work, 195
Average hours worked for latest year, 210, 214

B

Bankruptcy of partner, 9
Basis of assets, 29, 126–131, 137–141, 144, 146
Basis of distributed property, 132–134
Basis of partnership interests:
  alternative rule for determining, 143–144
  dates on which determined, 146
  distinct from basis of partnership assets, 137–141
  effects of liabilities, 141–143

  general rule, 47–48
  "in sync" with basis of partnership assets, 144, 146
  lost upon distribution, 146–147
  other causes of changes, 143
  sources, 141
Benefits, 27, 28
Billing, client, 189
Bill paying, 189
Bonds, 221
Bookkeeping function, upgrading, 190–191
Books, 249
Branch office:
  communication with main office, 176–179
    engagement, 177–178
    introductions, 178–179
    seminars, 178
    verbal, 177
    why problems arise, 176
    written, vices, 176–177
  contact with centers of influence, 168
  cost-benefit ratio, 183
  defections by personnel, 174–176
    case study, 175–176
    prevention, 174–175
  duplication of expenses, 182–183
  entering new market, 167
  equipment costs, 182–183
  following clients or patients, 168
  how acquired, 167–168
  image and quality, 179–180
    constant vigilance, 179
    specific controls, 179–180
  merger, 167
  space problem solution, 182
  staffing, 168–173
    case study on opening, 172–173
    large firms, 168
    problems, 171–172
    recruits or transferees, 169–170
    rotation of personnel, 170–171
    smaller firms, 169
  syndrome, 180–182
Breach of trust, 5
Business year, 24
Buy-out agreement, 223
Buy-sell agreement:
  disability invokes, 109–110
  essential provisions, 101
  funding with life insurance, 101–105
    borrowing, 102
    disposition of policies, 104–105

Buy-sell agreement (*cont'd*)
  funding with life insurance (*cont'd*)
    kind and amount, 102
    ownership, 102
    proceeds fund deferred payout, 105
  in force at time of death, 220
  need, 101

C

Calendar year, 43
Capabilities, 189
Capital:
  increases, 69–71
  not all on books, 67–68
  "off-balance sheet," 68–69
  shares, 46, 66–67
  varying ratios, 69
Capital account:
  accrual basis, 70–71
  defined, 65
  distinct from basis of partnership interest, 47–48
  distinct from drawing accounts, 65
  how created, 65–66
  interest, 72–73
  not all capital is on books, 67–68
  "off-balance sheet" capital, 68–69
  opening inequality, 71
  shares, 66-67
Capital contributions, 39
Capital gains, 22, 28, 74–75, 234
Capital ratios, 77, 79–80
Capital sources:
  cash and property, 45–46
  encumbered property, 46
Carried interest, 246
Cash basis, 70
Cash flow, 220, 221, 246
Cattle feeding and breeding, 249
Charitable contribution, 27, 226
Cleanliness, office, 189, 191
Close corporations, 220
Closing partnership year, 116–118
Coal, 249
Collection, client, 189
Common property, 10
Communication, 176–179, 197–198
Compensation:
  disability, 109
  portion specified, 40
  profit sharing not substitute, 75–76
  records, 203–204
  services, 71-72
  tax-shelter limited partnership, 241–242
Conduit concept, 8
Conflicts, motives, 198–200
Conflicts of interest, 246–248
Construction period interest, 269–270
Constructive distributions, 89
"Continuation of Partnership," 152–153

Contraction, 40
Contributed asset, sold, 82–83
Contributions of property, 80–83
Contumacy, 111
Corporations:
  attributes conferred by law, 3
  characteristics, 25–31
  compared with partnership, 19–31
  Subchapter S, 22, 23, 25–31
  tax shelter, 236–237
Cost-benefit ratio, 183
Costs, branch office, 182–183
Covenant not to compete, 41
Credit:
  investment, 52, 161–162, 235–236
  use, 26
Credit recapture, 52

D

Dealings, partnerships and partners, 90–91
Death of partner, 9, 40, 110–111
Debit, 157–158
Deceased partners, 115, 118
Decedent, income in respect of, 223–227
Defection, branch office personnel, 174–176
Deferred payout, 105
Deferring taxes, 233–234, 254–256
Democracy, 188
Departing partner, 112–114
Depletion, 14
Depreciation, 14, 82
Depreciation recapture, 52
Dictatorship, 187
Disability:
  causes, 108
  compensation, 109
  defining, 108–109
  invokes buy-sell agreement, 109–110
  pay, tax aspects, 109
  provision made, 40, 91–92
Disability insurance, 41, 223
Disagreement with partner, 111- 112
Disallowed expenses, 31
Disclosure, 262–264
Disloyalty, branch office, 181–182
Dissolution:
  causes, 151–152
  distribution of assets and liabilities, 40–41
Distributed property, basis, 132–134
Distributions:
  constructive, 89
  exceptions to general rule, 89
  guaranteed payments, 89
  no gain or loss recognized, 88–89
  nonliquidating, 89
  partnership affected, 89
  taxation, 27
Distributive shares, 89–90, 261–262
Dividend income, 28
Double taxation, 22, 224–225

Drawing accounts:
    distinct from capital accounts, 65
    partnership agreement defines, 65
Duration of entity, 25
Duties of partners, 44

E

Earnings:
    accumulations, 24, 27
    taxability, 26
Earnings and profits, 22
Economic circumstances, 221–222
Economic considerations, 13
Elections:
    adjust basis of distributed property,
        132–134
    adjust basis of partnership assets, 126–131
Employees, 98
Encumbered property, 46
Engagement, 177–178
Entity, 8, 10
Equipment costs, 182-183
Equipment leasing, 249, 258
Equity, underlying assets, 220
Estates, 3, 4, 5
Estate tax instructions, 220
Estrangement, branch office, 180–182
Exchange for services, 30, 52–55
Executive committee, 40, 62
Expanding, 168
Expenses:
    branch offices, 182–183
    construction period interest, 269–270
    guaranteed payments, 75
    obtaining financing, 270–271
    organization, 55, 268–269
    partners', 40
    pre-opening, 268–271
    start-up, 270
    syndication, 268–269
Expense-sharing, 11–12
Expulsion of partner, 111–112

F

Fair market value, 113, 219, 220
Family partnership, 32–34
Farming, 249
Fees, syndication, 55
FICA tax, 28
Filing requirements, 14, 15–16
Financial records, 202
Financing, cost of obtaining, 270–271
Fiscal year, 43, 117–118
Flexibility, 3
Formation, ease, 20, 25
Founding partners, 97–98
Function, organization by, 197
Funding, buy-sell agreement, 101–105

G

Gain, 14
General partner, 241–242, 243–244, 246
General partnership:
    benefits and pitfalls, 9
    compared to limited, 7–8
    tax shelter, 236
    Uniform Partnership Act, 4
    unlimited liability, 5–6
    written or verbal agreement, 6
Gifts of partnership interests, 227
Gift tax instructions, 220
Gift tax returns, 33
Goals:
    firm, 194
    individual, 194
    meetings, 192–193
    partnership, 193–194
    well-defined, 192
Good will, 45, 105–107, 220
Government units, 3
Gross income, 83–84
Group 4, 5
Guaranteed payments:
    capital gains, 74–75
    deductible if expenses, 75
    defined, 73
    distribution, 89
    former partners, 75
    normal choice, 105
    not best choice, 105–106
    reasonable, 75
    receipt, 74
    retired partners, 115
    tax news, 115
    tax-saving options, 225–226

H

Holding company, 27
Holding period, 52
Housekeeping, 189

I

Illness, 40
Image, 179–180
Inclusion in probate estate, 14
Income:
    election affects computation, 86–87
    gross, 83–84
    in respect of decedent, 115–116
    sharing, 246
    special treatment items, 84–85
    time for inclusion of items, 86
    value of partnership interest, 221
Income in respect of decedent:
    guaranteed payments, 225–226
    partnership income, 224–225
    payments for interest in partnership,
        226–227

Income in respect of decedent (*cont'd*)
    reducing double tax, 225
    taxed twice, 223–224
    transfers of interest, 115–116
Income-sharing, 10
Income taxation, 9, 251–273 (*see also*
    Tax-shelter partnership)
Incorporation:
    legal counsel, 154
    tax-free, 153–154
    tax implications, 153
    transferring assets, 154
Inflation, 234
Insurance, 41, 101–105, 111, 223
Intangible assets, 114
Interests:
    basis, 135–148
    capital accounts, 72–73
    transfers, 93–134 (*see also* Transfers of
        interest)
    valuation, 219–223 (*see also*
        Valuation of partnership interest)
Interest to be paid, 39
Internal Revenue Code, 4–5
Inter vivos agreement, 221
Introductions, 178–179
Inventories, appreciated, 118
Investment credit, 235–236
Investment credit, recapture, 52, 161–162

J

Joint ownership, 10
Joint tenancy, 10
Joint venture, 4, 5

K

Keogh-type plans, 24, 27

L

Leave of absence, 40
Legal considerations, 13
Legal counsel, 154
Leverage, 234–235, 248
Liability:
    disposition, 154–159
    exposure, 9,40
    limited, 19
    limits, 25
    unlimited, 5–6
Life insurance, 41, 101–105, 111, 223
Limited partners, 240–241, 243–244, 247
Limited partnership:
    benefits and pitfalls, 9
    compared to general, 7–8
    defined, 6
    tax-shelter, 231–232, 236–237, 240–249 (*see
        also* Tax-shelter partnership)
    Uniform Partnership Act, 4, 6

Liquidation, 30
Long-term capital gain, 234
Losses:
    capital, 31
    dividing, 40
    IRS Section 704(c)(3), 14
    limitation, 26
    net operating, 29
    person who reports, 30
Loss on investment, 24

M

Management:
    administrative partner, 189–191
    communications, 197–198
        absorption, 198
        hazards of lack, 197–198
        systematic, 198
    democracy, 188
    dictatorship, 187
    dominant partner resists change, 187–188
    executive committee, 62–63
    individual capabilities, 189
    limited partners excluded, 240–241
    managing partner, 189–197
        assigning responsibility, 189–190
        attitudes toward work, 195
        bookkeeping function, 190–191
        firm goals, 194
        good administrator, 196
        how he functions, 191–192
        individual characteristics, 193–194
        individual goals, 194
        make clean sweep for profit, 191
        meetings as goal-setters, 192–193
        partnership goals, 193–194
        payroll function, 190
        qualities, 192
        recognize productivity, 195
        requisites, 196–197
        routine tasks, 190
        selfishness, 195
        upgrading, 190–191
        well-defined goals, 192
        who, 196–197
    method, 39–40
    motives, 198–200
        conflicts, 199–200
        partnership motivators, 199
        resolution of conflicts, 200
    oligarchies, 188
    organization by function, 197
    partner, 62
    partnership vs. tenancies, 14
    record-keeping, 202–216 (*see also*
        Records)
    responsibility, 25
    shifts in positions, 200–202
    tax-sheltered investments, 235
    what partners want, 188–189

Mark-up/down, 205, 208, 209
Meetings, 40
Merger, 167-168
Metals, 249
Mining, 249
Minutes, 203
Mortgaged property, 48-50
Motives:
   conflicts, 199-200
   partnership motivators, 199
   resolution of conflicts, 200
Movies, 249
Municipal bond interest, 22

N

Name of partnership:
   general partnership, 9
   limited partnership, 9
   partnership agreement, 39
Negative tax shelter, 264-265
Net fees per partner, 210
Nonliquidating distribution, 89
Nonrecourse, term, 248

O

"Off-balance sheet" capital, 68-69
Oil and gas drilling, 243, 244-246
Oligarchies, 188
Operations, 57-92
Organization by function, 197
Organization expenses, 268-269
Organization of partnership:
   capital sources, 45-46
      cash and property, 45-46
      encumbered property, 46
   duties and responsibilities, 44
   expenses, 55
   interest, 46-55
      exchange for services, 52-55
      infusions of property, 46-52
   partnership agreement, 39-43
   rights, 44-45
   syndication fees, 55
   taxable year, 43-44
Outside activities:
   case, 63
   embarrassment, 64
   limitation, 63-64
   negative defense, 64
   ounce of prevention, 64
   positive defense, 64
   too much of good thing, 63-64

P

Partner, definition, 4
Partners:
   admission, 9, 97-100 (*see also*
      Admission of partners)

dealings with partnerships, 90-91
death, 9, 40, 110-111
deceased, 115, 118
departing, paid for interest, 112-114
disability, 91-92
disagreement with or expulsion, 111-112
dominant, 187-188
duties and responsibilities, 44
economic circumstances, 221-222
former, guaranteed payments, 75
founding, 97-98
guaranteed payments, 115
managing, 62
payroll taxes, 72
retirement, 9, 40, 41, 107-108, 115
rights, 44-45
salaries, 71-72
successors in interest, 115
Partnership:
   admission of partners, 9
   aggregate of partner, 8, 10
   bankruptcy of partner, 9
   basis of assets, 137-141, 144, 146
   basis of interests, 135-148 (*see also*
      Basis of partnership interests)
   benefits and pitfalls, 9
   branch offices, 165-183 (*see also*
      Branch offices)
   "breach of trust," 5-6
   compared with corporation, 19-31
      accumulated earnings, 24
      allocating taxability, 22-23
      characteristics, 25-31
      conclusions, 21
      deducting loss on investment, 24
      ease of formation and operation, 20
      liability, 19
      no double taxation, 22
      nontax considerations, 19-21
      nontax disadvantages, 20-21
      retirement plans, 24
      selecting business year, 24
      tax considerations, 21-24
      transferability, 21
   complex, 16
   "conduit" concept, 8
   dealing with partners, 90-91
   death of partner, 9
   definitions, 3, 4-5
   depletion, 14
   depreciation, 14
   entity, 8, 10
   exposure to liability, 9
   family, 32-34
   filing requirements, 14, 15-16
   flexibility, 3
   form of agreement, 9
   gain or loss, 14
   general, 4, 5-6, 7-8, 9
   gifts of interests, 227
   group, 4, 5

Partnership (*cont'd*)
  inclusion in probate estate, 14
  income in respect of decedent, 223–227
  income-sharing, 10
  income taxation, 9
  intent to form, 3
  intent to make profit, 3
  interest is personal property, 4
  Internal Revenue Code, 4–5
  joint venture, 4, 5
  legal and economic considerations, 13, 15
  legal nature of interest, 14
  limited, 4, 6, 7–8, 9, 231–232, 236–237,
    240–249, 256–258, 271–272 (*see also*
    Tax-shelter partnership)
  management, 14
  name, 9
  penalties for failure to recognize, 15
  pool, 4, 5
  professional, 165–183 (*see also*
    Branch offices)
  retirement of partner, 9
  silent partners, 13
  syndicate, 4, 5
  taxable as associations, 34–36
  tax-shelter, 222, 229–250, 251–273 (*see also*
    Tax shelter partnerships)
  tenancies, 10
  term, 9
  termination, 149–163 (*see also*
    Termination)
  Uniform Partnership Act, 3–4
  unincorporated organization, 4, 5
  unlimited liability, 5–6
  valuation, 14
  valuation of interest, 219–223 (*see also*
    Valuation of partnership interest)
  when to choose, 17–35
Partnership agreement, 39–43, 99–100
Partnership interest:
  exchange for services, 52–55
  infusions of property, 46–52
Partnership year, 116–118
Part ownership, 10
Pass-through of tax attributes, 261–265
Payments:
  easy payment plan, 240
  guaranteed, 73–75, 115
Payout:
  deferred, 105
  retiring partner, 103–104
Payroll function, upgrading, 190
Payrolls, 189, 190
Payroll taxes, 72
Penalties, 15
Percentage depletion, 235
Percentage income statement, 210, 213
Personal property, 4
Personnel, branch offices (*see also*
  Branch office)
Points, 271

Pool, 4, 5
Positions shifts, 200–202
Premiums, 103
Pre-opening expenses, 268–271
Price, 113–114
Probate estate, 14
Proceeds, 103, 105
Productivity, 195
Professional partnerships, 165–183 (*see also*
  Branch offices)
Profitability, records to maximize, 204
Profit and loss sharing ratios, 75–80
Profits:
  potential for future, 220
  shares, 46, 66–67
Profits and losses, 40
Profit-sharing, 10
Property:
  combined with cash, 45–46
  distributed, basis, 132–134
  encumbered, 46
  high-value, low-basis, 46–47
  holding period, 52
  infusions, 46–55
  mortgaged, 48–50
  tax distinction, 53
  tax effects of contributions, 80–83
  tax problems with contribution, 52
  undivided interests, 50–51
Proprietors, sole, 155–157
Proprietorship, 3, 236
Prospectus, tax shelter, 239, 247–248

Q

Quality, 179–180
Quorum, 40

R

Real estate, 221, 260–261, 267–268
Real estate partnership, 242
Recapture:
  depreciation, 52
  investment credit, 52, 161–162
Receivables, unrealized, 107, 118
Records:
  accounting, 40
  average hours worked for latest year, 210,
    214
  financial, 202
  maximize profitability, 204–216
  minutes, 203
  net fees per partner, 210, 212
  nonfinancial, 203
  partner compensation, 203
  percentage income statement, 210, 213
  policy manuals, 203
  statistical profile, 210, 211
  substantial mark-up/down, 205, 208, 209
  supplemental, 202

time and efficiency, 204–216
time card, 205, 206
work in process, 215
work in process detail ledger, 205, 207
Recruits, 169–170
Relatives, 98
Relocating, 168
Research, 249
Responsibility:
  assigning, 189–190
  partner, 44
Retirement of partner:
  general and limited partnerships, 9
  guaranteed payments, 115
  partnership agreement, 40, 41
  reward or exile, 107
  scheduled, 107
  transfers of interest, 107–108
  transition controlled, 108
Retirement plans, 24
Retiring partner, payout, 103–104
Retroactive allocations, 87–88
Reversionary interest, 246
Rights of partner, 44–45
Rotation of personnel, 170–171

S

Salaries, 40, 71–72
Schedules, work, 201–202
Securities laws, 238
Security factors, 222–223
Selfishness, 195
Seminars, 178
Services:
  compensation, 71–72
  exchange, 30, 52–53
Shares:
  capital and profit, 66–67
  distributive, 89–90
Shifts in positions, 200–202
Silent partners, 13
Sole proprietors, 155–157
Sole proprietorship, 3, 236–237
Staffing, branch offices, 168–173
  (see also Branch offices)
Start-up costs, 270
Statistical profile, 210, 211
Stocks, 221
Subchapter S corporation, 22, 23, 25–31
"Substantial economic effect," 78–79
Successors in interest, 115
Syndicate, 4, 5
Syndication expenses, 55, 268–269

T

Tangible assets, 113
Tapes, 249
Taxability of earnings, 26
Taxable year, 43–44

Tax-exempt income, 29
Tax-free incorporation, 153–154
Tax-shelter partnership:
  arrangements, 236–237
  "at risk" rules, 265–268
    delayed effect, 266
    1978 changes, 265–266
    other effects, 266–267
    prior to 1976, 265
    real estate, 267–268
  attractive, 232–236
  benefits, 233–236
  buying on easy payment plan, 240
  changing form of taxation, 258–260
  deferral of taxation, 233–234
  deferring taxes, 254–256
  definition, 231
  equipment leasing, 258
  how sold, 237–240
  image conjured, 231
  income tax aspects, 251–273
  inflation, 234
  investment and other tax credits, 235–236
  IRS, 239–240
  leverage, 234–235
  limited, 231–232, 236–237, 240–249,
    256–258, 271–272
    adversary roles, 243–244
    art, 249
    books, 249
    carried interest, 246
    compared, 236–237
    compensation, 241–242
    conflicts of interest, 246–248
    costs shared, 244
    deductions allocated, 244
    economic hazards, 248–249
    equipment leasing, 249
    exclusion from management, 240–241
    farming, 249
    fill the bill, 237
    general partner, 241–242, 243–244, 246
    ideal, 231–232
    large, 256–258
    leverage, 248
    limitations, 237
    limited partners, 240–241, 243–244, 247
    mining, 249
    movies, 249
    oil and gas drilling, 243, 244–246
    organization and operation, 240–249
    prospectuses, 247–248
    real estate, 242
    records, 249
    research and development, 249
    reversionary interest, 246
    sharing income and cash flow, 246
    tapes, 249
    taxed as association, 271–272
  long-term capital gain, 234
  pass-through of tax attributes, 261–265

Tax-shelter partnership (*cont'd*)
  pass-through of tax attributes (*cont'd*)
    disclosure, 262–264
    negative tax shelter, 264–265
    partner's distributive share items,
      261–262
    Schedule K-1, 262
  percentage depletion, 235
  pre-opening expenses, 268–271
    construction period interest, 269–270
    costs of obtaining financing, 270–271
    organization, 268–269
    start-up, 270
    syndication, 268–269
  professional management, 235
  prospectus, 239
  real estate investment, 260–261
  securities laws, 238–239
  simplest and safest, 231
  talent and money, 237–238
  tax savings not enough, 232–233
  valuing interest, 222
  who can benefit, 233
Tax trap, 15
Tenancies, 10, 13, 14
Tenancy by entireties, 10
Tenancy in common, 10, 12
Termination:
  disposition of assets and liabilities,
    154–159
  incorporation, 153–154
    legal counsel, 154
    tax-free, 153–154
    tax implications, 153
    transferring assets, 154
  recapture of investment credit, 161–162
  statutory provisions, 151–152
  tax hazards, 160–162
  two general rules, 152–153
  unwanted, avoiding, 159–160
Term of partnership, 9
Time and efficiency records, 204–216
Time card, 205, 206
Timing, 222
Transferability, 21, 25
Transferees, 169–170
Transfers of interest:
  adjust basis of distributed property,
    132–134
  adjust basis of partnership assets, 126–131
  admission of partners, 97–100 (*see also*
    Admission of partners)
  appreciated inventories, 118–126
  buy-sell agreements, 100–105 (*see also*
    Buy-sell agreements)
  closing partnership year, 116–118
  death of partner, 110–111
  disability, 108–110
  disagreement with partner, 111–112
  expulsion of partner, 111–112
  founding partners, 97

good will, 105–107
guaranteed payments, 115
income in respect of decedent, 115–116
payment of departing partner, 112–114
retirement of partner, 107–108
unrealized receivables, 118–126
Trusts, 3, 4, 5

U

Underlying assets, 221
Undivided interests, 80–82
Uniform Partnership Act:
  general partnerships, 4
  intent to form partnership, 3
  intent to make profit, 3
  interest is personal property, 4
  limited partnerships, 4
  termination, 151–152
Unincorporated organization, 4, 5
Unlimited liability, 5–6
Unrealized receivables, 107, 118
Upgrading, 190–191

V

Valuation, estate or gift tax, 14
  appropriate date, 219
  cash flow, 220
  economic circumstances of partner,
    221–222
  equity in underlying assets, 220
  fair market value, 219, 220
  gifts of partnership interests, 227
  income and cash flow, 221
  income in respect of decedent, 223–227 (*see
    also* Income in respect of decedent)
  IRS rules, 220
  no established market, 219
  potential for future profits, 220
  practical aspects, 220–221
  rarely an active market, 219
  special situation 220
  tax shelter partnership, 222
  three prices to consider, 219
  timing and security factors, 222–223
  value of underlying assets, 221
Value, 113–114
Varying interests, 87–88
Verbal communication, 177
Votes, 40

W

Withdrawal, 40
Work in process, 205, 206, 215
Written communication, 176–177

Y

Year, taxable, 43–44